The Study of Culture

L. L. LANGNESS

UNIVERSITY OF CALIFORNIA

LOS ANGELES

Chandler & Sharp Publishers, Inc.

San Francisco

✓ **Library of Congress Cataloging in Publication Data**

Langness, Lewis L
    The study of culture.

    (Chandler & Sharp publications in anthropology)
    Bibliography: p.
    1. Ethnology—History.   2. Culture.   I. Title.
GN17.L36   301.2   74-88
ISBN 0-88316-507-4

THE STUDY OF CULTURE

CHANDLER & SHARP PUBLICATIONS IN ANTHROPOLOGY

GENERAL EDITORS: L. L. Langness and Robert B. Edgerton

For Joany, with love

CONTENTS

ILLUSTRATIONS

PREFACE

This book is intended to be an introduction to the study of cultural anthropology or, for that matter, any course of study that deals with the concept of culture. It presents a brief overview of the history of anthropology, with focus on the history of the culture concept. It is not meant to be a definitive, comprehensive history of anthropology but, rather, a first introduction to the significant figures in this history and to the terms and concepts of cultural anthropology, more or less in the order in which they emerged.

It also attempts to correct some of the untruths, half-truths, and oversimplifications that have up to now been passed uncritically from one generation of anthropology students to the next: for example, that all of the early anthropologists believed exclusively in unilineal evolution; that Franz Boas and his followers did not believe in evolution at all; that Edward B. Tylor was alone responsible for introducing the concept of culture into the English language, that A. R. Radcliffe-Brown did not believe in history, and many others. It must be noted that only because of recent work in the history of anthropology—most importantly by George W. Stocking, Jr. and Marvin Harris, but also by A. Irving Hallowell, Margaret T. Hodgen, and others—has it become possible to attempt a shorter and more precise version of these events. The debt owed to these scholars is apparent on virtually every page and, as this volume is meant for the general student rather than the professional, I have often favored these recent sources rather than the originals.

I have used quotations liberally. In some cases the quotation makes the point far more parsimoniously than I can make it, in others I believed it was better to let the author speak for himself, and in still others I simply felt the quotation was interesting or provocative enough to stimulate students to want to look further.

Contemporary interest in the history of anthropology is only part of a broader interest in the history of science in general which has produced some recent books of much value in the preparation of this volume. The collection *The Wild Man Within*, edited by Edward Dudley and Maximillian E. Novak, Ernest Becker's stimulating work *The Lost Science of Man*, and Sidney Pollard's *The Idea of*

Progress come particularly to mind. There are also *The Idea of Prehistory* by Glyn Daniel (1962), *Growth of a Prehistoric Time Scale* by William Berry (1968), and Muhsin Mahdi's *Ibn Khaldun's Philosophy of History* (1971).

This historical approach has been deliberately chosen. It is important for students not only to understand the concept of culture as it is presently employed, but also to understand that it developed out of a series of real problems that people were attempting to cope with in the eighteenth and nineteenth centuries. Many of these problems are with us yet. Further, it is necessary and worthwhile to emphasize that no science, cultural anthropology included, developed independently of other sciences or of the important inventions and discoveries that were being made during the period of its emergence. Suggested links between developments in the history of anthropology and other disciplines have been pointed out whenever possible. Finally, the exceedingly comprehensive scope of anthropology itself must be made clear. Cultural anthropology is only one subfield of the larger whole which also includes archeology, physical anthropology, and linguistics. Although these other subfields are not dealt with directly, an attempt has been made to show how developments in each of them have affected the others.

I have attempted to present the history of the culture concept in such a way as to illustrate the arguments and counterarguments that were involved in its emergence and change. Naturally there was more overlapping of ideas and arguments over time than I have been able to make clear. And, concededly, the views presented in this account are somewhat oversimplified. By focusing on the concept of culture I have tried to eliminate the problem of having to be encyclopedic. Most courses in the history of anthropology start with Herodotus and move forward slowly from there so that by the time they actually reach the culture concept the history of anthropology since then becomes a mere afterthought. But anthropology does have its own history, however brief—a very interesting history worthy of treatment in its own right. Thus I believe it is important for those who are interested in anthropology to be exposed to a brief overview of this type. Too often we hear from students that they do not see how things fit together, or why certain things are important, or why they should study anthropology at all. If this book gives them a broader perspective and helps them to answer these questions it will have fulfilled its purpose. If it stimulates them to pursue their studies in anthropology further, so much the better.

L.L.L.

ACKNOWLEDGMENTS

I am indebted to many friends and colleagues who have read this manuscript and given advice and encouragement. In particular I am most grateful to Professor Robert B. Edgerton, who has been more than generous with his help from the very beginning. I am also grateful to Ms. Ceel Edgerton, Dr. Carol Eastman, Dr. Thomas Weisner, Mr. Paul Preuss, and Mr. Richard Mase, all of whom have read the manuscript and offered useful comments. Mr. George Guilmet has been not only an able critic, but also of great help, both practically and logistically. Mr. Gilbert Herdt has, likewise, offered several cogent and insightful criticisms. Finally, I must thank my secretary, Ms. Jae Stewart, for her diligence, patience, and cooperation at all times.

Naturally, I am alone responsible for whatever shortcomings the book may have.

L. L. L.

THE STUDY OF CULTURE

INTRODUCTION **THE SCIENCE OF MAN**

Anthropology is the scientific study of man. *Man* is a term of uncertain origin, the primary meaning of which is *human being*—that is, the human creature viewed in the abstract: male, female, all colors and shapes, prehistoric, ancient, and modern. Anthropology, then, most fundamentally viewed, is simply the attempt of human beings to study and hence to understand themselves at all times and in all places.

Cultural anthropology, the subject of this book, is only one part of man's efforts to know himself—that part which deals with *culture*. Although the concept of culture was introduced into the English language only in the 1880's by Matthew Arnold and Edward B. Tylor, the study of cultural anthropology has existed for much longer than that. It has been suggested, for example, that the metaphysical foundation upon which the definition of culture depended can be found in John Locke's *An Essay Concerning Human Understanding* (1690), and the concept itself was first given clear expression in Europe in 1750 by Anne Robert Jacques Turgot:

> Possessor of a treasure of signs which he has the faculty of multiplying to infinity, he [man] is able to assure the retention of his acquired ideas, to communicate them to other men, and to transmit them to his successors as a constantly expanding heritage. (quoted in Harris, 1968:14)

This definition does have a surprisingly contemporary character.

Muhsin Mahdi's study of Ibn Khaldun, however, discloses roots of the idea of culture at least as early as the fourteenth century. Ibn Khaldun, an Arab historian, he proposes, founded a science of culture at that time. Ibn Khaldun's idea of culture has the same surprisingly modern character as Turgot's:

> . . . Culture is not an independent substance, but a property . . . of another substance which is man. Hence the natural character of culture must have reference to what is natural to man, i.e., to his nature and to what differentiates him from the rest of the animal world.
> The essential differentia of man is the power or faculty of intellect or mind

1

. . . reflection . . . or deliberation. . . . Through his intellect man can understand; he can know both particular objects embedded in matter and universals abstracted from matter. (Mahdi, 1971:173)

No doubt one could find evidence for some notion of culture even further back, in Herodotus or Tacitus for example. Even so, the history of cultural anthropology as we now conceive of it is scarcely more than one hundred years old, a brief period indeed in the course of human history and prehistory.

In the slightly more than one hundred years since its introduction into English, the culture concept has come to be regarded as "the foundation stone of the social sciences" (Chase, 1948:59), and as "the most central problem of all social science" (Malinowski, 1939:588). A. L. Kroeber and Clyde Kluckhohn, two of America's most distinguished anthropologists, argued in their definitive survey of the concept (1963:3) that "in explanatory importance and in generality of application it [culture] is comparable to such categories as gravity in physics, disease in medicine, evolution in biology." Julian Huxley (1960:19) has asserted that man's acquisition of culture "enabled him to cross the barrier set by biological limitations and enter the virgin fields of psycho-social existence [which implies that] man's true destiny emerges in a startling new form. It is to be the chief agent for the future of evolution on this planet." More recently has appeared a volume, *The Idea of Culture in the Social Sciences* (Schneider and Bonjean, 1973), which emphasizes the enormous influence of the concept of culture on sociology, political science, geography, and history. It also makes clear that there is a budding field of cultural economics!

Thus the study of culture must be seen not as the unique occupation of a few professors interested in the academic and esoteric but rather as one of the major ingredients in any basic educational program and as one of the keys to the understanding of man's place on earth and in the biosphere.

Although humans must always have been interested in reflecting upon themselves, what we now consider the "scientific" study of man—that is, anthropology—could not have come into being until realistic notions had been formed about the age of the planet and the myriad things found upon it. Geology, stimulated early primarily because of the economic interests of mining, was developing rapidly throughout the nineteenth century. As the various strata of the earth were exposed along with occasional accompanying fossils, it became apparent to some that the earth was much older than was popularly supposed. The new evidence did not fit well with the established idea of an independent creation of fixed and unchanging species. Also increasingly demanding explanation were the stone and bone tools being unearthed by a number of scholars who were then generally referred to as *antiquarians*. As men were not believed to have been on earth for very long, and as no human fossils had been recovered up to this time, there was no satisfactory explanation for the presence of such artifacts deep in the earth. Midway in the seventeenth century, Archbishop James Ussher had worked out a Biblical chronology in which the six-day creation of all things had taken place in 4004 B.C. and the flood had occurred in 2501 B.C. Charles Lyell, one of the foremost British scientists of his day, noted in his *Principles of Geology* in 1830 that remains of life were rare in the deepest geological strata, that immediately above these came shells and vegetable remains, then bones of fishes and reptiles, then remains of birds and, finally, remains of four-footed creatures. Human beings were much more recent.

As far as fossil men were concerned:

Ignorance and prejudice combined to assert that man was created a few thousand years ago in a state of physical perfection. The possibility of the discovery of fossil man was therefore inconceivable to most people, and those early writers who entertained the idea were generally inclined to deny it. Cuvier, limiting the age of the earth to the orthodox 6000 years, had stated that fossil bones of man did not exist. Moreover, up to the time of his death (1832) nothing had been found to disturb this generally received opinion. (Haddon, 1934:48)

But the geologists of the time knew the earth had to be older than 6000 years. And they also knew that Biblical chronologies of man did not fit properly into the scheme they were busily developing. But they were also for the most part very religious men. It was a controversial situation in which the scholars of the day moved slowly and with caution; the churchmen were powerful. Scientists were aware of what had happened to Copernicus (who allowed his "heretical" view of the universe to be published only while on his deathbed), to Giordano Bruno (who had been burned alive for his impiety), to Galileo (imprisoned and humiliated), to Kepler and Newton (both bitterly attacked and denounced for challenging scriptural authority), and to others less well known. But even so:

. . . The most conservative geologists were gradually obliged to admit that man had been upon the earth not merely six-thousand, or sixty-thousand, or one-hundred-and-sixty thousand years. And when, in 1863, Sir Charles Lyell, in his book on *The Antiquity of Man*, retracted solemnly his earlier view—yielding with a reluctance almost pathetic, but with a thoroughness absolutely convincing—the last stronghold of orthodoxy in this field fell. (A.D. White, 1955:241)

Even more pathetic were the last-ditch attempts being made to somehow reconcile the findings of geology with those of scripture. Perhaps the best example of this is the book *Omphalos* by Philip Henry Gosse (1857) which attempted to argue that although the Almighty had in fact created everything in six days He made it appear (for reasons that are never quite explained) that it had taken much longer. Thus glacial marks, various kinds of tilted and uplifted strata, fossils of all kinds, and all other geological data were believed to have been created overnight. Using capital letters, Gosse closed his book, ''IN SIX DAYS JEHOVAH MADE

HEAVEN AND EARTH, THE SEA, AND ALL THAT IN THEM IS," his ultimate refutation of geology (A.D. White, 1955:242).

As another example of the climate of opinion, consider briefly the problems of Jacques Boucher de Perthes (1788-1868) who, according to Robert H. Lowie's *The History of Ethnological Theory* (1937), was largely responsible for bringing about the revolution in our ideas about the age of the earth. Boucher de Perthes was a French amateur antiquarian who, in the 1830's, argued that man must at one time have been contemporaneous with extinct mammals. In 1838 he argued that stone axes he had unearthed were proof of human craftsmanship in the Pleistocene (a geological period which, in the thinking of that time, antedated human creation). Most of the authorities were unconvinced. Some argued the artifacts had sunk to the strata where they were found simply because of their weight. Others doubted they were of human origin at all. Still others denied the stratum was as old as Boucher de Perthes claimed it was. Boucher de Perthes himself later commented on his experiences as follows:

Practical men disdained to look; they were afraid; they were afraid of becoming accomplices in what they called a heresy, almost a mystification: they did not suspect my good faith, but they doubted my common sense. (quoted by Lowie, 1937:7)

At last, in 1854, Dr. Rigollot, a countryman and an antagonist of Boucher de Perthes, after carefully examining the sites and the evidence, announced his conversion. Others followed suit and eventually, as we have noted, even the great geologist Charles Lyell, who had vigorously resisted the evolutionary theory of Lamarck as long as possible, announced his complete acceptance of the new view. If we remember the reaction that Charles Darwin's *Origin of Species* provoked when it was published at about this same time (1859), we glimpse the truly revolutionary nature of the changes that were occurring in man's thinking about himself: the belief in the immutability of species was being broken, the concept of evolution was becoming more widely accepted, the antiquity of man and the duration of culture were being extended backward to a more remote time. While it is convenient to say, as T. K. Penniman does (1935:20), "with Darwin, the history of anthropology as a single, though many-sided science begins," the statement grossly overemphasizes Darwin's contribution and ignores the many other scientists who labored to bring about this remarkable departure in human thought. In fact, the idea of evolution, in its primary sense of change over time, had been fundamental to virtually all philosophy at least since Lucretius in the first century B.C. Darwin's contribution was to bring the notion of evolution to biology from social science, where it had already gained prominence, not to discover it for the first time. (Harris, 1968:122)

Geology, antiquarianism, and Darwin were not the only challenges to traditional authority. The age of exploration had been under way for some time. Travelers were beginning to visit even the remotest parts of the globe. But since

Saint Augustine, about 400 A.D., had denied in *The City of God* that men could inhabit the far corners of the earth, the religious explorers of the day were confronted with a remarkably confused situation. There were people of some sort where none should have been; moreover, it was not clear whether they should be considered men or, more properly, animals. During the Middle Ages, descriptions had been circulated of men with only one eye in the center of their foreheads, hermaphroditic people, people without mouths, people with their feet backward, people with eyes in their shoulders and no heads at all, and still others who, instead of speaking, barked like dogs (H. White, 1972). These notions were still influential when the new world was being discovered:

Spanish captains went forth to their conquest expecting to encounter many kinds of mythical beings and monsters depicted in medieval literature: giants, pygmies, dragons, griffins, white-haired boys, bearded ladies, human beings adorned with tails, headless creatures with eyes in their stomachs or breasts, and other fabulous folk. For a thousand years a great reservoir of curious ideas on man and semi-men had been forming in Europe, and was now freely drawn upon in America. . . .

. . . Governor Diego Velazquez, despite his years of experience in Cuba, instructed Cortez to look for strange beings with great flat ears and others with dog-like faces whom he might expect to see in Aztec lands. Francisco de Orellana was so positive that he had encountered warrior women on his famous voyage of 1540 that the mightiest river in South America was named the Amazon. The Devil himself was to be found, some believed, on a certain island in the Caribbean Sea . . . (Hanke, 1959:3-5)

Likewise, the discovery of subhuman primates—gorilla, orangutan, chimpanzee, and others—posed unprecedented problems of classification and understanding. There were arguments over whether "savages" and orangutans could breed with each other, whether chimpanzees could use fire and dance, whether gorillas were some form of grotesque human or merely some kind of animal, and so on. Evenually, of course, as more and more information on people from other parts of the globe was accumulated, and as more was learned of various exotic animals, it became evident that the people, at least, were capable of taking over new ideas, including Christianity. Indeed, this ability was used to define humanness. So the question shifted from whether they were people to what their origins were. Paracelsus, in 1520, had first voiced the notion of a *polygenist* theory—that is, the idea that perhaps not everyone was descended from Adam and Eve. He suggested, rather, that a number of distinct races had been created. Around this issue, as well as the dispute over the age of the earth, the battle was joined and the science of anthropology began to emerge.

The first anthropological society—the Société des Observateurs de l'Homme—was formed in Paris in 1800. Although it had distinguished membership including Cuvier, Lamarck, Geoffroy Saint-Hilaire, Pinel, Bougainville, and others equally famous, it lasted only until 1804 when Napoleon apparently with-

A

UNVERIFIED HUMANOIDS, AS REP-
RESENTED IN WOODCUTS OF THE FIF-
TEENTH AND SIXTEENTH CENTURIES. (a,
b) From the *Prodigiorum* of Lycos-
thenem, 1557. (c) From Edward
Fenton's *Certaine Secret Wonders of
Nature*, 1569. (d) From Hartmann
Schedel's *Liber Chronicarum*, 1493.

B

C

D

E

drew his support—an early example of the continuing conflict between government and the social sciences. The ambitions of the Society's founders were large.
One, Jauffret, suggested in 1802 no less than a comprehensive classification of
races, a complete comparative anatomy, a comparative dictionary of all languages, a complete anthropological topography of France, and a museum of
comparative ethnography. It is interesting, if depressing, to speculate about how
all of this information might have helped to ease the genocidal colonialism that was
continually expanding at precisely this time. Jauffret also suggested an experiment
(which, fortunately, was not carried out):

> . . . possible only in "a century as enlightened as ours"—to determine the characteris-
> tics of "natural man" by observing through adolescence infants "placed from their birth in
> a single enclosure, remote from all social institutions, and abandoned for the development
> of ideas and language solely to the instinct of nature." (Stocking, 1964:135)

In the virtual absence of any reliable or systematic information about non-
European peoples, this experiment was in its way an advanced and humane
proposal.

A major effort during the short-lived existence of the Society was collaboration
in a grandiose but ill-fated scientific expedition to the south coast of Australia. One
of the expedition members was François Péron, a medical student and self-styled
"anthropologist." Interestingly enough, although information was sadly lacking,
both doctors and travelers were asserting at this time that "savages" were superior
in health, strength, and general physical perfection to Europeans. Simultaneously,
however, it was commonly accepted that the same "savages" were almost totally
lacking in manners, religion, and, above all, morals. Thus Péron set out to test his
hypothesis that "moral perfection must be in inverse ratio to physical perfection."
He also carried with him two outlines for how to study "savage peoples," one by
Citizen Degérando (Joseph Marie de Gérando), *Considerations on the diverse
methods to follow in the observations of savage peoples*, and one by Georges
Cuvier, *Instructive note on the researches to be carried out relative to the
anatomical differences between the diverse races of man*. Degérando's instructions were in many ways remarkably insightful. He insisted, first of all, on careful
observation; having made such observations, one could then proceed with comparisons. From careful comparisons one could derive general laws of human
behavior. It was easier to derive them by observing "primitive" people,
Degérando argued, because such people were less modified by outside influences.
He also believed, as anthropologists still believe, that one could understand
"savages" only by learning their language and becoming "fellow citizens." He
cautioned that numerous observations would be necessary; sex, age, and other
factors must be considered, and that one should not assume that all such peoples
would be of a single type (Stocking, 1968:23-24).

Though Degérando's memorandum had flaws, it was nonetheless very far ahead of its time. One of its most interesting features was its humanitarianism. It lacked any reference at all to the idea of race or the permanence of hereditary differences between peoples of the earth. Cuvier's memorandum, on the other hand, was little more than instructions for grave-robbing, being mainly a plea for skeletons and especially skulls, obtained "in any manner whatever." In the light of how little was available at the time for students of comparative anatomy, Cuvier's instructions made sense, but when they are seen from an ethical or even from a local point of view their ethnocentric and essentially racist character become obvious (Stocking, 1968:30).

Péron found on his journey, much to his satisfaction it appears, that the assertions of travelers and doctors were incorrect—that, in terms of his own work at least, Europeans were not only more moral but also stronger than savages. His conclusions are amusing now but at the time were taken more seriously:

> In interpreting his results, Péron argued that the lush bounty of their natural habitat had made the Malayans lethargic. But only the poverty of their social status could explain the weakness of the Australians and the Tasmanians. If "these disinherited children of nature gave up their ferocious and vagabond customs" and gathered in villages, if "the rights of property excited in them a happy emulation"—then the effective resources of their physical environment would multiply, their social state improve, and their "temperament become more robust." Nor were these the only virtues of the civilized state. Commenting elsewhere on the surprise evinced by Tasmanians at the sexual virility of a French sailor who ravished a Tasmanian woman immediately upon stepping ashore, Péron hypothesized that Tasmanian sexual desire was, like that of animals, periodic. The sustained ability and interest of the European were environmental—the product of warm rooms, good food, spirituous liquors, more complex social relations, and leisure. (Stocking, 1964:145)

That morals cannot be measured quite as easily as physical strength seems not to have occurred to Péron. He measured physical strength through a variety of tests he devised specifically for that purpose. He "measured" morals simply by arbitrarily comparing the "savage" to Europeans. This was a mistake which continued in anthropology for many years.

Sometime late in the seventeenth century a curious paradox arose in which two contradictory views of "savages" began to exist simultaneously. On the one hand was the traditional view of them as wild men, grotesque, nonhuman, immoral, disgusting, and variously objectionable. But a new view regarded such creatures as "noble savages"—happy, cooperative, carefree children of nature living lives uncluttered with the woes and cares of civilization. It has been suggested that the concept of the noble savage was created and popularized, mostly by Rousseau, as a convenient fiction that influential writers of the period could employ to make people aware of the flaws in their own culture (H. White, 1972). Be that as it may, it was this contradiction that oriented Péron's quest; and it was his work, and this period of time, that ushered in the decline of the concept of the noble savage. What

NOBLE SAVAGE. "Tragedy of the Stone Age," an engraving from an exhibit at the 1889 Exposition Universelle. (Print courtesy of David H. Spain)

is even more important is that Péron and others, unlike Degérando, increasingly hinted that the differences found between peoples were due to race. Prior to the fifteenth century the idea of race had not been employed as an explanation for cultural differences; the known world was not large and the differences could be regarded as being between Christians and non-Christians. By the nineteenth century the concept of race became more and more important and was increasingly invoked to explain the differences that were being constantly discovered. The concept of culture emerged against this background, in part at least, as an alternative to race for explaining differences in behavior.

It is highly important to recognize that cultural anthropology emerged in the nineteenth century as part of an attempt to create a new and comprehensive "science of man." It emerged out of a crisis of the eighteenth century, a crisis that continued into the nineteenth century and is still with us now in the twentieth century. The Industrial Revolution had brought with it changes in human behavior so unprecedented and drastic they have been described by at least one scholar as *qualitative* rather than quantitative (Polanyi, 1944)—different, that is, in kind, not just in degree. The structure and coherence of medieval society had collapsed. There was, as Ernest Becker has eloquently stated,

. . . a *moral* crisis. The medieval world view had loosened its hold on society, and now there was nothing to replace it. Whereas the Church had offered the one thing that man needs as much as the air he breathes—a dependable mode of behavior for himself and his fellow man—it was precisely this that was now wanting. Society was headed for the kind of chaos that *Homo sapiens* fears most: the chaos of undependable and immoral behavior in his fellow men, the chaos of unregulated, irresponsible social life.

The science of man, let it be emphasized once and for all, had the solution of this moral crisis as its central and abiding purpose. Why build a science of man in society? In order to have a sound basis for a new moral creed, an agreed, factual body of knowledge that men of good will could use to lay down laws for a new social order. (1971:111)

That anthropology or any wider ''science of man'' has not resolved this crisis is a different story, one which will become clearer as we proceed with our investigation. The concept of culture emerged from this crisis as an aid to the understanding of it, as a way of understanding human variation, and as a tool for the examination of human nature itself.

CHAPTER **I** DEGENERATION AND PROGRESS

This chapter deals with what can be regarded as the first substantial systematic body of anthropological theory. This is usually referred to as "evolutionism" and the scholars who promoted it as "evolutionists." To distinguish these scholars from contemporary evolutionists we often emphasize that they were "early evolutionists."

Before this period the existence of "savage" people was usually explained by saying such people had descended from ancestors who had fallen from grace. Even earlier, it had been denied by some that such peoples were human at all. The early evolutionists attempted to disprove the degeneration theory and substituted in its place a belief in "progress." The theory they suggested fitted nicely with other prevailing beliefs of the time and gave rise to a series of related ideas—among them, "survivals," the so-called "biogenetic law" (ontogeny recapitulates phylogeny), the idea that it was possible to compare existing "savages" with our earliest ancestors. In this chapter I will attempt to show that many of the ideas of this formative period are with us yet, if not in anthropology then in related fields such as psychology and psychoanalysis. I will also mention examples of how evolutionary theory was applied to various dimensions of culture, particularly to religion.

The relationship of anthropology to the notion of evolution is a fact of great importance in the study of culture, not only because all of the early anthropologists were influenced by the belief in evolution, but also because it continues to affect the ways we think about ourselves to the present day. This influence was so pronounced during the formative years of anthropology that we typically refer to the founders of anthropology as *evolutionists*. It matters little which of the early anthropological scholars one has in mind, or even what, specifically, he happened to be interested in; he invariably used essentially the same evolutionary idea. The most basic form of this model can be shown simply as in the diagram.

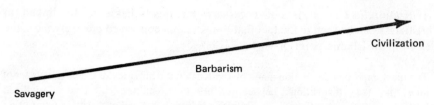

It was long taught in anthropology (as Marvin Harris points out; 1968:28), that this scheme was the brain child of Lewis Henry Morgan. Harris argues that it had been set forth much earlier (1748) by Montesquieu and elaborated by both A. R. J. Turgot (1750) and Adam Ferguson (1767). Though he is right, it also appears that a hierarchical view of this sort is virtually fundamental to human thought. All peoples must distinguish at least two categories, a "we" and a "they." And this distinction, as Hayden White has pointed out (1972:8), is essentially a difference between beliefs in an achieved and an imperfect humanity—very often a "we" who are humans or "people" and a "they" who are nonhuman or nonpeople. The idea that *all* people are fundamentally the same, if it is conceived of at all, is usually seen as meaning only all people of a single group. In Christianity this view is given an even greater emphasis: (1) because of the belief that mankind had been originally created as one but had subsequently fragmented as the result of improper human actions; and also (2) because of the idea of a vertical chain of being, embracing all of creation, but leading up to the Creator himself. It is absolutely crucial to understand that this distinction between people is made most fundamentally on *moral* and *ethnocentric* grounds. This fact can be seen very clearly in the following:

> . . . As long as men appeared different from one another, their division into higher and lower forms of humanity had to be admitted; for, in a theonomic [one subject to the authority of God] world, variation—class or generic—had to be taken as evidence of species corruption. For if there was one, all-powerful, and just God ordering the whole, how could the differences between men be explained, save by some principle which postulated a more perfect and a less perfect approximation to the ideal form of humanity contained in the mind of God as the paradigm of the species? Similarly, in a universe that was thought to be ordered in its essential relations by moral norms rather than by immanent physical causal forces, how could radical differences between men be accounted for, save by the assumption that the different was in some sense inferior to what passed for the normal, that is to say, the characteristics of the group from which the perception of differentness was made? (H. White, 1972:9)

The scheme thus places people on a continuum which in this case is a scale of value with "savages" on the bottom, "barbarians" somewhat higher, and "civilized" people at the very top. As it was seen in the context of evolution, it implies a time dimension as well as a scale of value—"savages" changed over time into "barbarians" and eventually might attain the "higher" stage of "civilization." That it is not necessary for this scheme to be linked to Christianity can be seen in the fact that Ibn Khaldun conceived precisely the same idea from an Islamic point of view:

> The most important distinction made by Ibn Khaldun in his study of the development of culture is the distinction between "primitive culture" . . . and "civilized culture" . . . or "civilization." . . . Primitive culture is defined primarily in terms of an economic way of life, which, in turn, colours the other aspects of a community, and distinguishes it from civilization. (Mahdi, 1971:193)

It is most important that no one underestimate the significance of this basic mode of thought, for although it has tended to disappear more from anthropology than from elsewhere, it survives even now in many insidious guises in other disciplines. And, although it is obviously not Lewis Henry Morgan's creation, we can say for our purposes here that it was Morgan who developed and elaborated it into what we now regard as *evolutionary stages*.

Lewis Henry Morgan

Although it is questionable indeed to assert as does Carl Resek, Lewis Henry Morgan's biographer, that Morgan "created the science of anthropology," there is no question that he was a unique and towering figure in American history. Darwin called him the New World's first social scientist. Henry Schoolcraft said he was the greatest authority on Indians in America. Henry Adams went even further, saying Morgan's work was the "foundation of all future American historical scholarship." Some argued that he was a socialist, others that his work was, in fact, a defense of capitalism. The truth about Morgan is not easy to come by because most of his personal papers were, unfortunately, destroyed at the time of his death (Resek, 1960). But whatever he was, it was Morgan's *Ancient Society* (1877) that influenced Karl Marx and through him Frederick Engels, a development of significance to which we will subsequently return.

Morgan was a New Englander. He attended Union College in Schenectady, New York, taking his degree in law. But for a number of years he could find no work so he read widely, lectured on temperance, and wrote scholarly articles on philosophy, the nature of society, instinct, and other related subjects. He was a great organizer and lodge member, which led him in 1843 to form "The Great Order of the Iroquois," which was to be modeled on the customs of the Iroquois. At first it was mostly just youthful exuberance; members dressed in Iroquois costumes and even carried tomahawks to their meetings. But this soon gave way to a more serious interest in American Indians. A chance meeting in a bookstore with a young Seneca Indian, Ely Parker, gave additional impetus to what was to become Morgan's lifelong devotion to *ethnology*. With a curious mixture of

LEWIS HENRY MORGAN (1818-1881). (Smithsonian Institution; National Anthropological Archives)

scholarship, romanticism, and paternalism, Morgan worked diligently all his life for various Indian causes and was instrumental in aiding Indian education, in preserving Indian tradition, and insofar as it was possible during his time, in protecting Indians from the greed of those who were attempting to take over their lands. Although Morgan's evolutionary scheme was subsequently challenged and profoundly modified by succeeding generations of anthropologists, his impact upon American ethnology remains.

Some appreciation of the virtually unlimited application of the basic evolutionary scheme can be gained from considering *Ancient Society* itself. Morgan was interested in the evolution of a number of specific things. He listed them as follows: Subsistence, Government, Language, the Family, Religion, House Life and Architecture, and Property (1877:5). There is probably no clearer statement anywhere describing the model to be employed for investigating these diverse things than Morgan's opening statement:

The latest investigations respecting the early condition of the human race, are tending to the conclusion that mankind commenced their career at the bottom of the scale and worked their way up from savagery to civilization through the slow accumulations of experimental knowledge.

As it is undeniable that portions of the human family have existed in a state of savagery, other portions in a state of barbarism, and still other portions in a state of civilization, it seems equally so that these three distinct conditions are connected with each other in a natural as well as necessary sequence of progress. Moreover, that the status attained by each branch respectively, is rendered probable by the conditions under which all progress occurs and by the known advancement of several branches of the family through two or more of these conditions.

An attempt will be made in the following pages to bring forward additional evidence of the rudeness of the early condition of mankind, of the gradual evolution of their mental and moral powers through experience, and of their protracted struggle with opposing obstacles while winning the way to civilization. It will be drawn, in part, from the great sequence of inventions and discoveries which stretch along the entire pathway of human progress; but chiefly from domestic institutions, which express the growth of certain ideas and passions. (1877:3)

Morgan then went on to attempt to demonstrate that *subsistence* had developed through five successive "arts of subsistence": "Natural Subsistence Upon Fruits and Roots on a Restricted Habitat," "Fish Subsistence," "Farinaceous Subsistence Through Cultivation," "Meat and Milk Subsistence," and "Unlimited Subsistence Through Field Agriculture."

The family, Morgan argued, had likewise evolved through five forms: the first type, "Consanguine," was based on the "intermarriage of brothers and sisters in a group," the second, called "Punaluan," was based on the "intermarriage of several brothers to each other's wives in a group; and of several sisters to each other's husbands in a group (the term *brother* here included male cousins, the term *sister*, female cousins). The third form, an intermediate one called "Syndyasmian," was "founded upon the pairing of a male with a female under the form of marriage, but without an exclusive cohabitation." The "Patriarchal" type "was founded upon the marriage of one man to several wives," and, finally, "Monogamian" families were, predictably enough "pre-eminently the family of civilized society, and . . . therefore essentially modern" (1877:27-28). We need not go into all of the details of Morgan's specific arguments here, and his terminology is outdated, but notice in the diagram, again, the form of the argument.

It should not be assumed that Morgan's theory of cultural evolution was quite as simple-minded as it appears here. Morgan believed, as is currently believed by a great many scholars, that the most satisfactory criterion for creating classifications or divisions of mankind would ultimately be on the basis of subsistence (the *technoeconomic base*, as it is sometimes called in anthropology nowadays). He felt, however, that investigation had not been carried far enough

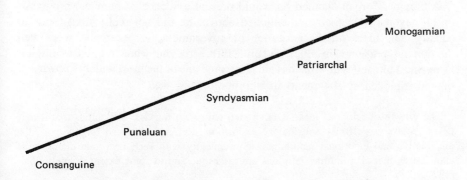

at his time to demonstrate this clearly. He thus attempted to link his stages of evolution to important inventions and discoveries and in the process of doing this he further subdivided each of the three main stages into a number of "statuses." The recapitulation of Morgan's scheme, as he presented it in *Ancient Society* (1877:12), is shown here.

RECAPITULATION.

Periods.	Conditions.
I.　Older Period of Savagery,	I.　Lower Status of Savagery,
II.　Middle Period of Savagery,	II.　Middle Status of Savagery,
III.　Later Period of Savagery,	III.　Upper Status of Savagery,
IV.　Older Period of Barbarism,	IV.　Lower Status of Barbarism,
V.　Middle Period of Barbarism,	V.　Middle Status of Barbarism,
VI.　Later Period of Barbarism,	VI.　Upper Status of Barbarism,

VII.　Status of Civilization.

I.　Lower Status of Savagery,	From the Infancy of the Human Race to the commencement of the next Period.
II.　Middle Status of Savagery,	From the acquisition of a fish subsistence and a knowledge of the use of fire, to etc.
III.　Upper Status of Savagery,	From the Invention of the Bow and Arrow, to etc.
IV.　Lower Status of Barbarism,	From the Invention of the Art of Pottery, to etc.
V.　Middle Status of Barbarism,	From the Domestication of animals on the Eastern hemisphere, and in the Western from the cultivation of maize and plants by Irrigation, with the use of adobe-brick and stone, to etc.
VI.　Upper Status of Barbarism,	From the Invention of the process of Smelting Iron Ore, with the use of iron tools, to etc.
VII.　Status of Civilization,	From the Invention of a Phonetic Alphabet, with the use of writing, to the present time.

(Morgan, 1877:12)

Although Morgan claimed he would present evidence of human "progress" on all seven of the themes mentioned above, he did not really treat them all equally. His ideas on the evolution of government, for example, were well thought out, presented in detail, and quite influential; but when he came to religion he excused himself with what has since become one of the most widely known and quoted ethnocentric statements in anthropology:

> The growth of religious ideas is environed with such intrinsic difficulties that it may never receive a perfectly satisfactory exposition. Religion deals so largely with the imaginative and emotional nature, and consequently with such uncertain elements of knowledge, that all primitive religions are grotesque and to some extent unintelligible. (1877:5)

As a further example of the fundamental theoretical position of evolutionism let us examine the work of perhaps the greatest early evolutionist of all, one who did not dismiss the subject of primitive religion in quite so cavalier a manner.

Edward Burnett Tylor

Edward Burnett Tylor was a Quaker, the son of a successful and liberal English Quaker father who owned a brass foundry. When threatened with tuberculosis in 1855 he was sent on a trip to the United States—to remove him from the English climate so that he might recover. While traveling in Cuba he met a somewhat eccentric but wealthy, enthusiastic, and intelligent antiquarian named Henry Christy. Christy was an avid collector of archaeological specimens and items of "primitive" art and manufacture. He soon interested Tylor in such things and the two of them set off on an adventurous journey through Mexico. Tylor, who, incidentally, had no university degree, soon wrote a successful book on the basis of his travels, *Anahuac or Mexico and the Mexicans, Ancient and Modern* (1861). This early interest, primarily in travel and sightseeing, led Tylor on to more serious but related interests. He eventually became keeper of the University Museum at Oxford University, Reader, and then Professor of Anthropology, also at Oxford (Haddon, 1930).

In a later book, Tylor provided what is usually understood as the first English-language definition of the culture concept:

> Culture, or civilization, taken in its wide ethnographic sense, is that complex whole which includes knowledge, belief, art, morals, law, custom, and any other capabilities and habits acquired by man as a member of society. (1903:1)

Like Morgan, Tylor appears to have been interested in virtually everything about man; but we will restrict ourselves here to a brief examination of his theory of religion. Like all of the scholars of his time, Tylor was naturally interested in

EDWARD BURNETT TYLOR (1832-1917). (National Portrait Gallery, London; Copyright Photograph)

evolution and also in *origins*—hence, in the origin of religion. His explanation for religion, correct or not, must be appreciated as a truly remarkable intellectual achievement.

Many of the scholars of Tylor's day had asserted that "savages" simply had no religious beliefs. Some of these writers, Tylor argued, gave evidence of inconsistency in their works. He decided their understanding of what constituted religion must be faulty—that it was ethnocentric:

. . . Lang, Moffat, and Azara are authors to whom ethnography owes much valuable knowledge of the tribes they visited, but they seem hardly to have recognized anything short of the organized and established theology of the higher races as being religion at all. (1871:419)

Tylor decided religion would have to be defined more generally, as "the belief in Spiritual Beings" (1871:419), and, although he was willing to concede that men could have emerged from some "non-religious condition," he knew of no contemporary men without religion (1871:425). He associated religion with the

THE BEAR DANCE: PREPARING FOR A BEAR HUNT. George Catlin (1796-1872). (Courtesy of the Smithsonian Institution; National Collection of Fine Arts)

fact that all men, everywhere, confronted directly two fundamental biological experiences: death and dreams. What was the difference between a live body and a dead one? And what, or who, were the creatures that appeared in dreams? Tylor postulated that humans, in reflecting upon these two experiences, would inevitably be led to invent the concept of the soul. His definition of the soul is worth quoting:

It is a thin unsubstantial human image, in its nature a sort of vapour, film, or shadow; the cause of life and thought in the individual it animates; independently possessing the personal consciousness and volition of its corporeal owner, past or present; capable of leaving the body far behind, to flash swiftly from place to place; mostly impalpable and invisible, yet also manifesting physical power, and especially appearing to men waking or asleep as a phantom separate from the body of which it bears the likeness; continuing to exist and appear to men after the death of that body; able to enter into, possess, and act in the bodies of other men, of animals, and even of things. (1871:429)

Tylor believed that "savages" thought about animals differently from "civilized" man, that they did not distinguish an absolute or qualitative difference between men and animals. From the idea of human souls, therefore, the idea of souls of animals would follow as a simple and natural step. And since plants likewise partake of life—they grow, reproduce, and die—it would not be unnatural to attribute souls to them also. Finally, since savages are *anthropomorphic*, they would also attribute souls to objects such as tools and weapons, sticks and stones. Likewise, Tylor believed that savages did not

THE
STORY OF MAN:

A HISTORY OF THE HUMAN RACE,

FROM THE CREATION TO THE PRESENT TIME, EMBRACING AN ACCOUNT OF THE ORIGIN OF RACES
AND THEIR DISPERSION OVER THE GLOBE;

ALSO,

The Wondrous Story of Prehistoric Man, the Cave, Lake and Tree Dwellers, and
the Strange Wild People who Inhabit Africa, Asia, Arabia,
Egypt, Syria, South America, and

THE ISLANDS OF THE SEA,

With a Thrillingly Picturesque Record of the Mighty Convulsions of Nature that
Destroyed Continents, Threw Up Mountain Peaks, Established Lakes and
Oceans, and Buried Beneath the Waves the Ancient Splendors of

THE LOST ATLANTIS;

Showing Man's Advancement from His Low Condition of Barbarism after the Sin
of Disobedience in the Garden of Eden, Including

THE AGES OF STONE, BRONZE, IRON AND STEEL,

Embracing also a Full History of the Ancient Druids, Celts and Norsemen, and those
Bold Rovers of the Sea—the Vikings.

EMBELLISHED WITH

Many Curious Facts Singular Customs, Wonderful and Weird Adventures, and a
Multitude of Marvellous Incidents Connected with

THE HISTORY OF ANCIENT PEOPLES AND WILD RACES OF MODERN TIMES.

BY J. W. BUEL,

AUTHOR OF

"The Beautiful Story," "The Living World," "Sea and Land," "The World's Wonders,"
"Exile Life in Siberia," Etc.

ILLUSTRATED WITH NEARLY 600 SPLENDID ENGRAVINGS,

From Scenes and Incidents Described in this Marvellous Record,

AND

MAGNIFICENT COLORED PLATES.

NORTH AMERICAN PUBLISHING CO.,
ST. LOUIS, MO.
1889.

TITLE PAGE, *THE STORY OF MAN*, BUEL, 1889.

distinguish subjective from objective experience: "Even in healthy waking life,
the savage or barbarian has never learnt to make that rigid distinction between
subjective and objective, between imagination and reality, to enforce which is
one of the main results of scientific education" (1871:445). In consequence of
this lack of judgment, savages would believe that the various phantoms and
figures who visited them during their dreams and trances were real. Eventually
these two beliefs—in souls and phantoms—would be joined together to produce
what Tylor termed *animism*. He believed that "Animism is, in fact, the
groundwork of the Philosophy of Religion, from that of savages up to that of
civilized men" (1871:426).

Animism eventually evolves into two great dogmas, forming parts of one consistent doctrine. The first is the belief in the souls of individual creatures which can survive after death and second, a belief concerning spirits up to the rank of powerful deities who are believed "to affect or control the events of the material world and man's life here and hereafter" (1871:426). The second, the belief in spirits, comes later in human development and can be traced to the belief in souls upon which it is based:

> It seems as though the conception of a human soul, when once attained by man, served as a type or model on which he framed not only his ideas of other souls of lower grade, but also his ideas of spiritual beings in general, from the tiniest elf that sports in the long grass up to the heavenly Creator and Ruler of the World, the Great Spirit. (1871:110)

Having thus established the basic evolutionary sequence involved in the history of religion, Tylor posed related questions. If one has a belief in souls this leads, of course, to further questions—what, for example, happens to souls after death? Tylor suggested that two general answers to this question had evolved. The first and earliest was the idea of the transmigration of souls; the second, the belief in the independent existence of souls after death. Transmigration, he thought, was a system of belief associated with the "lower levels of humanity," the independent-existence idea being associated with "higher" levels. A belief in the independent existence of souls leads to a further question: Where do they go? Tylor argued that three alternatives had been used to explain this: first, and most "primitive," a belief in a land of souls on earth; next, an intermediate notion, that of a subterranean Hades; and, finally, the highest-order belief, that of heaven.

The doctrine of spirits undergoes a series of changes, too, leading always, of course, from lower to higher. One who has evolved to the level of a belief in spirits must also, according to Tylor, come to believe they can "hover about" people, animals, and objects, and thus act through them and affect them. This idea, in turn, allows the "savage" to carry a useful spirit about with him (since it is believed to be hovering around some object he can move about—a charm, an amulet, an effigy, and so on). It also allows him to place a harmful spirit somewhere else if he wishes. This notion also allows him to set up a spirit (deity) for worship in the body of an animal, in a shrine, or in a temple. For Tylor, this chain of thought explained *Fetishism* and *Idolatry*, Fetishism being the "doctrine of spirits embodied in, or attached to, or conveying influence through, certain material objects" (1871:144). Idolatry was regarded by Tylor as being fundamentally the same, with Fetishism lower on the scale fading imperceptibly into Idolatry. Idolatry was regarded as an intermediate form of belief, being found neither among very "low" peoples nor among the "highest."

There are times, it seems, when a person's own soul serves him satisfactorily enough, but there are also times when he has a need for far more than that. This need led eventually, Tylor argued, to the idea of personal or guardian spirits—"the interventions of . . . a second superior soul" (1871:v. 2, p. 200). But "To the minds of the lower races it seems that all nature is possessed, pervaded, crowded, with spiritual beings" (1871:v. 2, p. 185)—a vast number of spirits of all kinds. There could be spirits of almost everything that "savages" used. Personality, we might say, was applied to natural things. This belief led, in Tylor's scheme, to tree worship, animal worship, water worship, patron animals, totemism, and the like.

At first a spirit was ascribed to each individual thing—each oak tree, for example, would be believed to have its own spirit. But this association gave way eventually to what Tylor called "species deities," an idea he developed from a clue he found in Auguste Comte, the famous French philosopher. Comte had distinguished deities from fetishes partly on the grounds that fetishes governed a single object and were inseparable from it, whereas deities (or gods) controlled a number of different objects simultaneously. "Thus . . . when . . . the similar vegetation of the different oaks of a forest led to a theological generalization from their common phenomena, the abstract being thus produced was no longer the fetish of a single tree, but became the god of the forest; here, then, is the intellectual passage from fetishism to polytheism, reduced to the inevitable preponderance of specific over individual ideas" (Tylor, 1871:243).

Ultimately out of polytheism arose the concept of a supreme deity, more powerful than the others and in some way having control of all of them. Tylor insisted that the notion of a supreme deity did not necessarily imply monotheism. He felt that any discussion of this problem would hinge on the definition of the relation of the Christian God to its host of supporting saints and angels, as well as the relation of the high god of polytheistic religions to the minor deities of those religions.

Tylor's theory of religion has been criticized as being overintellectualistic. That is, he was concerned almost solely with what people must have been thinking when someone died and paid too little attention to the practical, emotional, and social factors that must also have been involved. R. R. Marett, another distinguished English anthropologist, brought up the question of practical considerations:

. . . The mourner has to act as undertaker as well. Here is the dead man's body; what, then, are we to do with it? Here is the dead man's gear, with the smell of him, as the Australian natives say, still in it—that smell which itself testifies to his change of condition. Will he want this gear any longer; or, in any case, do we dare to use it ourselves? (1936:110)

Sigmund Freud and Emile Durkheim, respectively, brought up the questions of emotional and social factors. The point here, however, is not to dissect in detail Tylor's theory of religion, but rather to demonstrate again the ubiquitous evolutionary paradigm; observe the diagram (next page).

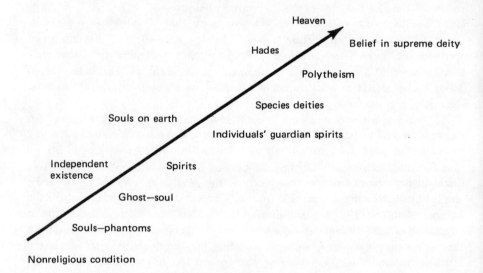

James George Frazer, J. J. Bachofen, Henry Maine, and Others

Bear in mind that Morgan and Tylor are here being used merely as examples of a way of thinking about culture and evolution. All of the scholars of the period thought in essentially the same way. James George Frazer, who had been stimulated by Tylor, in his classic work *The Golden Bough* (1890), not only set forth the principles of magic for the first time, but argued that magic was an early form of science based upon incorrect notions of cause and effect—basically that things which were similar or had once been in contact with each other could affect or continue to affect each other at a distance. Out of this faulty magical belief, Frazer argued, arose religion, a higher achievement but one still trying to cope with the question of causality. Finally, he felt, science would inevitably emerge as the correct way of dealing with this question. Indeed, Frazer ends *The Golden Bough* with this rather optimistic prose which gives much insight into the mood of the period:

The abundance, the solidity, and the splendour of the results already achieved by science are well fitted to inspire us with a cheerful confidence in the soundness of its methods. Here at last, after grasping about in the dark for countless ages, man has hit upon a clue to the labyrinth, a golden key that opens many locks in the treasury of nature. It is probably not too much to say that the hope of progress—moral and intellectual as well as material—in the future is bound up with the fortunes of science, and that every obstacle placed in the way of scientific discovery is a wrong to humanity. (1890:825)

It has been said that Frazer was "the last of the scholastics" and actually wrote *The Golden Bough* "as an extended footnote to a line in Virgil he felt he did not

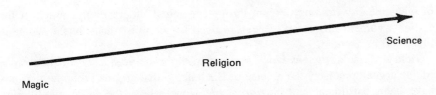

understand . . . ." (LaBarre, 1954:344). It appears, however, that Frazer thought of himself more as a writer than as a scholar (Leach, 1966), which role perhaps explains his remarkable prose style. It also makes the point that anthropology in this early period was less a profession than the hobby of a number of gentlemen of leisure. In fact, there was as yet no profession of anthropology. Nevertheless, at that same time more and more data about non-Western peoples were accumulating, more and more information from geology and archeology, and more and more knowledge in general.

At this time the term *culture* was used only in the singular and synonymously with the term *"civilization."* But if there was only a single grand tradition—civilization—how was it that people could be so different from one another? Why had some people attained the apex of civilization while others remained as "savages" or "barbarians"? The primary concern of all of the scholars of the period was to explain the process of becoming "civilized," and to reconcile, classify, and make sense out of the wealth of information that was so rapidly accumulating. Modern anthropology is much indebted to the gentlemen scholars who attempted to do this, whatever their excesses and shortcomings.

One piece of information acquired by these early students of man was that in some places people did not inherit rights in property and other things through their fathers, as "civilized" people did, but rather through females. J. J. Bachofen, another evolutionist, was the first person to attempt to deal with this question of *matrilineal descent*. In his 1861 book *Das Mutterrecht* (mother-right), Bachofen argued that social life for humans began with a period of sexual promiscuity. Women were entirely at the mercy of males. In such a situation the only parent relationship that could be determined with certainty was the physical (material) fact of motherhood. But women struggled to liberate themselves—and eventually succeeded because of their religiosity. Matrilineality now prevailed for a time and, in addition, female deities were believed to be more important than male: the moon was considered more important than the sun, the earth took precedence over the sky, and in general the order we now tend to think of was reversed. During this time women established the institution of the family by obliging men to marry them. But, as it turns out, according to Bachofen's speculations, the reign of women was predicated on an inferior principle—the basic and somewhat animal-like material ties between mother and child. Men established the higher religious principle of fatherhood and eventually took control. Thus *patrilineality* (tracing descent only through males) evolves out of matrilineality (tracing descent through females). Interestingly, much of this earlier argument has recently been revived by some of those in the women's liberation movement.

Henry Maine's *Ancient Law* appeared in the same year as *Das Mutterrecht*. Maine argued precisely the reverse of Bachofen—that originally the family must have been patrilineal and *patriarchical*! Nonetheless, the basic evolutionary point of view remained secure. Maine contended that whereas the unit of ancient society was the family, this evolved in such a way that in modern society the unit was the individual. There were corresponding changes from the common ownership of property to private ownership, and from a social organization based upon principles of kinship to a form based upon territory. It must be pointed out that these basic ideas set out by Maine are widely accepted today. Many scholars are attempting to deal with the implications of changing from kinship-based obligations to those that result from legal contracts. A great many more are still wrestling with the pros and cons of group versus individual ownership of land, the means of production, and the like. There are many in modern society who decry the breakdown of the family that they believe to have accompanied the process of becoming "civilized." Even Lewis Henry Morgan's basic findings about kinship remain current and constitute the basis for one important school of thought on that subject (Fortes, 1969).

There are many other examples of the scholarship of this period—Herbert Spencer, perhaps the greatest evolutionist of all, John Lubbock (Lord Avebury), J. F. McLennan, Andrew Lang, R. H. Codrington, Edward Westermarck, and more. But let us shift from the men and their particular interests to the questions, problems, and implications of the evolutionary scheme itself.

Questions and Problems of Early Evolutionism

Obviously, when dealing with such things as stages, development, periods, successions, and sequences, there is the problem of when one begins and when another one ends. It was not supposed by any of the evolutionist scholars that the changes they dealt with were clear-cut and precisely defined. Indeed, the fact that they were not was cleverly used itself as proof for the general evolutionary notion involved. This argument can be seen in the concept of *survivals* first employed by Tylor:

Among evidence aiding us to trace the course which the civilization of the world has actually followed is that great class of facts to denote which I have found it convenient to introduce the term "survivals." These are processes, customs, opinions, and so forth which have been carried on by force of habit into a new state of society different from that in which they had their original home, and they thus remain as proofs and examples of an older condition of culture out of which a newer has been evolved. (1903:16)

The notion of survivals allowed the evolutionists to explain the presence of certain things—"processes, customs, opinions, and so forth"—in European societies in particular, that would otherwise seem totally inconsistent with their evolutionary framework. If, for example, religion and science had evolved out of a previous belief in magic, how did one explain the fact that in Europe many people nailed iron horseshoes over their doors? Tylor was able to show that in European folklore iron doors kept away fairies and rendered them powerless. This fact he could relate in turn to earlier beliefs about witchcraft. Thus he could argue that the custom of nailing up horseshoes was a survival of previous beliefs in magic and witches. Likewise, he was able to explain palmistry, astrology, and indeed the entire range of superstitious beliefs and practices of his day. He could also explain the presence of many other things such as buttons on the sleeves of men's coats or the continued existence of bows and arrows. Some of these things may have been more useful than others, it is true, which becomes a point of contention later on, but they all fitted nicely in this way into the grandiose reconstruction of history the evolutionists were undertaking.

Another question which arose from the use of stages and periods had to do with the order of various steps. Was it necessary for certain stages to precede others? Could a society simply bypass one stage altogether? Did all societies necessarily evolve through all of the same stages? Were the sequences fixed? Was the process, in short, one of *unilineal evolution*? This was an obviously crucial issue but one that has never been completely clarified in the history of anthropology. The early evolutionists have often been accused, rather unjustly, of being invariably unilineal evolutionists. The facts are not so simple. Some of the scholars of the period, such as J. F. McLennan (1876), appear to have been fairly insistent upon fixed sequences; others, such as Maine, Morgan, and Tylor, were either not certain or not completely consistent on this point.

Considerable consequences follow from a belief that the stages of evolution are fixed and immutable so that one of them must be attained before the next one becomes possible. Such a belief, for example, allows one to predict accurately not only the direction of change but also what form each change would take. Further, although not absolutely crucial to either of them, the belief in fixed sequences is particularly congruent with both the monogenic and polygenic theories (that man descended from either one or several origins). It is also consistent with what came to be known as the *psychic unity of mankind*, a position we will discuss later.

But all of the above notions—evolution, survivals and unilineal stages—were linked to still another, namely the idea of *progress*. As Marvin Harris has indicated, the word *progress* was a standby of the Enlightenment, being used to convey "a sense of moral satisfaction with certain evolutionary trends" (1968:37). The term implies, then, not only that demonstrable change is present but also that it is in a specific direction—and this direction is arbitrarily defined as good. Here is the moral dimension of which we spoke earlier. Even though some of the evolutionists did not insist on unilineal steps, they almost all appear to have assumed progress. The progress they saw, of course, led from a previous condition (a "state of nature," "savagery," or the like) out of which the contemporary one (nineteenth-century European society) was believed to have evolved. Thus nineteenth-century Western European civilization was the standard by which change was evaluated—and thus also science was "higher" than magic, monogamy "higher" than polygyny, patriliny more "progressive" than matriliny, and territory a more desirable criterion for political organization than kinship. It is a powerful and insidious notion and one that influences our thinking even yet. The problem is that the notion of progress is fairly easily applied to those closely interrelated aspects of Western European culture we call technology, science, and knowledge (although even here there are difficulties), but far less easily applied to anything else. One of the better descriptions of this is from the economic historian Sidney Pollard:

> Improvement, or progress, has been understood in many different senses. Since the Renaissance, few men in the West, at least, have doubted the continued progress in knowledge of the environment of man, in the natural sciences, and more recently, few have doubted the continued improvement in technology derived from them. This is the base of the pyramid of the believers in progress and includes all those who believe in progress of some kind. There are almost as many who would add that this technological improvement will also lead, in the future, to greater wealth, to an improvement in the material conditions of life, and this may be said to form the next higher, and scarcely narrower, layer of the pyramid . . . .
>
> There would, however, be considerably fewer, and perhaps a minority only, who would feel equally persuaded that the tendency of the past, to be continued into the future, includes the improvement of social and political organization, and that human societies will become better governed, more just, freer, more equal, more stable or in other ways better equipped to permit a higher development of the human personality. (1971:12)

Pollard goes on to observe that there would be still fewer who believe that people will actually learn to control their institutions more effectively or that human nature will change for the better, or that people will become kindlier or more moral. As he says, too little change has been observed along these lines to give cause for this type of optimism.

Nevertheless, to our earlier paradigms we must add direction—the further dimension, "progress," as in the combining diagram.

All of this outlook becomes more clear, perhaps, when we consider how these scholars used the basic *comparative method* involved. This method is based most fundamentally upon the assumption that present-day cultures bear resemblances to cultures of the past. Some present-day cultures ("savages" and "barbarians") resemble those of the past much more clearly than do others ("civilizations"), so the former, it was argued, could be used to understand the evolutionary processes

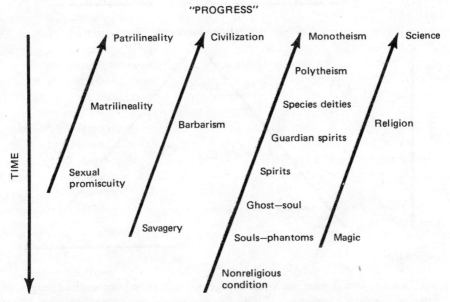

involved in the development of the latter. To do so it is first necessary to arrange contemporary cultures along a continuum from more recent to more ancient. Such a series, as in the next diagram, would have been widely acceptable to the evolutionists. And, as the basic idea is that some societies are more ancient than others, the line on which societies are arranged in space must also slope downward a bit to indicate time.

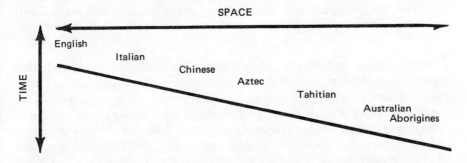

When the distance-ethnic axis and the progress-culture axis are joined at their high points, the resulting scheme exhibits space-ethnic categories and progress-culture categories in what appear to be corresponding levels, as the combined diagram shows (next page).

With this scheme in mind, the evolutionists suggested, the inquirer desiring to know something about the earliest stages of modern European culture

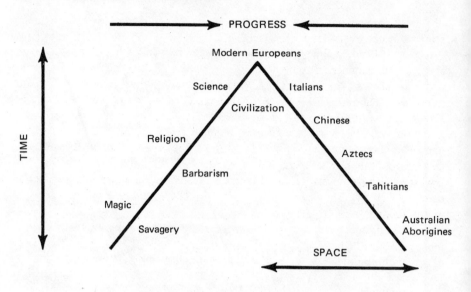

(civilization) could gain such knowledge by examining the current stages of existing "savage" societies—Tahitians, Australian Aborigines, or other. That is, one could equate existing "primitives" with prehistoric cultures. This position can be seen clearly in the following by A. Lane-Fox Pitt-Rivers, a well-known English archeologist:

> . . . the existing races, in their respective stages of progression, may be taken as the bona fide representatives of the races of antiquity . . . . They thus afford us living illustrations of the social customs, the forms of government, laws, and warlike practices, which belong to the ancient races from which they remotely sprang, whose implements, resembling with but little difference, their own, are now found low down in the soil . . . . (1906:53)

Archeologists had conclusively demonstrated that stone tools and other implements of the past did appear in a certain sequence and were also still being used by contemporary peoples. And, since paleontologists had likewise shown that many extinct animals could be understood only through a knowledge of contemporary animals found in distant parts of the globe, the equation of savages with ancestors came to be widely accepted and firmly held. This is not to say that all of the evolutionists accepted this equation literally. Many of them—certainly Morgan, Tylor, and Lubbock/Avebury—knew that existing peoples could be regarded only as *approximating* ancestral groups. In any case, in a revised form, we still retain and use this idea, and there are contemporary evolutionary theories in anthropology that are considerably more sophisticated.

The difficulties with the comparative method, as the early evolutionists employed it, had less to do with the method itself, perhaps, than with the absence of solid information about non-Western peoples and with the blatantly ethnocentric, even downright racist, tendencies of the anthropologists themselves. Lord Avebury is usually cited as the best example of both. His works abound with instances of the uncritical acceptance of the statements of travelers and missionaries. The fact that he could accept such statements must be attributed to his beliefs about racial superiority. Thus in *The Origin of Civilization and the Primitive Condition of Man* (1870) we find him asserting that "savages" often have "absurd reasons for what they do and believe" (p. 5), and he acceptingly quotes another "authority" that: "The mind of the savage then appears to rock to and fro out of mere weakness, and he tells lies and talks nonsense" (p. 7). "The lowest races have no institution of marriage; true love is almost unknown among them . . ." (p.54). They have "no religion" (p. 184), and are "entirely wanting in moral feeling" (p. 324). And so on. We have already noted Lewis Henry Morgan's attitude, even though unlike his contemporaries he had actually encountered "savages" first hand, that "all primitive religions are grotesque and to some extent unintelligible" (1877:5). Morgan also argued, in a different context, for the intellectual inferiority of Negroes, saying "It is too thin a race intellectually to be fit to propagate . . ." (Resek, 1960:63). Ironically, one might observe that the anthropologist's ethnocentrism was mild when compared to some of the more popular accounts of "odd" people:

> In his personal habits no human being is more filthy than the Fuegian. He never uses water for washing purposes; nor cleans the dirt from his skin in any way. He has no more idea of putting water to such use, than he has of drowning himself in it; and in respect to cleanliness, he is not only below most other savages, but below the brutes themselves: since even these are taught cleanliness by instinct. But no such instinct exists in the mind of the Fuegian; and he lives in the midst of filth. The smell of his body can be perceived at a considerable distance; and Hotspur's fop might have had reasonable grounds of complaint, had it been a Fuegian who came between the "wind and his nobility." To use the pithy language of one of the old navigators, "The Fuegian stinks like a fox." (Reid, 1861:460)

Mayne Reid, author of the above, seems to have been a traveler and writer. It is difficult to assess the influence of such people but certainly there were many of them during the nineteenth century and much of what people think they know of each other must have come from their popular literature.

The ubiquitous racism of the time enabled the evolutionists to ignore what would otherwise have been a number of more troublesome questions. Virtually all of the early anthropologists seem to have believed in racial determinism, however implicit rather than explicit it may have been in their work. The effect of this belief was on the one hand to keep them from seeing the limitations of their evolutionary theory and on the other to let them ignore questions they might well have had to ask had they not assumed racial superiority.

To understand this distortion properly it is necessary to look at the

A FUEGIAN ATTACHING A BONE HEAD TO A HARPOON. (Smithsonian Institution; National Anthropological Archives; from Hyades and Deniker, *Mission Scientifique du Cap Horn*, vol. II, Paris, 1891)

criticisms of those who followed the evolutionists. But note that the concept of culture, although introduced and defined for the first time, is not further developed. "Culture," as used by the evolutionists, is no more than a synonym for "civilization." The scholars we have discussed do not speak of individual cultures but, rather, of the evolution of culture, or aspects of it, in a generic sense. They were primarily interested in how they, Europeans, arrived at their "higher," "civilized" state. It remains for those scholars who follow to speak of cultures—that is, to speak in the plural, to concentrate on individual cases, and to further elaborate the concept of culture.

Implications of Evolutionism

The influence of this evolutionary mode of thought cannot be overstated. It influenced not only anthropology but also psychology, and particularly psychoanalytic psychology. As the notions involved here survive to the present day, and are related to current racist positions, we need to consider how this mode of thought came about.

When a powerful new theory comes along it inevitably generates a number of related ideas. One such idea generated by the theory of evolution was Haeckel's "biogenetic law." This was based upon work in embryology, in which it had been observed that features in the embryonic development of individual organisms sometimes resemble those which appear in adult individuals of earlier zoological form. For example, the human fetus at one period of development has gill slits similar to those of fishes. And, because such features sometimes appear in the individual in the same order in which they arose in the ancestral series, the phenomenon was generalized as the "recapitulation hypothesis"—"ontogeny recapitulates phylogeny." That is, the development of an individual organism (ontogenetic development), repeats the development of the species (phylogenetic development). This idea was quickly extended to the postnatal period as well. It was said by some, for example, that the grasping reflex in newborn human infants was a "simian phase in development as well as proof of the arboreal ancestry of man," and that the explanation for children sometimes walking on all fours is that this behavior represents an earlier mode, and the like (Hallowell, 1955:15). It was further suggested that the development of the child exhibited recapitulation with respect to thinking as well as other forms of behavior. Thus the development of thought in the child could be equated with the development of thought in the species—the evolution of intelligence, that is.

Once the scholars of the time had this idea it was a simple step to link it to the evolutionary paradigm we have already discussed. This association allowed people to believe that the idea of development sequences found in individuals, particularly in the development of thinking, was supported by anthropology:

Contemporaneously with the formulation and application of the recapitulation hypothesis, some anthropologists of the late nineteenth century were attempting to apply the biological concept of evolution to nonbiological phenomena. It was thought that human culture had evolved through a unilinear series of stages culminating in occidental civilization. Hence the aboriginal peoples that still survived represented arrested stages of cultural development that the more advanced races had passed through.

Usually the backwardness of these savage peoples, implicitly, if not explicitly, was interpreted as an index of their limited mental capacities. Hence, the idea of different levels of mental development within the human race as a whole was supported by anthropology, despite the fact that there was no direct evidence that this was true and that the stages of evolutionary cultural development postulated were arrived at by analogical reasoning rather than by actual historical investigation. (Hallowell, 1955:15)

In the hands of certain psychologists of the period—most notably G. Stanley Hall, who was the first child psychologist to give explicit psychological content to such stages as infancy, childhood, and adolescence—this idea permitted the direct equation of "savage" thought with the thought of children. And it allowed people to believe that children's drawings, for example, were like the drawings of "primitive" people. This likening, in turn, was associated with the Lamarckian belief in the inheritance of acquired characteristics.

It is possible to see how simple patterns of behavior in the postnatal period might be accounted for via inheritance without the idea of acquired characteristics—such things, for example, as simple reflexes. But it is difficult indeed to understand how more complicated types of behavior, including thought, can be thus accounted for. If the development of thought and behavior in children parallels the evolution of culture, what can the mechanism be that allows that to happen? The easiest answer, of course, is that the infant inherits acquired characteristics that were developed by his ancestors in the past. As the recapitulation theory came into prominence and was developed at the end of the nineteenth century and prior to the discovery of modern genetics, this was by no means an untenable assumption.

It is from this procedure that people have developed the ideas of such things as memory traces in the species (Freud, 1939), archetypes (Jung, 1959), and so on. This is seen clearly throughout the work of G. Stanley Hall:

. . . We are influenced in our deeper, more temperamental dispositions by the life-habits and codes of conduct of we know not what unnumbered hosts of ancestors, which like a cloud of witnesses are present throughout our lives. . . . Our souls are echo-chambers in which their whispers reverberate. . . . We have to deal with the archaeology of mind, with zones or strata which precede consciousness as we know it, compared to which even it, and especially cultured intellect, is an upstart novelty. (1904:61)

As for stages of development, Hall felt they were a function of maturation and racial inheritance:

. . . Adolescence is a new birth, for the higher and more completely human traits are now born. The qualities of body and soul that now emerge are far newer. The child comes from and harks back to a remoter past; the adolescent is neo-atavistic, and in him the later acquisitions of the race slowly become pre-potent. Development is less gradual and more saltatory, suggestive of some ancient period of storm and stress when old moorings were broken and a higher level attained. (Hall, 1904:xiii)

Hall did not give much weight, if any at all, to social, cultural, or environmental factors in development. He believed the individual became what he was because of his racial past and his level of maturity. He also held, as crucial to his theory, the notion that the child had to pass through each stage in order, as one was the necessary stimulus for the next. This is similar to what we find in psychoanalytic theory and obviously parallels the belief in unilineal cultural evolution. While there may well be some stages of development in children as a result of the limitations of physical maturation, this is a matter entirely different from the evolution of "civilization." Nonetheless, the original theory was constructed by analogy with the idea of cultural evolution and not on the basis of independent work.

G. Stanley Hall was a very influential psychologist and this mode of thinking about the development of children became widespread. But even more unfortunate is the fact that Freud himself fell under the influence of the evolutionists' theorizing. It is no accident, perhaps, that G. Stanley Hall was responsible for first inviting both Freud and Jung to the United States.

Freud had read all of the major anthropologists of his day; these were, for the most part, those mentioned in this chapter. There is no doubt that he was familiar with evolutionism. That he was familiar with and used both the recapitulation hypothesis and the notion of the inheritance of acquired characteristics is demonstrated repeatedly throughout his work:

. . . The era to which the dream-work takes us back is "primitive" in a two-fold sense: in the first place, it means the early days of the *individual*—his childhood—and, secondly, in so far as each individual repeats in some abreviated fashion during childhood the whole course of the development of the human race, the reference is phylogenetic. (Freud, 1920:177)

And again:

. . . The experiences undergone by the ego seem at first to be lost to posterity; but, when they have been repeated often enough and with sufficient intensity in the successive individuals of many generations, they transform themselves, so to say, into experiences of the id, the impress of which is preserved by inheritance. Thus in the id, which is capable of being inherited, are stored up vestiges of the existences led by countless former egos; and, when the ego forms its super-ego out of the id, it may perhaps only be reviving images of egos that have passed away and be securing them a resurrection. (1935:52)

There is no need to dwell upon the overwhelming influence of Freud and psychoanalytic theory on the twentieth century. Some of Freud's followers, particularly Sandor Ferenczi and Marie Bonaparte, have carried the recapitulation notion to even further extremes. Indeed, Otto Fenichel, in his influential *The Psychoanalytic Theory of Neurosis* (1945) goes so far as to assert: "Animal crackers, loved by children, are significant remnants of early cannibalistic fantasies'' (1945:63). Jung's commitment to this point of view is also well known and can be seen throughout his work, from the earliest to the latest:

> As the evolution of the embryonic body repeats its prehistory, so the mind also develops through a series of prehistoric stages. The main task of dreams is to bring back a sort of "recollection" of the prehistoric, as well as the infantile world, right down to the level of the most primitive instincts. (1968:89)

Although this idea still survives, many psychoanalysts and psychiatrists in recent years accept it only implicitly, being unaware, it seems, of its importance to the theories that inform their work. Since, unfortunately, much of the work of psychoanalysts and psychiatrists has become divorced from theory, this does not constitute the problem for them that it should.

G. Stanley Hall, Freud, and Jung are by no means the only important figures to have been influenced by these early evolutionary ideas. Jean Piaget, by far the most influential contemporary student of child development, began his remarkable career in the early part of the twentieth century, just at the time psychoanalytic theory was coming into prominence. There is no doubt that he was influenced by both Freud and Jung (Ginsberg and Opper, 1969:3).Thus, although it is true that Piaget does attempt to link mental development to actual studies of children and their physical growth more precisely than do other theorists before him, he also incorporated the notion of "stages" and "levels" of development which are unfortunately often spoken of as "higher" and "lower." He also was interested "in relating the increase of knowledge in the individual to the increase of knowledge in a society," a position he refers to as "genetic epistemology" (Ginsberg and Opper, 1969:210). Because of the great mass of his work, produced over such a long period of time, it would be difficult to assess just how much this "genetic epistemology" has influenced his theory of intelligence. But there is no doubt that it is closely identified with the recapitulation hypothesis.

Thinking in terms of higher and lower stages of thought is characteristic of virtually all students of intelligence and development—even though it is perfectly obvious that such conceptualizations make sense as "higher" or "lower" only in accordance with some arbitrarily imposed standard of measurement. Thus we find ourselves speaking of "concrete" modes of thought which are "lower" than "abstract" modes of thought, prelogical as opposed to logical modes, animistic as opposed to scientific modes, and the like. In fact, little has been accomplished so far in studies of intelligence, especially cross-culturally, and even if it were possible to demonstrate clearly different "styles" of thought it would still be impossible to rank them as higher or lower except in the same arbitrary way we have defined and come to believe in "progress." The decision to classify one task as somehow higher than another is fundamentally an arbitrary one, and it is relative

BUSHMEN, KALAHARI DESERT. The hierarchical outlook in a headline. (Copyrighted 1929 by American Weekly Incorporated, Great Britain)

to the culture in which the decision is made. Likewise, the ability to perform well on any given task is also strongly influenced by culture. It is the failure to recognize this relationship that allows people like Arthur R. Jensen (1969) to argue from intelligence-test scores to inherited intellectual inferiority. All such tests are culturally biased, mostly towards literary, verbal skills, reading ability, context, exposure to certain kinds of information, and other like things. Furthermore, they assume that everyone taking them solves problems in precisely the same way, in the same amount of time, and that, indeed, they are all equally interested in solving them in the first place. Memorizing a long list of numerals is deemed more intelligent than memorizing the location of seal breathing holes in the ice, or the migratory habit of caribou, only because our own culture values the one skill more than the other—there is nothing intrinsic about the tasks that makes one fundamentally more intelligent or "higher" than another. Piaget and others have, it appears, established different styles of thought. No one, however, has devised an acceptable standard for rating the styles as higher or lower. This statement is just as true for the thought of children (where a way of thinking is "higher" only because it in general appears later) as it is for cross-cultural differences in thought (where thinking is higher the closer it approximates our own).

It would seem that most people, at least most Western Europeans, find it virtually impossible to think of intelligence as contextual rather than hierarchical. This incapacity, as we have seen, is an intellectual legacy from as far back as we can remember; but it was these early evolutionists who presented it in its most articulate form. The effects of this way of thinking about development and intelligence are well summarized by George A. Miller:

Every culture has its myths. One of our most persistent is that nonliterate people in less developed countries possess something we like to call a "primitive mentality" that is both different from and inferior to our own. This myth has it that the "primitive mind" is highly concrete, whereas the "Western mind" is highly abstract; the "primitive mind" connects its concrete ideas by rote association, where as the "Western mind" connects its abstract ideas by general relations; the "primitive mind" is illogical and insensitive to contradictions, whereas the "Western mind" is logical and strives to attain consistency; the "primitive mind" is childish and emotional, whereas the "Western mind" is mature and rational; and so on and on. In its most frightening form, this myth includes the claim that these differences are genetically based and derives from this fact that other people are just not as intelligent as Caucasians.

The dangers inherent in this hodgepodge of half-truths do not derive solely from the blunders they inspire in our relations with the Third World. The same stereotype is likely to be applied to ethnic minorities living in the West. Foreign and domestic policies based on such beliefs are paternalistic at best, and at worst can degenerate into frank repression and exploitation. It is of practical importance, therefore, to establish the true facts of the matter. (Miller, 1971:vii)

That this is not merely idle accusation can be seen in the following statement on what has come to be called "Jensenism":

One of Jensen's basic assumptions is made explicit in the comment printed with his approval in The New York Times Magazine (Sept. 21, 1969, p. 14). In this he clearly regards "intelligence as the ability to adapt to civilization," adding that "races differ in this ability according to the civilizations in which they live." Building on this, he further assumes that "the Stanford-Binet IQ test measures the ability to adapt to Western civilization." An ability in which he claims American Negroes to be inferior to "Orientals," with the clear implication that, as a blanket category, they are far less well-endowed than American whites. For an educated man to hold such beliefs is regrettable, but for a presumed "scientist" to be allowed to publish them in a popular journal without informed editorial supervision is an example of the unfortunate failure of intellectual responsibility. (Brace and Livingstone, 1971:69)

Summary

The marriage of anthropology to evolutionary theory would seem to have been inevitable. It was a development of great significance, not only to anthropology.

but to other academic disciplines as well. Although the early view of cultural evolution has been discredited, there are survivals of it even now—in anthropology, psychology, psychoanalysis, and elsewhere. All of the early scholars who dealt with the subject of man employed the same evolutionary perspective, spelled out in its clearest form in Lewis Henry Morgan's *Ancient Society*. Edward B. Tylor gave us one of the earliest English-language definitions of culture. He also made popular the notion of survivals. The prevailing view of "primitive" people before the evolutionists held that they had simply fallen from grace and hence were "degenerates." "Progress" came to be seen as possible, not only for Western Europeans, but for others as well. But even though they held out hopes of progress for all, the scholars of the period remained ethnocentric, racist, and paternalistic. The concept of progress was associated with evolution in such a way as to allow Western Europeans to compare themselves, always favorably, with all others. They equated present-day nonliterate people with people of the ancestral past and were led thereby to attempt comparisons of "primitives" with children and even neurotics and the retarded. This misdirection was made possible, in part, by the misapplication of Haeckel's so-called biogenetic law—"ontogeny recapitulates phylogeny." Although anthropologists themselves quickly gave up this early, grandiose, evolutionary scheme, its effects linger on, sometimes in an acceptable and useful form as we shall see later, but sometimes, sadly, in a most unacceptable and vicious form. Both will become clearer as we proceed.

Further Readings

Marvin Harris's *The Rise of Anthropological Theory* is a must for anyone interested in the history of anthropology, as is George W. Stocking, Jr.'s, *Race, Culture, and Evolution*. For information on the earlier period see Margaret Hodgen's *Early Anthropology in the Sixteenth and Seventeenth Centuries* and the volume edited by Dudley and Novak, *The Wild Man Within*. Andrew D. White's detailed account, *A History of the Warfare of Science with Theology in Christendom*, is especially good on the degeneration theory and the resistance to Darwin and other scholars. The best discussion of the recapitulation doctrine can be found in A. I. Hallowell's *Culture and Experience*. Sidney Pollard's *The Idea of Progress* is a good recent account of that particular idea. The best statement on the question of race is the collection *Race and Intelligence*, edited by Brace, Gamble, and Bond.

To gain a better appreciation of the period discussed in this chapter, try reading some of the originals: Morgan's *Ancient Society*, Tylor's *Primitive Culture*, Frazer's *The Golden Bough*, or perhaps even McLennan's *Studies in Ancient History*. For even more enlightenment, try reading any of the more popular accounts of the time—Mayne Reid's *Odd People: Being a Popular Description of Singular Races of Man*, or Buel's *The Story of Man*, for example.

A very readable popular history of anthropology is Hays, *From Ape to Angel: An Informal History of Social Anthropology*.

CHAPTER II HISTORICALISM AND DIFFUSION

Here we deal with the reaction to the early evolutionary theory we discussed in the previous chapter. The so-called historical particularists, inspired by the dynamic and forceful Franz Boas, began to systematically undermine the evolutionary argument. They argued that the search for grand laws of evolution or progress was at least premature and perhaps not even possible. Anthropology, they believed, was essentially history; but history and evolution were often confused. As there were many existing Indian peoples in America it was possible to establish a tradition of actual fieldwork, to get to know "savages" first hand. This first-hand observation led to the realization that such things as intelligence, morals, progress, and the like were relative rather than absolute. Other anthropologists during this period argued that the proper subject of investigation for anthropology should be diffusion—the process whereby one culture acquires things from another. These people argued that man was by nature uninventive and most things must have been invented only once. Boas, with his relativistic position, was the first to use the term *culture* in the plural—*cultures*. His students, with Alfred Kroeber in the forefront, began to explore the concept of culture in greater and greater detail. In the previous chapter we dealt with the early period in the formation of anthropology; here we deal with the formative years of what was to become American anthropology.

The evolutionists had attempted a scheme whereby culture, or civilization, *in general*, had evolved following a uniform pattern. This scheme implied that when an institution, an artifact, or a belief occurred in similar form in more than one place, that fact could be explained by the uniformity of the process involved in bringing it about—that is, by *parallel evolution*. And if different cultures passed through similar stages in roughly uniform ways, the people themselves must also be potentially similar. They must be intellectually able, for example, to cope with the same processes, discoveries, and changes. This notion of intellectual equality was generally referred to as the *psychic unity of mankind*. In addition to being a critical correlate of the concept of parallel evolution, it was also a necessary belief for all monogenists and thus had a long and respectable history. But how was it possible to reconcile a belief in the psychic unity of mankind with the prevailing beliefs about racial inferiority? This seeming paradox did not really trouble the evolutionists a great deal because they believed that intellectual capacity evolved in tandem with cultural evolution. Indeed, the first chapter of Morgan's *Ancient Society* is entitled "Growth of Intelligence Through Inventions and Discoveries," and we have already commented on the intellectualism of Tylor. An even bettter example might be seen in the writings of Frazer, who was interested specifically in the evolution of magic, science, and religion essentially as a cognitive phenomenon (as, that is, attempts at explanation). This culture-intelligence relationship which all three scholars assumed meant that the psychic capacity of human beings could be assumed to be fundamentally similar, *provided they were on the same stage of development*. Thus, at any given moment in time, there could be some people who were intellectually (as well as culturally) inferior to others since they had not yet attained the higher levels of civilization.

Much of this theoretical position can be understood by reminding ourselves that for the most part evolutionists were "armchair" anthropologists. With rare exceptions such as Tylor and Morgan, virtually none of the fathers of anthropology had ever seen any "savages" or "barbarians" and had no first-hand knowledge of such peoples. In any event, they were interested, not in particular peoples or cultures but, rather, in the "grand design," the master scheme whereby the evolution of civilization out of savagery could be comprehended and explained in its entirety.

Progress and Degradation

But built into the concept of culture itself, as it had been introduced by Tylor and by Arnold (1869), was the idea of "progression." Where later conceptions of culture became relativistic, Tylor's was absolutistic. In this way it was similar to Matthew Arnold's view, to what has been referred to in the past as the "humanistic" view of culture, the view that comes to mind when one thinks of etiquette, the fine arts, nobility, and the like. Tylor's great contribution, contrary to what generations of anthropology students have been told in the past, was not to separate the scientific view of culture from the humanistic but, rather, to "fit the notion of culture into the framework of social evolutionism" (Stocking, 1968:87). Tylor's work addressed itself most fundamentally to the refutation of the Archbishop of Dublin, Richard Whately, who had argued in 1854: "No community ever did or ever can emerge unassisted by external helps from a state of utter barbarism into anything that can be called civilization" (A. D. White, 1955:304)

ALICE CUNNINGHAM FLETCHER (1845-1923). (Smithsonian Institution; National Anthropological Archives; photograph by Anty Emilio, Editions Napoleón, Barcelona)

FRANK HAMILTON CUSHING (1857-1900). In Zuñi costume. (Smithsonian Institution; National Anthropological Archives; photo by John K. Hillers)

Tylor was thus a "progressivist," and was responding to the "degradationists." It was absolutely crucial to his argument that he not distinguish between "culture" and "civilization"—"Culture or Civilization, taken in its widest ethnographic sense . . ."—that the whole history of mankind be viewed as progressive and as leading "upwards," towards Western European civilization. Thus "savages" could be thought of as moral, provided they were not deemed as moral as Europeans, as religious but not of the higher religions, as intelligent but not at the same level as Englishmen. And, inasmuch as the prevailing humanist view was similar to that of the clergy, at least in that it would not accept that savages could be civilized or cultured at all, this view also was challenged by Tylor. In some ways, however, the humanists were closer to the modern view of culture than was Tylor. They tended to view culture more as a "way of life," as something ideational and integrative, something that was internalized and that gave direction and meaning to life, whereas Tylor's view was of something much more materialistic and fragmentary. The great humanists of the time, like Matthew Arnold, were social critics; dissatisfied with their society as it was, they suggested a more "cultured" life in its place. The evolutionists were not interested in a rejection of contemporary values but rather in how the values had come about and how others could attain them. Tylor's work defined new conditions for thinking about culture which helped to bring about the modern view.

In the United States a different situation existed. There were readily available large numbers of aborigines, and there was at least some tradition of *fieldwork*. Henry Schoolcraft had worked intensively with American Indians as early as the 1830's (P. P. Mason, 1962). Lewis Henry Morgan, as we have already mentioned, was one of the few evolutionists who was not merely an armchair theorist. He had spent considerable time with the Iroquois. Morgan had also greatly influenced Adolph F. Bandelier, who in 1880 began intensive field work in New Mexico (L. White, 1940). Frank Hamilton Cushing was conducting his well-known work in Zuñi at about the same time (Gronewold, 1972). Erminnie Smith and Alice Cunningham Fletcher had both conducted independent field research as early as 1884 (Lurie, 1966). There were others as well. Even so, it is Franz Boas who stands as the significant figure in American anthropology and who is generally credited not only with establishing fieldwork as an integral and necessary part of anthropology but also with establishing anthropology as a legitimate academic subject in the United States.

Franz Boas

Boas, born and educated in Germany, first encountered "savages" in 1883 when he traveled to Baffinland. This was an important encounter for Boas, trained in physics and geography, as the experience helped to head him into an-

ESKIMO WOMAN AND CHILD, NUNIVAK. Although posed more than forty years later and more than a continent distant, this picture suggests something of the culture that impressed Franz Boas in Greenland. (1928 photograph by Edward S. Curtis, 1868-1952)

thropology. How Boas's "relativism" contrasted with the "absolutism" of Tylor is revealed in one of his Baffinland notebooks:

Is it not a beautiful custom that these "savages" suffer all deprivation in common, but in happy times when someone has brought back booty from the hunt, all join in eating and drinking. I often ask myself what advantages our "good society" possesses over that of the "savages." The more I see of their customs, the more I realize that we have no right to look down on them. Where amongst our people would you find such true hospitality? Here, without the least complaint people are willing to perform *every* task demanded of them. We have no right to blame them for their forms and superstitions which may seem

KWAKIUTL OF THE NORTHWEST COAST OF NORTH AMERICA. Dancing to restore an eclipsed moon. This culture was of continuing interest to Franz Boas. (1914 photograph by Edward S. Curtis)

ridiculous to us. We "highly educated people" are much worse, relatively speaking. The fear of tradition and old customs is deeply implanted in mankind, and in the same way as it regulates life here, it halts all progress for us. I believe it is a difficult struggle for every individual and every people to give up tradition and follow the path to truth. The Eskimo are sitting around me, their mouths filled with raw seal liver (the spot of blood on the back of the paper shows you how I joined in). As a thinking person, for me the most important result of this trip lies in the strengthening of my point of view that the idea of a "cultured" individual is merely relative and that a person's worth should be judged by his *Herzenbildung* [roughly, "education of the heart"]. This quality is present or absent here among the Eskimo, just as among us. All that man can do for humanity is to further the *truth,* whether it be sweet or bitter. Such a man may truly say that he has not lived in vain. But now I must really get back to the cold Eskimo land. (Boas, quoted in Stocking, 1965:61)

After his initial field experience Boas returned to Germany. By 1886 he was again doing fieldwork, this time with the Kwakiutl of the Northwest coast, who were to occupy much of his time from then on. Three years later he accepted his first job in the United States and went on from that to completely dominate American anthropology.

To understand what Boas accomplished, it is necessary to understand the uncritical and speculative use of the comparative method and evolutionism by the Americans of his time. It was a period of the most vulgar racism that attempted to make "savages" as close to subhumans as possible, that arranged everything in stages always leading towards Western European society, and towards democracy, that glorified the wildest speculations with virtually no respect for facts, and that attempted to reduce anthropology to a simple-minded formula explaining everything and nothing at all. Boas's determination to set high standards for fieldwork, to make fieldwork a necessary part of anthropological training, and to collect ethnographic facts diligently and patiently, was a refreshing response to the excesses of others. Remember that anthropology was not yet recognized as a science or, for that matter, even as a university subject. Thus virtually anyone and everyone who wished could submit his or her views on man and culture to whatever audiences would listen. There was often little regard for scientific objectivity. The *American Anthropologist*, the principal anthropological journal then as now, contains many examples of this undisciplined and imaginative procedure:

> The cleared spaces . . . in the African forests . . . are . . . used by the chimpanzees to build immense bonfires of dried wood gathered from the neighborhood. When the pile is completed one of the chimpanzees begins to blow at the pile as if blowing the fire. He is immediately joined by others, and, eventually by the whole company, and the blowing is kept up until their tongues hang from their mouths, when they sit around on their haunches with their elbows on their knees and holding up their hands to the imaginary blaze. (Büttikofer, 1893:377)

And again:

> It is a remarkable fact that the centre of civilization has shifted from near the equator towards the poles. Today the most progressive races inhabit the temperate zone, while the stolid and stationary ones are in the frigid and torrid where there is little variation of temperature. It would almost seem that a diversified climate, one of sharp contrasts of hot and cold, of rain and snow, was essential to a progressive civilization, and at all events it is in such that the intellect attains its most vigorous growth. In Europe the Germans and English are in advance of the Italians and Spaniards, and in our own country the people of New England claim to be ahead of their fellow-citizens in the south. (Ferree, 1890:148)

Boas's respect for facts, more than any other thing, has led people to argue that he was the father of "scientific anthropology" (Mead, 1959:35). His revolutionary work in physical anthropology, based upon careful quantitative data, led the way to the destruction of the commonly held beliefs in racial superiority and *racial determinism* that were so much a part of anthropology before him. His early Eskimo experience led him to abandon *geographical determinism* (the idea that geography determines cultural forms) and he brought to American anthropology an eclecticism which enabled his students to develop in a variety of directions—which, as we shall see, they soon did.

In his famous paper on "The Limitations of the Comparative Method of Anthropology" (1896), Boas attacked the uniformity of change as presented by

THE ANDAMANS AND ANDAMANESE.—In an article entitled "The Andamans and Andamanese" (*Scottish Geographical Magazine*, Vol. 5, No. 2, Feb., 1889, pp. 57–73) Col. T. Cadell, Chief Commissioner of the Andaman Islands, gives an interesting general account of these very primitive savages. Perhaps the most striking thing in the article is the favorable account he gives of the appearance and disposition of these people, who have generally been presented to the world in a very unfavorable light. He scouts the idea of their ever having been cannibals, and goes on to describe them as " well-made, dapper little fellows," with " smiling, innocent faces," and " pleasant to look upon "—" such jolly, merry little people. * * * You cannot imagine how taking they are. Every one who has to do with them falls in love with them." By kindness and liberality the English have succeeded in gaining the affections of all the inhabitants of Great Andaman except the Járáwas, who speak a " totally different language" and differ in their customs and weapons, and friendly relations are gradually being established with the people of Little Andaman.

JOHN MURDOCH.

CURIOUS MARRIAGE CUSTOM IN THE ISLAND OF ROTTI.—In this island, one of the Malay Archipelago near Timur, the bride wears a girdle round her waist fastened with nine knots, which, to make them still harder to untie, are covered with wax. Before the bridegroom may enjoy his marital rights he must untie all these knots, using only the thumb and forefinger of his left hand. Two old women are detailed to watch the bridal couple and see that this is done fairly. If the bridegroom should, for instance, try to tear the girdle off, his father-in-law would have the right to claim a heavy penalty from him. It is said that sometimes a month, or even a whole year, is spent in this process. (Mittheilungen der geographischen gesellschaft zu Jena, 1890, p. 168.)

EARLY ANTHROPOLOGICAL REPORTING. The paragraph concerning the Andamans was published in *American Anthropologist*, Vol. III, p. 236, 1890; the note on curious marriage custom appeared in *American Anthropologist*, Vol. IV, p. 160, 1891.

the evolutionists. He argued that even though some aspect of culture—say, *shamanism,* the bow and arrow, or masks—could be widely found around the world, this did not have to mean they came into being everywhere for the same causes and were everywhere part of precisely the same evolutionary process:

> The fact that many fundamental features of culture are universal, or at least occur in many isolated places, interpreted by the assumption that the same features must always have developed from the same causes, leads to the conclusion that there is one grand system according to which mankind has developed everywhere; that all the occurring variations are no more than minor details in this grand uniform evolution. It is clear that this theory has for its logical basis the assumption that the same phenomena are always due to the same causes. (Boas, 1896:275)

The view of Tylor and the other evolutionists was one of parallel evolution. That is, if a particular pattern existed in two or more places, it could be explained as a parallel development stemming from a common cause and process. Boas wanted to separate *convergent* from parallel evolution. He went on to carefully demonstrate that in a great many cases the assumption of parallel evolutionary stages was incorrect—that it was entirely possible for the same thing to have come about for different reasons. Using specific examples of social organization, art, folktales, and other items of culture, he demonstrated his thesis repeatedly. The result of this review was not to destroy evolutionism entirely but, rather, to demonstrate that the presumed regularity of history had been grossly exaggerated. Boas felt it was necessary to have detailed historical and ethnographic information on particular cases before any generalization could be permitted, hence the label *historical particularism* is sometimes attached to this "school" of anthropology. He believed anthropology should be historical, and that it should be *inductive* rather than *deductive*. He felt that individual cases of historical development were valuable and necessary in and of themselves and that, somehow, they would eventually and in normal course lead to generalizations. This led Boas and his students into a rather fruitless series of arguments over "what anthropology really was." Was it history or was it science? Should it seek for *laws*—regularities in the way cultures developed over time—or should it seek merely to concentrate on individual cases—that is, specific histories of specific cultures? Should it attempt to generalize, or was generalization pointless? As Marshall Sahlins has since shown, the argument was generated largely because of the failure to see that there is both a *specific* as well as a *general* evolution. The individual historical cases, of which Boas was so fond, are examples, in Sahlins's view at least, of specific evolution; the progression of forms through stages of over-all progress is general evolution (Sahlins, 1960:43). Later we will discuss the modern evolutionists, of which Sahlins is one of the foremost. And we will also return to the concept of "over-all progress." Thus, the anthropology of Boas, as many have observed, was *idiographic* (it dealt with particular or specific cases) as opposed to *nomothetic* (dealing with generalization from a number of cases).

During Boas's time there was also a belief on the part of many that because American Indians (and other ''savages'') were rapidly disappearing it was crucial to gather as much material as possible. There was a tendency to think there was no time for theory, that theorizing could come later. But Boas's influence on anthropology, in spite of his failure to leave a coherent theory of culture, was direct and profound, since he was almost singlehandedly responsible for the training of the first generation of American anthropologists—Alfred Kroeber, Robert Lowie, Edward Sapir, Fay-Cooper Cole, Alexander Goldenweiser, Melville Herskovits, Ruth Benedict, Leslie Spier, Paul Radin, Clark Wissler, J. Alden Mason, E. Adamson Hoebel, Margaret Mead, Erna Gunther, Ruth Bunzel, Jules Henry, Frank Speck, Alexander Lesser, and others as well.

Although Boas never offered a precise definition of culture, it seems clear that his use of the concept was quite different from that of Tylor and that it led the way for the emergence of modern versions. Tylor consistently used the term only in the singular—*culture*. In this sense there was one single phenomenon, synonymous with civilization, which some people had and some people were somewhere on the way to having. Boas's fieldwork experiences, along with his *relativism*, apparently led him to perceive particular *cultures*, in the plural, and to appreciate that each one had a unity, coherence, and history of its own. Boas attributed this to ''the genius of the people,'' an idea which we will see was developed later by some of his students.

Invention and Diffusion

If some item of culture is found in two or more places in the world, one explanation for it is that the same thing was *independently invented* in both or all places. The notion of psychic unity, a necessary assumption of parallel evolutionism, is supported by such cases, and for that reason the notion of independent invention was of great importance to the evolutionists. There is, of course, another explanation—namely, that one group received the item from another through a process that came to be designated as *diffusion*. Much of the work of Boas, but more particularly of his students, revolved around the concept of diffusion and these two possibilities.

Although Tylor and others of his general persuasion were perfectly aware that borrowing occurred and was of importance, this awareness was sometimes overlooked by the historicalists in the United States who were eager to destroy the grand speculative evolutionary theories. It was likewise overlooked, or even denied, by the German and English *diffusionists*, although the latter, as we shall see, were not taken seriously for very long.

W. H. R. Rivers, the founder of British diffusionism, seems to have been the first to formally attack the evolutionists. But the extreme diffusionistic position that developed is more usually associated with the names G. Elliot Smith and W. J. Perry. Smith and Perry believed that virtually everything on earth had originated in Egypt and had diffused outward from that point (Smith, 1928). Prior to about 6000 years ago, in their scheme, the earth had been inhabited by "natural man" who possessed no clothing, houses, ceremonies, or the like, and more importantly, no agriculture. In approximately 4000 B.C., according to their simple-minded scheme, the residents of the Nile valley adopted an agricultural mode of life and then quickly invented everything. As Egyptian civilization grew and progressed the Egyptians began to travel over increasingly larger distances looking for raw materials, precious metals, and other things they felt they required. This exploration resulted in the spread of the original civilization. The existence of Aztec and Mayan civilizations in the New World, among other things, was offered as evidence for their view. Smith and Perry did not believe that civilization could have been invented more than once because, they argued, man was basically "uninventive."

The work of G. Elliot Smith is another example of the lack of professionalism that characterized anthropology during its formative period. While Smith was a well-known anatomist, he had no training in anthropology, becoming interested in it only because of a trip to Egypt. He was fascinated by the process of mummification and believed it was so complicated it could only have been invented once—which apparently led him to believe that most everything else could also be invented only once. He determined, on the basis of no acceptable evidence whatsoever, that there was a *culture complex*—consisting of sun-worship, stone monuments, mummification, the symbol of the swastika, serpent-worship, ear-piercing, the couvade, and a number of other things—that could be found virtually all around the world. On the basis of his belief, and very little else, he influenced W. J. Perry, who then helped him to spread his "gospel." These two had little actual influence on academic anthropology itself, though their views, as they found a popular audience, may have somewhat embarrassed and inconvenienced the growing number of professional anthropologists. Such things still occasionally happen today, as is attested by the writings of Robert Ardrey, Desmond Morris, and a few others.

The German diffusionists, the *Kulturkreis* (culture circle) school, was a far more sophisticated development. F. Ratzel was skeptical of human inventiveness and argued that contact between groups had to be completely ruled out in every case before independent invention could be granted. He was interested in *migration* and other diffusionary processes and sought to understand their general principles (Ratzel, 1896). Out of this, primarily through Leo Frobenius (1898), Fritz Graebner (1911), and Wilhelm Schmidt (1939), developed the major ideas of *diffusionism*. It was suggested that not only did similarities exist between individual elements of culture but also between whole *culture complexes* and *culture circles*. It was necessary, they believed, to understand the migration of a number of *traits* simultaneously, traits which were linked as part of a particular culture complex or culture circle. This is clear in the following:

One of the facts which has been established by culture history beyond all peradventure of doubt is that not only discrete culture elements or small groups of elements migrate and exert an influence, but also whole compact culture complexes. If such a culture complex embraces all the essential and necessary categories of human culture, material culture, economic life, social life, custom, religion, then we call it a "culture circle," because returning into itself, like a circle, it is sufficient unto itself and, hence, also assures its independent existence. Should it neglect or fail to satisfy one of the more important human needs, then a substitute for this must be called from another culture—the greater the number of such substitutes that are required, the more it would cease to be an independent culture circle. (Schmidt, 1939:176)

The two most basic rules followed by the diffusionists were fairly simple: (1) the "criterion of quality" (or form) holds that when characteristic similarities are found between two culture elements, no matter how far apart they are, if the likeness does not arise from the nature of the object itself, or from the material of which it is made, we must postulate a historical connection (Schmidt, 1939:143), (2) the "criterion of quantity" says simply that the greater the number of items shared by two cultures the greater the likelihood that any one item is a result of a historical connection (Schmidt, 1939:150).

Graebner and Schmidt, by looking at distributions of contemporary culture traits, reconstructed a small number of original culture circles or *Kreise*, For Schmidt there were four major "grades" of culture circles, Primitive, Primary, Secondary, and Tertiary, and within each of these were two or three different *Kreise*. These were not always very clear but nonetheless everything was believed to have diffused from these original places. In the process, cultures mixed and changed:

. . . All the American Primitive cultures, the South American (Fuegians, Gez-Tapuya) and the North American (north central Californians, the Algonkins) once formed an old culture together with the Arctic culture (Samoyedes, Koryaks, Ainu, Ancient Eskimo), whose habitat was somewhere in (North) Eastern Asia. To the southwest, the Pygmy culture joined it and it was the first to separate from there and split up into an African and a (South) Asiatic group. On the Southeast, the preparatory stages of the later Southeastern Australian Primitive culture joined, which migrated from there over the present Indonesia and New Guinea to Australia. (Schmidt, 1939:223)

This, of course, is speculative historical reconstruction with a vengeance. Also, despite some confusion over this matter in the past, it is basically an evolutionary scheme, for the "grades" can readily be equated with the "stages" of the evolutionists. Various methods and principles were developed by the diffusionists which, they felt, allowed them to establish measures of time and chronology. But in the United States, although the scholars of the time were vitally interested in historical reconstruction and diffusion, they wanted little to do with speculation or evolutionism and thus took a somewhat different direction.

Culture Areas

One of Boas's first arguments, upon his beginning to work in the United States, was with Otis Mason and John Wesley Powell. It had to do with the principles of arrangement in ethnological museums. In brief, Mason and Powell wanted to display *artifacts* according to their presumed position on an evolutionary scale, regardless of where they came from, and also in terms of which particular human "needs" or "wants" they were believed by Mason to be designed to satisfy. Boas insisted that all of the materials from a single tribe or tribal region should simply be grouped together. Classifications, Boas felt, should follow, not precede the study of ethnographic materials. He argued that there was a danger in classifications based upon "analogies of outward appearance" when further investigation might uncover less superficial criteria, that only in the context of the whole could the individual specimen be understood:

> From a collection of string instruments . . . of "savage" tribes and the modern orchestra, we cannot derive any conclusion but that similar means have been applied by all peoples to make music. The character of their music, the only object worth studying, which determines the form of their instruments, cannot be understood from the single instruments, but requires a complete collection of the single tribe. (Boas, 1887:486)

Implicit in the argument between Boas, Mason, and Powell was the idea of *culture areas*, which came to occupy the attention of American ethnologists throughout the early 1900's. Although Kroeber (1931:249) has suggested that the concept of culture areas was developed by American anthropologists as a "community product," and probably as a result of the greater uniformity of aboriginal culture in the New World and the absence of a documentary history, the term was first employed in 1894 by Otis T. Mason in his presidential address to the Anthropological Society of Washington, "Technogeography, or the Relation of the Earth to the Industries of Mankind" (1894:148). Mason expanded the idea in the following year, and it was also elaborated by Holmes (1914).

It is Clark Wissler, however, one of Boas's first students, who is the most strongly identified with the notion of culture areas. In his book *The American Indian* (1917), Wissler named, described, and then formalized culture areas for the entire Western hemisphere. At first he designated eight areas on the basis of the characteristic food available in each; later he elaborated these into

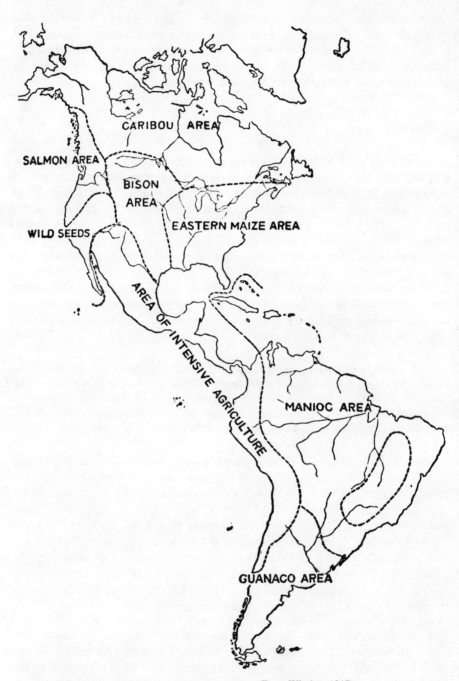

FOOD AREAS OF THE NEW WORLD. (From Wissler, 1917)

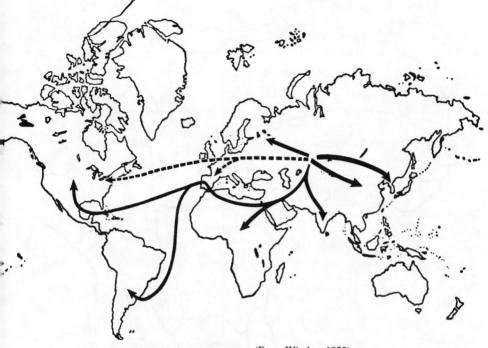

SPREAD OF THE HORSE COMPLEX. (From Wissler, 1923)

fifteen. Thus the Plains culture area was dependent upon the bison, the North Pacific Coast and Plateau areas on the salmon, the California area on wild seeds, and so on.

To arrange groups of people geographically in this way is a simple enough and useful idea. But to link them to a particular food supply suggests a form of geographical determinism. Neither Boas nor Wissler were geographical determinists but, in any event, they were more interested at this time in describing trait distributions and *culture centers* than in explaining them. It remained for later scholars, as we shall see, to add the dimension of technology to environment and thereby convert this basic idea into one with more explanatory significance.

For Wissler the concern is with the typical culture of the area as defined by the presence of a large number of *culture traits*. Thus in the Plains area a number of tribes possess the traits believed to be characteristic of the area (skin teepee, round shield, sun dance, absence of pottery, absence of agriculture, stone ceremonial pipes, and others). On the periphery of this group of tribes are others which have most but not all of the traits. A culture area is an arbitrary division and contains within it *a culture center* "which coincides with the habitat of the most typical tribes." Culture centers, then, are not precise points but, rather, extensive nuclei. Social units such as *tribes* are different from *culture complexes*, which are "aggregations of culture material" (Kroeber, 1931:252).

CULTURE AREAS OF AFRICA. (From Herskovits, 1949)

The concept of a culture area should not be confused with the idea of *age area*. The age area is a concept employed to infer time sequences from space distributions. Whereas *culture area* refers to culture traits as they aggregate, the age-area idea is applicable to separate traits as well as to clusters of traits. The fundamental principles here are that one can infer areas of origin from concentrations of distribution and can infer antiquity from peripheral distributions. That is, the more prevalent a trait is in a given area the greater the probability that it originated there, and the further from the origin point it is found, the older it is likely to be. This statement assumes Wissler's "law of diffusion" (that traits tend to diffuse in all directions from their centers of origin). (1926:182)

TABLE 4

OCCURRENCE OF TRAITS IN SOUTHERN NORTHWEST COAST SUB-AREAS

C, N. W. California; O, S. W. Oregon; L, Lower Columbia; P, Puget Sound
x, trait present; o, absent; –, no data

	C	O	L	P
Body and Dress				
1. Head deformation	o	o	x	x
2. Universal	o	o	x	o
3. General	o	o	x	x
4. Sign of free birth	o	o	x	o
5. Tattooing	x	x	x	x
6. Women on face	x	x	o	o
7. 3 stripes on chin	o	x	o	o
8. Almost solid on chin	x	o	o	o
9. Men, measuring lines on arm	x	x	–	–
10. Women's hair in 2 clubs	x	x	o	–
11. Parted, but flowing	o	o	x	–
12. Dentalium nose ornament	x	x	x	o
13. Women's basketry hat	x	x	x	x
14. Brimless cap	x	x	o	o
15. Brim, peak, and knob	o	o	x	x
16. Flattened cone	o	o	o	x
17. Men's basketry hat	o	o	x	x
18. Brim, peak, and knob	o	o	x	x
19. Flattened cone	o	o	o	x
20. Men's deerskin shirt	o	x	o	o
21. Men's leggings, limited use	x	x	x	–
22. Men's robe	x	x	x	x
23. Of deer fur	x	x	o	o
24. Twined or woven	o	o	x	x
25. Fur strips or mountain goat wool	o	o	x	o
26. Cedar bark or dog hair	o	o	o	x
27. Women's petticoat	x	x	x	x
28. Fringed deerskin	x	o	o	o
29. Fiber	x	x	x	x
30. Fiber for profane use	o	x	x	x
31. Women's deerskin gown	o	x	x	–
Houses				
32. Material redwood	x	o	o	o
33. Sugar pine	o	x	o	o
34. Cedar	o	x	x	x
35. Bark	o	x	x	o
36. Planks vertical	x	x	x	o
37. Breadth 12 feet	o	x	o	o
38. 20 feet	x	o	(x)	o
39. Up to 30 or 40 feet	o	o	x	(x)
40. Up to 60 feet	o	o	o	x

AN EXAMPLE OF A TRAIT LIST. (Portion of a table in Driver and Kroeber, 1932)

Despite whatever shortcomings American anthropologists perceived in this general scheme, it was their major focus for a considerable period of time. Perhaps the most important theoretical elaboration of the methods to be employed by diffusionists was an early article by Edward Sapir, "Time Perspectives in Aboriginal American Culture" (1916). Melville J. Herskovits, another of Boas's students, applied it to Africa (1924). A. L. Kroeber began a comprehensive survey of Indian cultures west of the Rocky Mountains using a massive trait list and statistical techniques that he hoped would give him coefficients of similarity—that is, a statistical measure of how alike two different groups were on the basis of how many traits they shared (Driver and Kroeber, 1932). He eventually substituted the term *culture climax* for culture center.

Problems and Implications

While culture traits, areas, centers, and climaxes may be useful concepts for initial fact-finding and description, they are not very useful for the development of nomothetic explanations. Indeed, Harris refers to diffusion as a "nonprinciple" and argues: (1) that cultural differences and similarities cannot be explained by geographical-historical propinquity; (2) that diffusion cannot account for the origin of traits, (3) that if independent invention has occurred widely, as archeology now tends to demonstrate, diffusion is a superfluous concept; and (4) that even if independent invention is rare, there is still differential receptivity to cultural influences independent of distance. As diffusion proved to be a sterile notion, it became increasingly apparent that investigators must consider "all the factors of environment, technology, economy, social organization, and ideology" which must be involved in nomothetic explanations (Harris, 1968:377-78).

But note that Harris does not mention psychological factors. Thus, while most of this argument is true, diffusion is "superfluous" only if your sole concern is with origins. And surely it is an overreaction to refer to diffusion as "the very incarnation of antiscience" (Harris, 1968:378). Likewise, although Harris perceives that "a diffused innovation, no less than an independently invested one, must withstand the selective pressures of the social system if it is to become a part of the cultural repertory," he asserts that there is a single process in the adoption or rejection of an innovation whether the item is invented by the people themselves or borrowed from others (1968:378). Psychologically, this would appear unlikely —the source of an innovation appears to have an influence on whether or not people will accept it; the circumstances in which it is presented can also be influential; so also can the particular values held by the receiving group (Barnett, 1953).

It is interesting to note that Schmidt thought of culture and cultural processes in psychological terms. Consider this definition of culture:

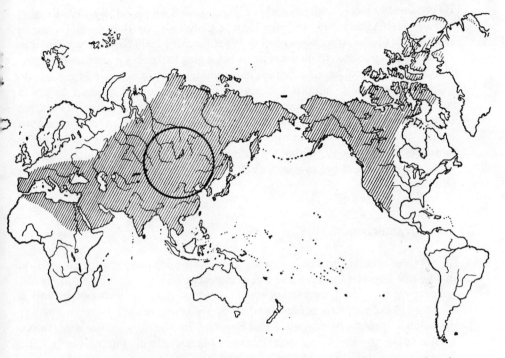

DISTRIBUTION OF THE SINEW BOW. Maps of this kind were often used by diffusionists to show the dispersal of culture traits. (From Wissler, 1923)

Culture consists in the inner formation of the human mind and in the external formation of the body and nature in so far as this latter process is directed by the mind. (1939:347)

He defined a culture circle as "a culture complex which embraces all the essential and necessary categories of human nature" (1939:347). This is actually fairly close to Malinowski's "psychological functionalism" which we will discuss in the next chapter. But Schmidt and the diffusionists, like the historical particularists, were more interested in the distribution of culture traits than in pursuing the psychological dimension of culture. We will return to psychological considerations in the study of culture in a later chapter.

Tylor linked the culture concept to evolution; Boas began the separation of the concept of culture from that of civilization; students of Boas began seriously reflecting upon what "culture" means. A. L. Kroeber, the first of Boas's students to take his degree, is perhaps the best example of this.

Kroeber had just finished taking his master's degree in literature and was teaching his first classes when in 1896 he met Boas, who had arrived at Columbia, where he had been appointed the first lecturer in anthropology. With only two others, Kroeber enrolled in Boas's first course—in American Indian languages.

He became fascinated with the study of language and with Boas. By 1898 Kroeber had become Assistant in Anthropology at Columbia. In 1899 he did summer fieldwork with the Arapaho Indians in Wyoming. By 1900 Kroeber was hired as Curator for a collection of museum items belonging to the San Francisco Academy of Sciences. Immediately, he began doing ethnographic work among the Klamath Indians of northwest California, being given the sum of one hundred dollars to cover all of his costs including collecting further museum specimens! Kroeber never again left the West Coast except for brief periods in the East to visit relatives or give lectures. He went on to become one of the most significant figures in American anthropology. Although he retained a strong personal attachment to Boas, the two did engage in academic disputes of various kinds from time to time (Kroeber, 1970).

Superorganicism

In spite of several disputes, it appears that Kroeber departed seriously from Boas in only one important respect, but a very important one it was. Whereas Boas had believed the individual, interacting with his environment, was an important unit in the study of culture, Kroeber argued that individuals were entirely subordinate to the culture. It might be suggested that Kroeber, like Tolstoy in *War and Peace*, wanted to destroy the "great man" theory of history. In his famous paper "The Superorganic" (1917), he put forward the following thought-provoking statements:

Here, then, we have to come to our conclusion; and here we rest. The mind and the body are but facets of the same organic material or activity; the social substance—or unsubstantial fabric, if one prefers the phrase,—the existence that we call civilization [culture], transcends them utterly for all its being forever rooted in life. The processes of civilizational activity are almost unknown to us. The self-sufficient factors that govern their workings are unresolved. The forces and principles of mechanistic science can indeed analyze our civilization; but in so doing they destroy its essence, and leave us without understanding of the very thing which we seek. The historian [anthropologist] as yet can do little but picture. He traces and he connects what seems far removed; he balances; he integrates; but he does not really explain, nor does he transmute phenomena into something else. His method is not science; but neither can the scientist deal with historical material and leave it civilization, nor anything resembling civilization, nor convert it wholly into concepts of life and leave nothing else to be done. (1917:212)

Here one sees not only Kroeber's *superorganicism* but also his contention that anthropology is history rather than science. For his antiscience and *reification*, Kroeber has been criticized so regularly that we lose sight of the fact that this was one of the earliest articles to really attempt to understand the meaning of the culture concept, to formally separate cultural from organic evolution, and to suggest the

We may sketch the relation which exists between the evolutions of the organic and of the social (fig. 8). A line, progressing with the flow of time, rises slowly, but ever gatheringly. At a certain point, another line begins to diverge from it, insensibly at first, but ascending ever farther above it on its own course; until, at the moment where the curtain of the present cuts off our view, each is advancing, but far from the other, and uninfluenced by it.

In this illustration, the continuous line denotes the level inorganic; the broken line, the evolution of the organic; the line of dots, the development of civilization. Height above the base is degree of advancement, whether that be complexity, heterogeneity, degree of coördination, or anything else. A is the beginning of time on this earth as revealed to our understandings. B marks the point of the true missing link, of the first human precursor, the first animal that carried and accumulated tradition. C would denote the state reached by what we are accustomed to call primi-

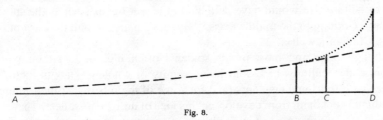

Fig. 8.

tive man, that Neandertal *homo* who was our forefather in culture if not in blood; and D, the present moment.

It is inevitable that if there is any foundation for the contentions that have been set forth, an arguing from one of these lines to the other must be futile. To assert, because the upper line has risen rapidly just before it is cut off, that the one below it must also have ascended proportionally more in this period than in any before, is obviously uncompelling. That our institutions, our knowledge, the exercising of our minds, have advanced dizzyingly in twenty thousand years is no reason that our bodies and brains, our mental equipment and its physiological basis, have advanced in any corresponding measure, as is sometimes argued by scientists and generally taken for granted by men at large.

CULTURE AS SUPERORGANIC. A page from Kroeber, 1917, with his diagram.

extragenetic or nonbiological quality of culture. Kroeber's attitude to the individual follows from his concept of culture:

> The reason why mental heredity has nothing to do with civilization, is that civilization is not mental action but a body or stream of products of mental exercise. Mental activity, as biologists have dealt with it, being organic, any demonstration concerning it consequently proves nothing whatever as to social events. Mentality relates to the individual. The social or cultural, on the other hand, is in its very essence non-individual. Civilization, as such, begins only where the individual ends. . . . (1917:192)

Kroeber spent much of his life attempting to demonstrate "how patterns of art, religion, philosophy, as well as of technology and science, waxed and waned, acquired their characteristic content and kept rolling majestically along, quite independently of particular individuals" (Harris, 1968:328). Perhaps his most famous demonstration of this was his comprehensive study of fashion in which he showed how the basic features of style recur periodically, are distinguished from short run "modes," and are largely independent of particular designers. *Patterns* and *configurations* of culture, identified with Kroeber, remain important in the study of culture. He would have delighted in recent trends such as the spread of "hippie" clothing to the middle class, "Beatles" haircuts, and the current popularity of Indian jewelry.

Although Boas and most of his students often indicated in their work an awareness that cultures had, somehow, a unity or wholeness about them, their concern with traits and elements (and for some of them perhaps, their interest in individuals) kept them from developing this idea of unity to its fullest. There was a tendency to fractionate—to view cultures as made up of bits and pieces—and a corresponding implication of a lack of coherence or integrity. Robert Lowie, another of the most famous of American anthropologists trained by Boas, is usually singled out as being the most guilty of this fragmenting because of the concluding statement in his *Primitive Society*:

> Nor are the facts of culture history without bearing on the adjustment of our own future. To that planless hodge-podge, that thing of shreds and patches called civilization, its historian can no longer yield superstitious reverence. He will realize better than others the obstacles to infusing design into the amorphous product; but in thought at least he will not grovel before it in fatalistic acquiescence but dream of a rational scheme to supplant the chaotic jumble. (1920:331)

However fairly or unfairly, it was to the "shreds and patches" notion that the next important development in anthropology addressed itself. It also addressed itself to the related question of anthropology as history.

Summary

As is often the case when a new idea comes into being and is promoted for a time, the reaction to it becomes an overreaction. This was the case with the historical particularists' reaction to the early evolutionists. The search for a grand theory that would explain all, they argued, was ill-advised if not useless. Anthropology was history. It was idiographic. If a person wanted understanding it could only come through patient, detailed study of individual cases of cultural growth and change. Boas, the giant of American anthropology, sent his students into the field to gather all the data they could —Indian cultures, like the buffalo and the passenger pigeon, were quickly disappearing; they could theorize later. When they did examine their materials it was mainly in terms of the diffusion and distribution of traits rather than in terms of their invention or discovery. If Tylor introduced the term *culture* into English, Boas was the one who perceived that "culture" had a plural form. His students, trained to be eclectic, began their own investigations out of which American anthropology was born and the culture concept came under more and more systematic scrutiny. Alfred Kroeber, Boas's first student, led the way.

Further Readings

In addition to Harris's very negative account of historicalism and diffusionism, two of the older histories of anthropology have much to say on the subject: Lowie's *The History of Ethnological Theory* and Haddon's *History of Anthropology*. The clearest exposition on the methods of the diffusionists can be found in Schmidt's *The Culture Historical Method of Ethnology*. For a discussion of the confusion over evolutionism see Sahlins and Service, *Evolution and Culture*.

For the ambitious, Matthew Arnold's *Culture and Anarchy* might be contrasted with Tylor's *Primitive Culture*, for two quite different treatments of the idea of culture. Some of the books of the time that present discussions of particular instances of diffusion are Wissler's *The American Indian*, Lowie's *Culture and Ethnology*, and Kroeber's *Anthropology*. The extreme and fanciful diffusionism of G. E. Smith and W. J. Perry can be found in their respective books *In the Beginning: The Origin of Civilization* and *Children of the Sun*. Ralph Linton's *The Study of Man* contains a marvelously readable chapter on diffusion, and Wissler's classic paper, "Influence of the Horse in the Development of Plains Culture," is still of interest as well.

CHAPTER **III** STRUCTURE AND FUNCTION

The next period in the history of anthropology is associated with two of the most distinguished figures in the profession: the Englishman A. R. Radcliffe-Brown, and the Pole, trained in England, Bronislaw Malinowski. It would appear inevitable that the theoretically sterile approach of the historical particularists would have to give way eventually to a more conceptually oriented anthropology. Gathering masses of data over long periods of time is all very well, but eventually it becomes imperative to have some way of ordering and interpreting such data. A theory is needed to generate hypotheses that can then be tested against further data. This theoretical vacuum was filled by the *functionalists*. Although we concentrate here mainly on Radcliffe-Brown and Malinowski, it is important to realize that each of them represents an approach in anthropology that was followed by many others. Radcliffe-Brown, for reasons that are not completely clear, tended to create more disciples than did Malinowski. But the brilliant Pole did not lack for students and was to make an impression on anthropology every bit as enduring as that of Radcliffe-Brown. The effect of their work is part of what has been described as a "Copernican revolution" in anthropology. We will discuss the other part of this revolution in the chapter to follow. Although both of these anthropologists were British-trained, their impact was as great on American anthropology as it was elsewhere.

It has been remarked that Boas and his students "forged a discipline out of a curiosity" (Murphy, 1972:43). Certainly Robert H. Lowie was one of the most significant figures in this accomplishment. Lowie was born in Vienna in 1883 but when he was ten his family emigrated to New York City. His precociousness and ambition can be seen in the fact that he received his B.A. degree from the City College in New York by the time he was eighteen. He then taught for a short time before taking summer courses at Columbia where, like Kroeber, he met Boas and decided on a career in anthropology, in so far as there was such a thing in those days. Clark Wissler, another of the early "greats" of American anthropology, had just been appointed to the chairmanship of the Department of Anthropology at the

American Museum of Natural History. He, along with Boas, directed Lowie's career. It was Wissler who arranged for Lowie's first fieldwork with the Shoshone in Idaho in 1906. And it was also Wissler who appointed Lowie as Assistant in the American Museum. Their association had lasted for fourteen years when Lowie joined the University of California faculty at Berkeley in 1921, after virtually all of his fieldwork with American Indians was finished (Murphy, 1972).

To understand his famous "shreds and patches" statement it is necessary to remember that Lowie, like all of his colleagues, was reacting to the only major anthropological theory of the time—evolutionism. And like Boas, Lowie brought with him to anthropology the same German interest in science, empiricism, and, above all, facts and caution. Lowie virtually made his career out of demonstrating over and over again that the stages of evolution postulated by Morgan, Tylor, and others simply would not stand up to the facts. He was a truly unusual and dedicated fact-collector. At his death he probably knew more about North American Indians than any other person, and he also had vast quantities of information on other parts of the world. Lowie believed that the demonstrable facts of diffusion completely negated the evolutionists. Thus he argued, with all kinds of ethnographic examples, that the evolutionists were misinformed:

. . . One of Lowie's favorite examples was that of the bow and arrow, which had been diffused throughout the New World and were used by the simplest of hunters and collectors as well as by the armies of great states. This was enough to place even the rudest of the American Indians in the stage of Upper Savagery, one notch above the Polynesians, whose islands had not been reached by the weapon. . . . Yet, the Polynesians were consummate navigators and skilled agriculturalists, possessing stratified societies of remarkable sophistication. Obviously, in this case the progress of the Polynesians had little to do with whether or not they used the bow and arrow. In other technological items, entire stages of evolution were simply bypassed. One common assumption of the evolutionists was that man emerged from the Stone Age to the use of copper, thence to bronze, and finally to iron. This sequence is borne out by Near Eastern archeology and undoubtedly represents the actual world-wide sequence of the emergence of the inventions. But, as Lowie pointed out, the Africans went directly from the Stone Age to an Iron Age through borrowing. . . . (Murphy, 1972:49-50)

This kind of all-out attack completely destroyed evolutionism for a time and earned Lowie a reputation for being destructive but not very constructive. Like many such accusations, this is a much oversimplified view. Lowie was well aware that the evolutionists recognized diffusion. But he felt they had not fitted it adequately into evolutionary theory. He was also aware there could be multiple origins for things and, in fact, argued that the *clan* had multiple origins. Lowie was not out to destroy evolutionism so much as he was to insist that the evidence must always come first.

Although he can be classified basically as a historical particularist and a diffusionist, Lowie's views went beyond these points of view to anticipate what was to follow, namely, the position known as *functionalism*:

. . . His early work on kinship predated the publications of Malinowski and the theoretical writings of Radcliffe-Brown, and his criticism of Morgan rested heavily on Morgan's failure to see facts in a contemporary relationship to each other. And, although it is well remembered that the great British functionalists were scathing in their denunciation of historical reconstructions, or "conjectural history," based upon alleged "survivals" of earlier stages of history, Lowie led the way in his attack upon Morgan's notion that kinship nomenclatures were, in themselves, survivals. He showed them, instead, to be living and vital parts of social organisms. But he was a cautious functionalist, whose aims were also historical. (Murphy, 1972:65)

That anthropologists should see cultural facts in their current relationship to each other rather than historically or in evolutionary perspective became the most basic tenet of functionalism, the development which followed historical particularism.

Lowie's position on culture, which he expressed early in his first book, *Culture and Ethnology* (1917), was similar to Kroeber's view—that culture was, somehow, a reality of its own, and the causes of culture would be found only in culture itself. This similarity indicates that Kroeber was not alone in beginning to question the meaning of the term *culture*. Anthropology was expanding and becoming more self-critical and reflective.

By 1911 eight people had received their degrees under Boas: Clark Wissler, Alfred L. Kroeber, William Jones, Albert B. Lewis, Robert H. Lowie, Edward Sapir, Alexander Goldenweiser, and Paul Radin. As this "first generation" of anthropologists moved out, finding jobs wherever they could, Boas trained others. Soon Columbia ceased to be the only university where anthropological training could be obtained. The University of California, Berkeley, created a department of anthropology, as did others: the University of Chicago, Harvard, Yale, Pennsylvania, Michigan. Still others followed. The number of professional anthropologists kept growing and, encouraged by the eclectic Boas and the similarly eclectic first generation, kept finding new problems and trying new methods and techniques. It was a period of rapid expansion and great activity.

The "second" and subsequent generations of American anthropologists continued their *"salvage ethnography"* with American Indians in an effort to record these cultures before they were destroyed, but they also began extending their research further afield. Ralph Linton was in the Marquesas by 1920. Margaret Mead did her first fieldwork in Samoa in 1925. Robert Redfield was doing his early work in Mexico in 1926. By the early 1930's many American anthropologists were doing fieldwork overseas, particularly in Oceania and Africa. The British, too, were conducting more and more field studies. Even so, until the 1930's no dominant orientation or clear-cut theoretical position emerged to replace historical particularism. And it was still believed by many that to be a successful anthropologist one had to be well versed in all areas of anthropology. Thus the same person was often cultural anthropologist, physical anthropologist, linguist, and archeologist all joined into one. Linton, in fact, went to the Marquesas as an archeologist, but changed his interest while in the field and reported on the living Marquesans instead. Several of the anthropologists of this time combined archeology with their ethnological studies of remnant American Indian groups. Alfred Bowers, who did both archeological and ethnological work with the Mandan and Hidatsa, is a good example of this combination (Bowers, 1950). All of this was soon to change.

In their attempt to show the inadequacies of the early evolutionists the historical particularists did at times tend to overreact. Whereas the evolutionists dealt with the over-all process that had led to civilization (culture), the particularists argued that it was necessary to study individual cultures. Where the evolutionists presented a grand, all-encompassing theory, the particularists became virtually antitheoretical, cautioning always that adequate theory would follow only after the painstaking collection of all the facts. Where the evolutionists reconstructed history the particularists demanded accurate, detailed, historical data. It was a relatively simple matter for the particularists to demonstrate, in case after case as Lowie and others did, that the evolutionary paradigm was incorrect. They produced cases where, in the evolutionists' view, people who should have been matrilineal were in fact patrilineal. They found people who should have been polytheistic but who were monotheistic. They also produced cases demonstrating that the same custom could arise in two different places for quite different reasons, thus destroying the notion that similarities were necessarily the result of parallel evolution. But in all this criticism they failed to come up with a coherent body of theory of their own. The world we observe being exceedingly complex, it can be comprehended only through adequate concepts that fit together and give it meaning. But this conceptualization was precisely what was missing in the work of Boas and the first generation of particularists. Melford Spiro has put it very well:

That the method of radical empiricism (historical particularism) should have led, too, to scientific agnosticism is not at all surprising. Cultural phenomena are indeed complex, as Boas rightly cautioned; but this method could hardly have decreased the impression of their complexity. The fact is, of course, that the phenomenal world—the physical no less than the cultural—is always complex; it is, as William James put it, a "booming, buzzing, confusion." Hence, it is at least arguable that the order and simplicity now perceived to characterize the physical world are conceptual rather than phenomenal, and that the absence of order and of simplicity that seems to characterize the cultural world may similarly be conceptual rather than phenomenal. For we anthropologists are no exception to a universal law of perception: *viz.*, that any stimulus field becomes a perceptually meaningful field only when it is structured. But having decided to collect all the ethnographic facts, and to collect them as objectively as possible—that is, without explicit theory —anthropology was confronted with an enormous corpus of unstructured ethnographic material. And, as in any other unstructured situation, the resultant perception was one of enormous complexity. (Spiro, 1972:577)

ANDAMAN ISLANDERS. Turtle catching. (Smithsonian Institution; National Anthropological Archives)

Two of the developments to emerge out of this background, at virtually the same time—the 1920's—were *structuralism* and *functionalism*. More precisely we should term these *structural-functionalism* and *psychological functionalism*. The first of these is always identified with the name A. R. Radcliffe-Brown and the second most usually with Bronislaw Malinowski. It is strange, perhaps, that the two major influences on American anthropology at this time both came from British-trained anthropologists. But however strange, the impact of these two scholars was by far the most important and exciting development in anthropology since Tylor.

A. R. Radcliffe-Brown

At the same time that Boas was turning out the first generation of his students in America, A. R. Radcliffe-Brown was studying anthropology at Cambridge under W. H. R. Rivers. He also trained with A. C. Haddon, said to be "the father of scientific fieldwork in British anthropology" (Fortes, 1949:viii). In 1906 he began the fieldwork in the Andaman Islands that was to become the basis for his book *The Andaman Islanders*. His preliminary account of this work was accepted as his Ph.D. dissertation; but partly because of the first World War it was not published in book form until 1922. Radcliffe-Brown spent the years 1910-1912 in western

Australia doing further fieldwork. From 1916 to 1919 he was Director of Education in Tonga. From there he went to South Africa and thence to Australia. During most of this time he wrote and lectured profusely. Some of his most important papers were published between 1922 and 1926. Thus when he arrived as Professor of Anthropology at the University of Chicago in 1931 he brought with him an impressive, semilegendary background. Being handsome, urbane, and sociable, he quickly attached to himself a wide following. Ralph Linton was teaching at the University of Wisconsin and establishing his own reputation at the time. Being somewhat isolated in Madison, Linton spent much of his time with colleagues at the University of Chicago and there encountered Radcliffe-Brown. Some idea of that time can be gathered from the following:

Personal animosity did not prevent the two men from offering a joint seminar session at the University of Wisconsin in 1936. Radcliffe-Brown came to Wisconsin University accompanied by a collection of his devoted followers, and the session turned into a confrontation and was one of the most stimulating events that Wisconsin social sciences had produced. The two men provided quite a contrast on the rostrum: Radcliffe-Brown, tall and arrogant in beautifully tailored English clothes, a monocle, and a long cigarette holder; Linton, big and burly in rumpled unmatched tweeds and smoking a pipe. Linton did not attack Radcliffe-Brown's functional theories in total, but he did reject his rather arbitrary formulations of so-called structural-functional laws as not being based upon empirical fact but upon intuitive speculation. Furthermore, Linton, both by training and personal inclination, disliked the imposition of any elaborate theoretical system such as that Radcliffe-Brown was trying to achieve. He also felt that Radcliffe-Brown in his sociological search for "laws" was ignoring the biological and psychological reality of man. . . . (A. Linton and Wagley, 1971:39-40)

Even so, Linton, like many other American scholars of the period, accepted the basic tenets of functionalism, and *social anthropology* (Radcliffe-Brown's label for his type of anthropology) became firmly established in the United States with the University of Chicago as its headquarters.

Although its proponents tried to dismiss the concept of culture as irrelevant to the mainstream of anthropology, structural-functionalism is of importance to us here because of the effect it had on developments to come. Radcliffe-Brown, following a tradition established by the great French sociologist Emile Durkheim, believed that anthropology should study *social systems* rather than culture:

This brings us to a fundamental axiom of the science of society, as I see it. Is a science of culture possible? Boas says it is not. I agree. You cannot have a science of culture. You can study culture only as a characteristic of a social system. Therefore, if you are going to have a science, it must be a science of social systems. (Radcliffe-Brown, 1957:106)

But Boas's belief that a science of culture was not possible grew from his beliefs about the historical processes involved in the formation of cultures, not from his objection to the concept of culture as such. Not so Radcliffe-Brown, who attempted to demonstrate that the culture concept was less meaningful than the concept of social systems. The simplest way to understand what Radcliffe-Brown had in mind is to consider his organic analogy.

> . . . it is convenient to use the analogy between social life and organic life. An animal organism is an agglomeration of cells and interstitial fluids arranged in relation to one another not as an aggregate but as an integrated system of complex molecules. The system of relations by which these units are related is the organic structure. As the terms are here used the organism is *not* itself the structure; it is a collection of units [cells or molecules] arranged in a structure, i.e., in a set of relations; the organism *has* a structure. Two mature animals of the same species and sex consist of similar units combined in a similar structure. The structure is thus to be defined as a set of relations between entities.
>
> As the word function is here being used the life of an organism is conceived as the *functioning* of its structure. It is through and by the continuity of the functioning that the continuity of the structure is preserved. If we consider any recurrent part of the life-process, such as respiration, digestion, etc., its *function* is the part it plays in, the contribution it makes to, the life of the organism as a whole. (Radcliffe-Brown, 1952:178-179)

In somewhat simpler terms: just as an individual human being constitutes a finite system with a distinctive structure—each organ performing a particular activity, the function of which is to contribute to the maintenance of the system as a whole (the secretion of gastric fluid is an activity of the stomach, the function of which is to change protein into a form in which it can be absorbed and distributed by the blood to the tissues) (Radcliffe-Brown, 1952:179)—so a human society constitutes a similar system with its distinctive structure and functions. A "natural science of society" must recognize the natural system, discover its structure, and perceive how each part functions in relation to the system. Radcliffe-Brown was able to explicate, using this analogy, a number of previously less well-understood facts about kinship and social structure.

In spite of his rejection of a science of culture, and although it is by no means completely clear what he meant by *culture*, Radcliffe-Brown did employ a concept of culture. For him, culture was considered (1) a set of rules for "fitting human beings together into a social system," (2) "common symbols and common meanings attached to them" (1957:99), and (3) "a certain common set of ways of feeling and a certain common set of ways of thinking" (1957:102). But, he argued, as these rules, symbols, and common ways could not exist independently of real, living, interacting human beings, all an investigator could do was study specific acts of behavior. Language was used by Radcliffe-Brown as an example of this proposition:

> Culture cannot exist of itself even for a moment; certainly it cannot continue. What, for example, is the basis of the continuity of a language? . . . A language you recognize as a

body of speech usages, and you can describe it in terms of a set of rules. It is quite clear that a set of speech usages does not remain unchanged, even for a comparatively short period. But English today is still English, though not that spoken in the eighteenth century. We recognize a certain fundamental continuity. What is the basis of it? It is that at any moment of time between the eighteenth century and the present day we could have put our finger on a certain body of human beings who constituted the English-speaking community of that time *and had a structural continuity as a group*. The continuity of the language depends on continuity of the social structure. Just so does the existence and continuity of the whole of culture as a characteristic of the group. You cannot have coaptation without culture and you cannot have the continuity of culture without continuity of social structure. The social structure consists of the social behavior of actual individual human beings, who are *a priori* to the existence of culture. Therefore, if you study culture, you are always studying the acts of behavior of a specific set of persons who are linked together in a social structure.

On that basis I would say no science of culture is possible, that even a science of language is part of the total science of which I am speaking. (Radcliffe-Brown, 1957:107-108)

But the social structure—which is not the actual behavior of human beings in Radcliffe-Brown's theory but, rather, an abstraction from behavior—could also exist only if there were individuals *a priori* to the behavior. Radcliffe-Brown, like many creative scholars, was not always completely consistent in his views. In any case, the fact that rules, symbols, and common ways, including languages, exist only if people exist does not mean they do not exist at all. And if they exist, presumably they can be studied. Surely Radcliffe-Brown did not mean to tell us we cannot study dreams, thoughts, stories, geometry, religion, and their likes, all existing only if people exist *a priori*? That the implications of his rejection were not completely clear in Radcliffe-Brown's own mind can be seen if we continue the quotation above:

. . . I can qualify that statement a little in this way: while no complete science of culture is possible by itself, you can have an independent scientific treatment of certain aspects, of certain portions of culture. They will not give you the final scientific conclusions, but they will give you a certain number of quite important provisional ones. (1957:108)

Unfortunately, Radcliffe-Brown never told us what an incomplete science might be as distinguished from a "complete science," or precisely what "portions of culture" might be amenable to scientific treatment, or what "final scientific conclusions" may be, or what he meant by "important provisional ones." The above qualification is all the more confusing when one finds Radcliffe-Brown elsewhere arguing that it is permissible to use "logical fictions":

Force is a logical fiction, a convenient concept by which we can describe a certain type of physical phenomena. *Interest* is a similar logical fiction for describing biological phenomena; it is a shorthand description of a series of acts of behavior—not itself a real entity, but valuable in describing phenomenal reality. (1957:44)

Apparently one can study and use logical fictions—''not themselves real entities''—but one cannot study culture or language because ''it cannot exist of itself.'' But both language and culture, and social structure as well, are precisely what Radcliffe-Brown meant by ''a logical fiction''—''a shorthand description of a series of acts of behavior.'' As has been noted above, Radcliffe-Brown was given at times to grandiose pronouncements that are often as incomprehensible as they were ambitious. Consider Lowie's remark on Radcliffe-Brown:

> The grandiloquent use of the term ''law'' is most regrettable and in some circumstances leads to absurdity, as when Radcliffe-Brown writes of ''a universal sociological law though it is not yet possible to formulate precisely its scope, namely that in certain specific conditions a society has need to provide itself with a segmentary [clan] organization.'' Whoever heard of a universal law with an as yet undefinable scope, of a law that works in certain specific *but unspecified* conditions? Is it a law that some societies have clans, and others have not? Newton did not tell us that bodies either fall or rise. (Lowie, 1937:225)

But even Lowie admitted, somewhat begrudgingly, that when Radcliffe-Brown set aside his theoretical pronouncements and set to work on data he did bring order to what had previously appeared chaotic. Thus he wrote insightful articles on such topics as joking relationships, taboo, totemism, law, the relationship of mother's brother to sister's son, and many other customs of interest to anthropologists. Although not all of his work has survived the test of time, it was always stimulating and exciting. It would appear that Radcliffe-Brown was at his worst when he came to the subject of either culture or psychology.

It seems in retrospect, as Audrey Richards has stated, that whatever Radcliffe-Brown and his colleagues were not interested in they subsumed under the term culture and thus arbitrarily eliminated from anthropology:

> It was argued that social structure should be clearly separated from the other aspects of man's social heritage. These came to be subsumed under the title ''culture,'' a word which has often been used in the post-war years almost in a pejorative sense to describe a sort of rag-bag of odds and ends in which to thrust all facts and ideas in which the social anthropologist was not at the moment interested. (Richards, 1957:29)

These particular obfuscations, however, were probably less misleading to the further development of anthropology than were Radcliffe-Brown's well-known pronouncements on the relationship of anthropology to psychology:

> How do I meet the criticism that social science and psychology both observe the same entities, acts of behavior of individuals? If the subject matter, the data, constituted the only difference between two sciences, then there would be no difference between the sciences of the psychologist and the sociologist. You can, however, take an act of behavior and observe it in two totally different systems. The social scientist and the psychologist are not concerned with the same system and its set of relations. The social scientist is concerned

with relations he can discover between acts of diverse individuals; the psychologist with relations between acts of behavior of one and the same individual.

Psychology deals with the system we call *mind*. Mind . . . is the name of a system of mental relations, a system of which the units, individual acts of inner and outer behavior, are connected with one another by relations of interdependence. You do not have to bring in the body, which I believe exists always with the mind. . . . The physiologist studies the body; the psychologist, the mind; the physiological-psychologist, the system mind-and-body. (1957:45-46)

Aside from arbitrarily excluding much of what most anthropologists, psychologists, social psychologists, psychiatrists, and psychoanalysts believe they are interested in, the above statement has to stand as one of the best examples of what Ernest Becker has called the "fetishist reaction":

It is the "fetishist" reaction to the protean problem of a science of man that has lasted up to the present day and continues to trouble us. I call it "fetishist" because it is just that: an attempt to cope with an overwhelming problem of conceptualization by biting off very tiny pieces of it and concentrating on them alone, even, to push the analogy, deriving all one's sense of self, all one's delight in life and work, from the feverish contemplation of a ludicrously limited area of reality. Of course, this does not characterize all the disciplinarians, and especially not those we are going to talk about, but it does characterize the discipline as a whole. (1971:81-82)

It certainly characterizes Radcliffe-Brown who, in his attempt to define the boundaries of social anthropology, went so far as to claim:

No relationship *between two persons* can by my definition be a psychological relation. The only psychological relations are those which exist within one mind—unless you admit telepathy. (1957:47)

Anyone is free to define psychology or culture as he wishes. But Radcliffe-Brown did more—he specifically outlawed the study of psychology and culture for those who would follow his social anthropology. Both Radcliffe-Brown's anti-psychological and anticultural orientation are doubtless related to his competition with Bronislaw Malinowski to dominate anthropology. Malinowski, as we shall see, depended heavily upon psychology and the concept of culture for his version of functionalism. Likewise, there was an increasing interest in psychology and in the individual by those American anthropologists who had not been won over by Radcliffe-Brown.

Radcliffe-Brown's antipsychological attitude is otherwise difficult to understand in that he studied psychology and was, in fact, the first student of W. H. R. Rivers, a psychologist famous for his Torres Straits expedition of 1898 (Fortes, 1949:viii). His abandonment of the culture concept, which he used in his famous early book *The Andaman Islanders* (1922), is perhaps not so difficult to understand, since he did attempt to include some of its content, however inadequately, in his subsequent definitions of social structure (Richards, 1957:16). But, in any case, it was certainly not Radcliffe-Brown's intention to be a "fetishist," inasmuch as he firmly believed in a science of man that would solve the increasingly pressing problems of this day:

> . . . Ever since his student days Radcliffe-Brown had held unwaveringly to the belief that the only road to the solution of the ills of human society is the long and arduous one of first building up the scientific knowledge upon which effective remedies can be based with some hope of success. This was the theme of all his extramural activities. He wrote for the press, gave public lectures, addressed many conferences of bodies concerned with education and social welfare, and most successfully of all, organized vacation courses in applied anthropology. (Fortes, 1949:x)

This belief he shared with Boas. He also shared with Boas a distaste for the evolutionists who had preceded them both. He did not share Boas's historical orientation; history, he asserted, was *idiographic* whereas anthropology should be *nomothetic*. That is, it should search for "acceptable generalizations," universal laws that would be the equivalent of laws of physics and would apply to human social behavior. But realize that he objected not to history as such but rather to the "reconstructed history" of the evolutionists—which he thought of contempuously as pseudohistory. Radcliffe-Brown pointed out, rightly, that most of the societies of interest to anthropology did not have any written history. Unfortunately, his lack of interest here led him not to utilize historical records even when they were available.

Radcliffe-Brown made his greatest contribution, not by actually discovering any general laws of human social behavior, but by helping to set anthropology in an entirely new direction and by insisting on higher standards of fieldwork and analysis. He insisted that anthropology use the standard scientific procedure of starting from a hypothesis, testing it by intensive fieldwork, modifying it if necessary, and continuing the process. This insistence meant that anthropology had to have a theory from which to derive testable hypotheses—precisely what was so conspicuously absent in the work of Boas and his followers.

Following Radcliffe-Brown's lead, a host of able fieldworkers produced a wealth of permanently valuable contributions to anthropology. Because Radcliffe-Brown taught at the major English universities (including Oxford where he held the first chair in Anthropology), founded a chair of Social Anthropology at the University of Cape Town, founded the chair of Social Anthropology at the University of Sydney, went to the University of Chicago as Professor of Anthropology, and shortly before his death was appointed the first Professor of Sociology at Farouk I University in Alexandria, he had, like Boas, a profound influence on the profession of anthropology. In the tradition of social anthropology established by Radcliffe-Brown are such distinguished figures as E. E. Evans-

Pritchard, Meyer Fortes, Raymond Firth, Lucy Mair, S. F. Nadel, Max Gluckman, Edmund R. Leach, Audrey Richards, Hilda Kuper, and many more.

Radcliffe-Brown took the concept of "function" from Durkheim. But he defined it in such a way that it could be applied only to "social structure"—hence structural-functionalism. The idea was, as we have seen, that one could study social structure—the relations between the members of groups—and one could then determine the function of any given behavior in terms of how well it promoted the well-being of the group. This was usually stated in terms of "unity," "harmony," "consistency," or "solidarity"—"a condition in which all parts of the social system work together with a sufficient degree of harmony or internal consistency" (Radcliffe-Brown, 1952:181). The idea of the functional unity of a social system, Radcliffe-Brown felt, was a hypothesis worthy of testing by the systematic observation of facts.

Although Radcliffe-Brown did have an idea of culture—really "ideology"—as did most of his followers, neither he nor his followers can be said to have contributed much to further development of the culture concept. Hence we will leave social anthropology by turning to a different kind of functionalism, one with different implications for the culture concept. It is interesting to note, however, that whereas structural-functionalism as such has virtually been abandoned, many, if not most present-day American anthropologists—and quite a few British as well—are now studying precisely those rules, symbols, and common ways of feeling and thinking that Radcliffe-Brown attempted to purge. Likewise, since the second World War there has been a renewed and intensified interest in history or, as it is often termed, *ethnohistory* (Carmack, 1972).

Bronislaw Malinowski

What Radcliffe-Brown was attempting to do can be better understood when we consider his "competitor," Bronislaw Malinowski. Born in Krakow (then in Austria though now in Poland), Malinowski received a Ph.D. in physics and mathematics but shortly thereafter was threatened with tuberculosis. He is reported to have walked from his university with Frazer's *The Golden Bough* under his arm, determined to read it in the original English to take his mind off his problem. As quoted by H. R. Hays, Malinowski later commented: "No sooner had I read this great work than I became immersed in it and enslaved by it. I realized then that anthropology, as presented by Sir James Frazer, is a great science, worthy of as much devotion as any of her elder and more exact sister studies and I became bound to the service of Frazerian anthropology." (Hays, 1958:314)

In 1910 Malinowski, whose health had improved, entered the London School of Economics, where he met Sir James Frazer and studied anthropology under A. C. Haddon, C. G. Seligman, and Edward Westermarck. In 1914 he was traveling in the Pacific. With the outbreak of the World War he became technically an "enemy

TROBRIAND ISLANDERS. Dancing, with yam huts in the background. (Smithsonian Institution; National Anthropological Archives)

alien'' because of his place of birth. He was allowed by the Australian government to stay in the Trobriand Islands and spent the next four years there doing fieldwork. This was a development of great significance for the science of anthropology, for out of it Malinowski fashioned not only a stimulating theory of culture but also a number of important books, now classics.

Malinowski cut himself off from the white traders entirely, set up a tent, and lived with the Trobrianders themselves. He learned their language and came to share in their feasts, ceremonies, amusements, and other life activities. This type of fieldwork went far beyond anything previously attempted and because of it Malinowski could later speak with great authority. The new standard for fieldwork he set has rarely been surpassed to this day.

Malinowski's theory of culture included many of Radcliffe-Brown's principles but went far beyond them. The basic building blocks for Malinowski were seven basic human ''needs.'' Culture was seen as the instrument through which these needs were met. Malinowski, however, insisted that these were individual, not group needs, and it was here that the greatest rift occurred between structural-functionalism and Malinowski's more comprehensive, more psychological functionalism, which he referred to as ''pure functionalism.'' The differences are well expressed in the following:

SYNOPTIC SURVEY OF BIOLOGICAL AND DERIVED NEEDS AND THEIR SATISFACTION IN CULTURE

A Basic Needs (Individual)	B Direct Responses (Organized, i.e., Collective)	C Instrumental Needs	D Responses to Instrumental Needs	E Symbolic and Integrative Needs	F Systems of Thought and Faith
Nutrition (metabolism).....	Commissariat	Renewal of cultural apparatus	Economics	Transmission of experience by means of precise, consistent principles	Knowledge
Reproduction...	Marriage and family				
Bodily comforts.	Domicile and dress	Charters of behavior and their sanctions	Social control		
Safety.........	Protection and defense			Means of intellectual, emotional, and pragmatic control of destiny and chance	Magic Religion
Relaxation.....	Systems of play and repose	Renewal of personnel	Education		
Movement.....	Set activities and systems of communication				
Growth........	Training and apprenticeship	Organization of force and compulsion	Political organization	Communal rhythm of recreation, exercise, and rest	Art Sports Games Ceremonial

MALINOWSKI'S BASIC HUMAN NEEDS. This table presents essentials of his "pure functionalism." (1939:938-964)

Professor Radcliffe-Brown is, as far as I can see, still developing and deepening the views of the French sociological school. He thus has to neglect the individual and disregard biology.

Functionalism differs from other sociological theories more definitely, perhaps, in its conception and definition of the individual than in any other respect. The functionalist includes in his analysis not merely the emotional as well as intellectual side of mental processes, but also insists that man in his full biological reality has to be drawn into our analysis of culture. The bodily needs and environmental influences, and the cultural relation to them, have thus to be studied side by side. (Malinowski, 1939:939).

This point was precisely the one, you will remember, that Ralph Linton and others were also trying to make. The functionalism of Malinowski consisted of showing how the various elements of culture contributed to the culture as a unified, consistent whole. This outlook entailed always attempting to correlate one set of activities with the whole. In this work he was doing what Radcliffe-Brown was attempting to do with social systems. But Malinowski was much more ambitious. In *Coral Gardens and Their Magic* (1935), for example, Malinowski focused on horticultural activities and attempted to relate them to the cultural whole—which included such things as the family, the kinship system, political organization, land tenure, technical processes, religion, and magic. He demonstrated how important it was to see customs, beliefs, and institutions in their cultural context, and he continually railed at those who attempted to pull out "traits" or artifacts and study them in isolation—thus dissenting from the "shreds and patches" notion of Lowie (Lowie, 1920:331). Nor did he believe you could readily compare items cross-culturally, not because each culture had a unique history, but because of the dangers of violating their proper context and hence changing them into something they were not.

At the same time that institutions or customs had to be shown as contributing to the culture as a whole, they also had to be shown as meeting specific human needs—for, after all, what was culture but a "vast instrumental reality," created precisely for that purpose. However we may look back on it today, it was a monumental and exciting scheme. Malinowski shared with Radcliffe-Brown the use of the concept "function," the belief that people were organized in "systems," that these constituted "wholes" of some kind, and that the parts therefore contributed something to their wholeness. They both believed in the importance of fieldwork and they also shared the belief that anthropology should be a science, not a pseudohistory. Above all, they both believed anthropology should be theoretical and not merely an exercise in random fact-gathering. Since they wrote and taught during precisely the same period, the combination produced an electrifying effect on anthropology. Audrey Richards gives us some idea of this when speaking of Malinowski:

The idea that rites, beliefs, and customs, however extraordinary they appear to an observer, actually fill "needs," biological, psychological, and social, became commonplace in anthropological teaching. It is difficult now to believe that Malinowski's teaching on this point could ever have struck his students as being brilliantly new. The changed outlook was probably due to the fact that discussions of the function of aspects or institutions of tribal life led directly into fieldwork material, either Malinowski's own extraordinarily rich collection of field notes or those of his first students. Those who listened to his lectures on the Trobriand Islanders will remember his intense absorption in the activities of the people he described and his stress on what actually happened as distinct from what anthropologists had guessed had happened in the past. This gave the work a vividness which the existing textbooks, and even the best contemporary missionary or anthropological monographs, lacked. Were kinship terms a survival of past stages in history? The answer lay, Malinowski would tell us, in the empirical material. How were the terms used? What was the index of emotional content? Or again, what was the function of myth or folk tale? The answer lay in a description of how these stories were actually recited; the occasions on which they were recited, and the manner of those who spoke, whether it was bragging, serious or lighthearted. In comparison with works such as those of Frazer, Crawley, Westermarck, or Durkheim which we read at the time, or with the ethnographic work produced by observers paying short visits to different tribes, such as that of Rivers or Seligman, the work seemed lively and stimulating, and we began actually to visualize ourselves "in the field." (1957:18-19)

It appears that one reason many of the British anthropologists entered the camp of Radcliffe-Brown rather than follow Malinowski lay in the sheer bulk and richness of the ethnographic materials that had to be presented as a description of a culture. They felt it was unmanageable and thus they chose to abstract one important feature, social structure, and attempted to make it the prevailing and only legitimate anthropological interest:

The complexity of primitive institutions that was revealed by such methods [Malinowski's] and their wide limits of variation began to strike with alarm those who were optimistic enough to believe that social typologies could be immediately constructed, and by those who hoped to reduce their material to a few simple abstract postulates. Malinowski and his pupils were considered to have collected too many facts of too many kinds to make simple comparative work possible. Gluckman described Malinowski's data as "too complex for comparative work" and he and Evans-Pritchard have constantly criticized it as being "overloaded with (cultural) reality." . . .
. . . They did not come to the conclusion that the comparisons they had in mind were too ambitious for the existing state of our knowledge, but decided instead that it would be better to have fewer facts, so as to make the comparisons easier. (Richards, 1957:28)

Thus it was Malinowski and a small minority of his followers that carried on and added to the study of culture in Great Britain. Although Malinowski did not improve much on Tylor's definition of 1871, his influence was overwhelming with respect to demonstrating the crucial significance of the concept. He was selected to write the article on "culture" in the American *Encyclopedia of Social Sciences* in 1931. In this article he wrote, "The social heritage (culture) is the key concept of cultural anthropology" (1931:621), and thus set forth a way of thinking about culture and anthropology that remains a key ingredient today.
In the culture concept of Malinowski, and to a somewhat lesser extent in the structural-functionalism of Radcliffe-Brown, we see clearly the influence of Matthew Arnold's view of culture as it contrasted with that of Tylor:

. . . Although Tylor thought rather more in terms of evolutionary product and Arnold of individual process, both men conceived culture in normative humanist terms as a conscious "cultivation" of the capacities which are most characteristically human. But while Tylor took humanistic culture and fragmented it for purposes of analysis, Arnold's culture . . . was, both for the individual and for society, an organic, integrative, holistic phenomenon. Tylor's analytic evolutionary purpose forced him to place great emphasis on the artifactual manifestations of culture, on those objects of "material culture" which were easily and convincingly arranged in hierarchical sequence; Arnold's culture, like that of most modern anthropologists, was an inward ideational phenomenon. For Arnold much more than for Tylor culture was a "way of life." . . . (Stocking, 1963:795)

Although both Malinowski and Radcliffe-Brown spoke critically of pseudohistory and historical reconstructions, it must not be thought that they were totally antievolutionary in their approaches. Radcliffe-Brown clearly accepted a type of evolutionism which he traced to Herbert Spencer; and Malinowski, having been influenced by Frazer and Westermarck, was even more heavily committed to an evolutionary view. But neither Radcliffe-Brown nor Malinowski can be said to have contributed to the further development of such theory.

Not only did both believe in evolutionism but both also failed to overcome the insidious notions of superiority-inferiority it implied. It is difficult to take exception to Marvin Harris's view of this:

. . . The judgment of history lies heavy on those anthropologists who believed themselves free of ethical involvement because they were advocates of the "Native" cause before the tribunals of the European racists while at the same time preaching moderation to the exploited and underprivileged.

Were it constructive in this context to plunge into a discussion of ethics, I should raise the question, never entertained by Malinowski, of why the Africans who had been invaded, conquered, enslaved, and exploited owed the Europeans anything else in return. The basic premise of Malinowski's position involved him in the assumption that the Europeans had a right to be governing the Africans and that every future adjustment rightfully demanded that the European interests be given their legal and customary due. Despite the admonitions to the Europeans that they had better be nice to the natives or the natives would go on misbehaving, there *is* a sanctimonious note in Malinowski's theory [of culture change] which helps to explain why anthropology is still a dirty word among many African nationalists. . . . (1968:557)

As for Radcliffe-Brown:

As late as 1950, Radcliffe-Brown's "Introduction" to *African Systems of Kinship and Marriage* included an opening quote from Gobineau advising Europeans who wish their civilization to spread, of the importance of knowing and comprehending those who were to be benefited. This is followed by the author's wish that "this book will be read not only by anthropologists, but by some of those who are responsible for formulating or carrying out policies of colonial government in the African continent." (Harris, 1968:517)

And, as one of the major flaws in the functionalists' approach was the inability to accommodate change in social systems or cultures, they have also been charged with complicity in maintaining the colonial status:

. . . Between 1930 and 1955 the overwhelming bulk of the contributions of the structural-functionalist school was based upon fieldwork in African tribal societies located in European, especially British, territories. Under such circumstances it is impossible not to draw a connection between the proposal to study social systems *as if* they were solidary and *as if* they were timeless, with sponsorship, employment, and indirect association of the members of this school by and with a now defunct colonial system. (Harris, 1968:516)

Here, however, is a good place to observe that there is a great difference between motives and functions. Even if it can be clearly demonstrated that the consequence (function) of twenty-five years of functionalism was to help perpetuate an unchanging colonial situation, it still does not follow that the functionalists' intention (motive) was that their approach should have that consequence. Perhaps for a few it was. But that most anthropologists had no such intentions is quite clear. That anthropologists are people of their own times and circumstances and that hindsight is better than foresight are also equally clear. The functionalists were avowedly ahistorical if not antihistorical. This outlook led them to deal with societies and cultures as if they were timeless, and they were accordingly unable to deal adequately with culture change. To argue that their failure to deal with change came from their being colonialists rather than from their being anthropologists, or vice versa, would take us far beyond the scope of this volume.

Interestingly enough, one of the major shortcomings of this functionalist view was precisely the failure to distinguish clearly between motives and functions. Motives were rarely considered at all by either Malinowski or Radcliffe-Brown, and thus was generated some unnecessary confusion. To observe, for example, that the function of marriage in tribal societies is to create political ties between two groups of people does not demonstrate that it was the intention of the people to do that. That the performance of the rain dance promotes social solidarity among the participants says nothing about the motives of the actors. Most certainly one is not justified in saying that people engage in religious rituals of various kinds because they wish to promote social solidarity even if, in fact, such rituals do have that function.

One final matter in this discussion: Malinowski shared with Radcliffe-Brown the firm conviction that the science of anthropology should be related to practical human affairs—to the moral crisis of which Ernest Becker speaks:

He looked upon his subject as a science, its role being "first handmaiden to a general theory of human society"; but he saw it also in its bearings upon human affairs—"a theory trying to achieve a deeper grasp of human nature and human history," perhaps capable of being used to influence the makers of policy but above all "useful in creating a saner attitude, finer and wider ideals in the minds of men." (Firth, 1957:7)

But unlike Radcliffe-Brown, Malinowski cannot be said to have been a disciplinary "fetishist." Indeed, he might well be considered one of the forerunners of what we now conceive of as an "interdisciplinarian," an early practitioner of a further development in anthropology often called "culture-and-personality," to which we will turn in the next chapter. Malinowski was a colorful and most influential scholar as well as a gifted teacher. He left an indelible mark on his students, many of whom were also students of Radcliffe-Brown. He was also, unlike most anthropologists, a gifted writer. That he was aware of having this skill, or at least was aware of his attempt to achieve it, is illustrated by a remark attributed to him by Mrs. B. Z. Seligman: "Rivers is the Rider Haggard of Anthropology; I shall be the Conrad" (Firth, 1957:6). Malinowski was one of those strong personalities who inevitably make enemies as well as friends. While he was intelligent and sensitive in most things, his enthusiasm often overcame him and aroused hostility in others. He is reported, for example, to have referred to the distinguished Fritz Graebner as "a museum mole" (Hays, 1958:325) and he tended always to ignore or minimize the importance of the contributions of other functionalists including, of course, Radcliffe-Brown. His accomplishments, however, must not be undervalued because of his personality characteristics. Some idea of the complexity of Malinowski the man, as well as what his experience in the Trobriands was like, can be gained from perusing the posthumously published *A Diary in the Strict Sense of the Term* (Malinowski, 1967).

Summary

The period from roughly 1915 to the early 1930's was one of intense growth and activity in anthropology. American and British anthropologists began doing fieldwork all over the globe. There was considerable innovation both in methods and in theory. The greatest intellectual stimulus came at this time from Radcliffe-Brown and Malinowski, who offered competing brands of an anthropological theory known as functionalism. Whereas Radcliffe-Brown's version came to be known as structural-functionalism, Malinowski claimed to have a "pure" functionalism. Malinowski's theory of culture was much more all-encompassing than was Radcliffe-Brown's "natural science of society." Whereas Malinowski emphasized psychological and biological needs as well as social needs, Radcliffe-Brown argued that there was no place for psychology or biology in anthropology. But both of these men felt that anthropology should be a science, that it should not be history, that it should not be primarily concerned with evolution, and that the parts of any whole, whether a social system or a culture, had to function for the maintenance of that whole. Since both of these figures were intelligent, dynamic, colorful personalities, and since they tended to compete vigorously with each other to dominate the field, it was an exciting time in the history of anthropology. Radcliffe-Brown attempted to ignore the culture concept as much as possible, with only limited success. Malinowski retained and promoted it and further clarified its meaning.

Further Readings

Marvin Harris's *The Rise of Anthropological Theory* has a detailed chapter on "British Social Anthropology" which discusses both Radcliffe-Brown and Malinowski. For a very different interpretation and point of view see the two books by I. C. Jarvie, *The Revolution in Anthropology* and *The Story of Social Anthropology*. Detailed articles on various aspects of Malinowski's work can be found in the collection edited by Firth, *Man and Culture*. For more details on Radcliffe-Brown see his *Festschrift* edited by Fortes, *Social Structure Studies Presented to A. R. Radcliffe-Brown*, and also Radcliffe-Brown's posthumously published statement of his position, *A Natural Science of Society*.

Malinowski's major books, *Sex and Repression in Savage Society, The Sexual Life of Savages in Northwestern Melanesia, Coral Gardens and Their Magic,* and *Crime and Custom in Savage Society*, remain as worthwhile and fascinating anthropological studies. Radcliffe-Brown's works were primarily theoretical. *The Andaman Islanders*, while not completely representative, is still of interest.

A few representative works in the tradition of British social anthropology, all worth reading, are Eggan, *Social Organization of the Western Pueblos*; E. E. Evans-Pritchard, *The Nuer*; Firth, *We, the Tikopia*; Fortes, *The Dynamics of Clanship among the Tallensi*; Fortune, *Sorcerers of Dobu*; Gluckman, *Order and Rebellion in Tribal Africa*; Hogbin, *Law and Order in Polynesia*; Leach, *Political Systems of Highland Burma*; Mair, *An African People in the Twentieth Century*; Meggitt, *The Lineage System of the Mae Enga of New Guinea*; Nadel, *A Black Byzantium*; Richards, *Economic Development and Tribal Change*; and M. G. Smith, *Government in Zazzau: 1800-1950*.

CHAPTER IV IDEALISM AND MATERIALISM

Not all anthropologists followed the functionalism of Radcliffe-Brown or Malinowski. There were other developments in anthropology, particularly in the United States. A number of investigators, stimulated primarily by the brilliant linguist Edward Sapir, became increasingly interested in individual human beings, in psychology, and in the question of how individuals were related to the culture of which they were a part. Ruth Benedict and Margaret Mead were also in the forefront of this culture-and-personality movement. In more recent years new interests have developed along these lines.

Other scholars rejected social anthropology and culture-and-personality studies in favor of a newer, more scientific brand of evolutionism with a basis in technoenvironmental determinism. One of these scholars, Leslie White, met with a great deal of resistance because of his identification with the thought of Karl Marx at a time when such identification was politically undesirable. Julian Steward, on the other hand, found a ready acceptance for his ideas which were very similar in their fundamentals to those of White.

This course of development has led to the contemporary situation in anthropology which, in a simplified version, sees the existence of two major and largely opposed points of view. We will refer to these, following Marvin Harris (1968), as cultural materialism and cultural idealism. Harris can be regarded as the chief spokesman for cultural materialism although other proponents of that point of view are important. The idealists, for convenience, can be subdivided into four main groups: (1) culture-and personality (also referred to as psychological anthropology), represented by such figures as John W. M. Whiting, Melford Spiro, Anthony F. C. Wallace, Francis L. K. Hsu, Robert LeVine, John Honigmann, and others, (2) structuralists, following Claude Levi-Strauss, (3) ethnoscientists, following developments in linguistics, and (4) symbolic anthropologists, represented by Clifford Geertz, Victor Turner, and others. The idealists can be said to share an interest in psychological phenomena and they tend to view culture in mental and symbolic terms. The materialists, on the other hand, tend to define culture strictly in terms of overt, observable behavior patterns, and they share the belief that technoenvironmental factors are primary and causal. They are, in general, antipsychological.

During the period when Radcliffe-Brown and Malinowski were reacting against evolutionary and historical reconstructions, demanding anthropology become a science, and developing their structural-functional approach, other important developments were taking place. One of these was labeled *culture-and-personality* and has more recently been termed *psychological anthropology*. Remember that both Linton and Malinowski criticized Radcliffe-Brown for omitting psychological and biological phenomena in his attempt to create a science of society. They were not alone in expressing such reservations and there was a growing interest in how the individual was related to his culture. This interest produced the second half of the so-called "Copernican revolution" in anthropology, mentioned previously.

. . . Despite the important differences that divided these schools [culture and personality and social anthropology], it should be observed that they also had much in common. First, in contrast to the earlier historical schools, both displayed almost systematic indifference to problems of a historical nature. This is not to say, as is sometimes charged, that they dismissed historical variables as irrelevant, but rather that they viewed the task of anthropology as something other than historical reconstruction. Second, in contrast to an older trait-list approach, both emphasized the primacy of context, pattern, configuration, and structure. Third, instead of a descriptivist approach, both were theoretically oriented. Primitive societies were to be studied for the light they could shed on theoretical issues: in the one case—and here they differed—sociological, and in the other, psychological. (Spiro, 1972:579)

This description does not refer merely to the difference between Radcliffe-Brown and Malinowski but rather to a newer and much more actively psychological point of view. Like structural-functionalism, these new culture-and-personality studies attempted to be scientific and nomothetic as opposed to historical and idiographic. They also attempted to consider wholes rather than merely parts. And they were avowedly theoretical.

Culture-and-Personality

Various writers have expressed different ideas as to where the beginnings of culture-and-personality are to be found. Milton Singer, in a survey of culture-and-personality theory and research, says that it was the encounter of anthropology with psychoanalysis that brought about the new development:

. . . It was in fact the encounter of anthropology, and to a lesser extent sociology and political science, with psychoanalysis, that gave rise to culture and personality studies. (Singer, 1961:10).

The early importance of psychoanalysis is evident by 1920 when Kroeber reviewed Freud's book *Totem and Taboo* (1918) in the *American Anthropologist*.

Although the review was not entirely critical it was, in general, much more negative than positive. Kroeber spent the bulk of the review demolishing Freud's attempt to find the origins of culture in the *Oedipus complex*. Nonetheless, Kroeber had been sufficiently taken by psychoanalytic theory to undergo analysis in 1917 and to practice as a lay analyst in San Francisco during 1918-1919 (Theodora Kroeber, 1970:105). Furthermore, when twenty years later Kroeber wrote another review of the same book he had somewhat changed his tone:

> He now thinks Freud's explanation of culture would deserve at least "serious considera-tion as a scientific hypothesis," if it were restated as a proposition about the constant operation of certain psychic processes—for example, the incest drive, incest repression, and filial ambivalence—in widespread human institutions. He still finds that psychoanalysis refuses to undertake such a restatement, because of its indifference to history and to accepted scientific attitudes, and its dogmatic all-or-none attitude which resists influences from without. (Singer, 1961:10)

C. G. Seligman, one of the important influences on Malinowski, took as his theme for his presidential address to the Royal Anthropological Institute of Great Britain and Ireland in 1924 the subject, "Anthropology and Psychology: A Study of Some Points of Contact." He discussed primarily Carl Gustav Jung's recently conceived types of personalities—introvert and extrovert—in relation to the study of anthropology. Europeans, he felt, were predominantly extrovert whereas Hin-dus were introvert. He also suggested the unconscious should be investigated among "non-European races" through the study of dreams. Seligman returned to the psychoanalytic theory of Freud and Jung, which he regarded as of importance to anthropology, in a later paper as well (1932).

The influence of psychoanalysis was also felt in early fieldwork. Thus while Malinowski was in the Trobiands (1914-1918) he received information and litera-ture from Seligman that stimulated him to pursue topics which were to have great impact on psychoanalytic theory and on anthropology. In his subsequent books, *Sex and Repression in Savage Society* (1927) and *The Sexual Life of Savages* (1929), he argued against a universal Oedipus complex as Freud had described it on the grounds that in matrilineal societies (like the Trobriands) the expression of Oedipal feelings and conflict would differ from that in Europe. Malinowski argued that in the Trobriand family it was the mother's brother who held authority and not the father—hence a boy's antagonism would be directed not toward his father but toward his mother's brother, a situation not considered by Freud.

Still another figure of importance with regard to the relationship of psychoanaly-tic theory to anthropology was the Hungarian-born scholar Geza Roheim. Roheim, a psychoanalyst, was as close to a psychoanalytic purist as it was possible to be. He had also done fieldwork of his own as early as 1927 in Africa and Australia. He argued that if anthropologists (like Malinowski) could not find oedipal feelings as Freud conceived of them, they, themselves, must be suffering from unresolved

AN AUSTRALIAN ABORIGINE WOMAN AND CHILD. (Smithsonian Institution, National Anthropological Archives)

Oedipus complexes! Needless to say Roheim did not endear himself to other anthropologists with this approach. And, because much of his own work depended upon an unquestioning belief in a theory of universal symbols which he got from Freud, his analyses of various myths and customs were not generally accepted by other anthropologists. Nonetheless, in spite of his excesses, Roheim did make a contribution to culture-and-personality studies. He suggested, for example, that *Homo sapiens* as a species has certain universal characteristics that could account for some kind of universal sexual complex. And he also suggested that such constant features of human life as these had to do with *"the origin and function of culture"*; the expression became the title of one of his most important works (1943). Thus, although he infuriated many of his colleagues, he was instrumental in laying the groundwork for the contemporary view of culture which assumes a number of psychobiological constants that give rise to and make inevitable a cultural mode of life for *Homo sapiens*. But even so, the more or less classical psychoanalytic approach of Roheim has generated little enthusiasm and has few practitioners, the most notable being George Devereux and Weston LaBarre.

Basic unsolved questions about human nature have also been suggested as the starting point for culture-and-personality studies, and they are obviously related to the impact of psychoanalytic theory on anthropology (and vice versa). Melford E. Spiro has suggested that culture-and-personality studies could have come about only when certain time-honored traditions of thought broke down. Modern science, Spiro argued (1951), is the heir to a tradition which has always elaborated dichotomies—real-ideal, means-ends, theory-practice, mind-body, matter-spirit, and many others. The clear separation between the individual and his society or culture, Spiro said, is another example of this dichotomizing. And this, he went on, was probably inevitable, given the belief in an inherent human nature which unfolded itself by a maturational process that was regarded as natural. However much people may have disagreed about what this human nature really was, they all agreed that for the most part society and/or culture were not involved in it. This notion is in evidence in psychoanalytic theory. It is found in G. Stanley Hall. And it clearly stimulated much of the work in culture-and-personality in the 1920's and 1930's. Margaret Mead, in the preface to the 1939 reissue of her book *From the South Seas*, graphically described the situation:

> It was the simple—a very simple—point to which our materials were organized in the 1920's, merely the documentation over and over of the fact that human nature is not rigid and unyielding, not an unadaptable plant which insists on flowering or becoming stunted after its own fashion, responding only quantitatively to the social environment, but that it is extraordinarily adaptable, that cultural rhythms are stronger and more compelling than the physiological rhythms which they overlay and distort, that the failure to satisfy an artificial, culturally stimulated need—for outdistancing one's neighbors in our society, for instance, or for wearing the requisite number of dog's teeth among the Manus—may produce more unhappiness and frustration in the human breast than the most rigorous cultural curtailments of the physiological demands of sex or hunger. We had to present evidence that human character is built upon a biological base which is capable of enormous diversification in terms of social standards. (1939:x)

Mead, however, just like a great many other anthropologists, although disavowing Freud's biological and ethnocentric point of view, in her later work took over and used much of psychoanalytic theory. This influence is perhaps most clear in her work with Gregory Bateson on *Balinese Character* (1942).

A third suggestion as to the beginnings of culture-and-personality studies has been offered by John Honigmann:

> Culture and personality studies began among North American Indians with the collection of personal documents, a category in which I include autobiographies, biographies, and psychological analyses. . . . (1961:96)

Although there had been numerous biographies and autobiographies of American Indians prior to the 1920's, there was, at this time, a more formal, deliberate attempt to use such materials in anthropology. Paul Radin and Edward Sapir, both students of Boas's, were the most important figures in this respect. But it should be made clear that Radin's attempt to use this kind of material, most notably in his well-known *Crashing Thunder* (1926), can be seen in the culture-and-personality tradition only in that he emphasized the individual as an important source for information—information which he ultimately would use to describe and understand *culture*—not psychology, personality, or even the "individual-in-culture." This was the dominant orientation of most life histories until about 1945 (Langness, 1965:8).

While opinions on the origin of culture-and-personality studies vary, all agree on the key role played by Sapir. As was previously noted, Sapir was one of the earliest of Boas's students. It has also been said that he was the most brilliant of all of them. Primarily a linguist, like so many of his contemporaries, he was well-versed in other aspects of anthropology as well. He was remarkably talented in general, being a poet, pianist, and composer of sorts, in addition to writing for a variety of sophisticated magazines. As early as 1917 Sapir reviewed a book on psychoanalytic method. In 1921 he reviewed, favorably, Rivers's *Instinct and the Unconscious* (1920). In 1923 he reviewed Jung's *Psychological Types* (1921). Both he and Radin were well-informed on Jung's work. He was also acquainted with the great psychiatrist Harry Stack Sullivan, a relationship of mutual intellectual stimulation which was instrumental in the rapprochement of anthropology and psychiatry. Although Sapir did not really write extensively on psychology, there is no doubt of his powerful influence on Ruth Benedict and Margaret Mead, who helped develop the new field of culture-and-personality.

To fully understand Sapir's significance in the development of culture-and-personality, and hence in the further development of the culture concept itself, one must understand his reaction to Kroeber's attempt to establish culture as a "superorganic." In retrospect, and in view of Becker's thesis, it might be suggested that Kroeber's attempt to define culture as a superorganic, as an entity existing independently in its own right and independently of individual men and women, was not only an attempt to define culture more precisely but was also an attempt to establish a distinctively anthropological subject matter as opposed to psychology, sociology, or some other discipline. David Bidney has commented on this point also:

. . . The older generation of anthropologists, whether evolutionists, diffusionists, functionalists, or culturologists, all agreed [implicitly] to maintain the independence and distinctness of anthropology as a science. They thought that if they could demonstrate the autonomy and reality of culture as a reality *sui generis*, then this would justify and validate their claim for an autonomous science of cultural anthropology. (1967:xvii)

Be this as it may, Kroeber's insistence on the unimportance of individuals represented a sharp break with Boas, who had always had an interest in the individual and in the individual's relationship to his culture. Although Boas had not pursued this interest himself, he had encouraged his students to do so.

Boas had also, as we have seen, converted the early notion of culture (civilization) from singular to plural. But he had not actually added or changed substantially the definition of culture that had come from Tylor and Arnold. Nor had anyone else, it appears, until Kroeber's ideas on the superorganic nature of culture appeared in 1917. This departure seems to have had the effect of stimulating others—most notably Sapir—to consider more carefully the meaning of the concept of culture. Sapir responded immediately in an article entitled "Do We Need a Superorganic?" (1917). He took Kroeber to task and accused him of using overly selective examples to make his point. He suggested that had Kroeber dealt with religion, aesthetics, philosophy, and things of that sort as well as with the realm of sciences and invention, he would not have been able so easily to denigrate the importance of the individual in history. What, he asked, of figures like Jesus? Mohammed? Were they, as individuals, unimportant to the further course of history? Would events have followed the same path had these particular individuals not existed? Sapir did not think so, and this opinion led him to define culture in a way importantly different from any that had previously been suggested. John Honigmann has commented most lucidly on this point:

Cultural anthropology, he [Sapir] said, emphasizes the group and its traditions but pays little regard to the individuals who make up the group and who actualize its traditions in individual variations of behavior. Anthropology might also focus on persons and see culture in its "true locus," namely, "in the interactions of specific individuals and, on the subjective side, in the world of meanings which each one of these individuals may unconsciously abstract for himself from his participation in these interactions"—in much the same way as psychiatry focuses on a whole individual and observes him in his world of social relationships. (1972:125)

By suggesting that culture might be something internalized by individual human beings as a "world of meanings," Sapir set the stage for more recent concepts of culture. What he had in mind here might be best illustrated by what later became known as the Whorf-Sapir hypothesis—basically, that the language a person internalizes affects the way he perceives the world around him. Language, of course, is a part of culture; hence it is possible to assume that one can internalize other aspects of culture as well as language. Sapir also forged a strong link between anthropology and psychiatry that is still developing. We now have, for example, a "cultural psychiatry" (Kennedy, 1973), a *Transcultural Psychiatric Research Review*, and so on, all ultimately resulting from the stimulating early work of Sapir and those he influenced.

Although it is well beyond the scope of this volume to demonstrate, I would like to suggest that the merging of psychology with anthropology, far from being an American innovation of the 1920's, has been characteristic of anthropology from its very beginning. What appears to have happened in the 1920's is that—first in response to Kroeber's "superorganic," later in response to Radcliffe-Brown's sociological dogmatism, and still later as a response to culturology—many anthropologists were forced to make their psychological perspective more and more explicit. Thus, by becoming more visible, a tradition that could be labeled psychological anthropology became more easily identifiable. In spite of the belief on the part of some that psychological anthropology (or culture-and-personality) was a fad that is now disappearing, the greater part of contemporary cultural anthropology is probably more psychologically oriented than ever before. This orientation will become more clear, I believe, as we proceed.

Sapir had also suggested two years previously in a well-known 1924 paper, "Culture, Genuine and Spurious," that it was possible to distinguish between culture as man's entire material and social heritage, and culture as "those general attitudes, views of life, and specific manifestations of civilization that give a particular people its distinctive place in the world" (1924:405). This latter, as Honigmann points out (1972:124), was a new version of what had interested certain historians—particularly in Germany—the notion of "national genius." It was an idea Boas subscribed to as well. Sapir's close friend Ruth Benedict was to carry this idea to its extreme anthropological fruition in her famous book, *Patterns of Culture* (1934).

Ruth Benedict, like Sapir, was a gifted poet. A student at Vassar, her background was in English and literature. After her graduation from Vassar in 1909, she taught English for a time and then married in 1914. She came to anthropology rather late in life, conducting her first fieldwork with California Indians in 1922 at the age of thirty-five. Benedict received her Ph.D. from Columbia in 1923 and began teaching at Columbia in the same year. She worked during the summers with the Zuñi (1924-1925), the Cochiti (1925), and the Pima Indians (1926). She was extremely close to Boas, her mentor, and, as mentioned, to Edward Sapir. Margaret Mead, her first student, also had a great influence on her (Kardiner and Preble, 1961; Mead, 1959). Benedict was roundly criticized by many of the anthropologists of her time for her overly humanistic, literary approach. Nonetheless, *Patterns of Culture* remains probably the most widely read book of anthropology, and Benedict made a significant impact on the discipline.

The core of *Patterns of Culture* is the contention that culture is patterned —that is, each culture selects from infinite possibilities only a few and these, which must be congruent with each other, constitute a configuration. This configuration is, then, an "integrated whole" that has consistency and is reflected, Benedict believed, in all of the various parts of the culture.

A culture, like an individual, is a more or less consistent pattern of thought and action. Within each culture there come into being characteristic purposes, not necessarily shared by

TERRACED HOUSES OF THE ZUÑI. (1903 photograph by Edward S. Curtis)

other types of society. In obedience to these purposes, each people further and further consolidates its experience, and in proportion to the urgency of these drives the heterogeneous items of behavior take more and more congruous shape. (Benedict, 1934:46)

Borrowing terms from the philosopher Friedrich Nietzsche, Benedict attempted to characterize the Zuñi Indians of the southwest as "Apollonian," the Apollonian character being restrained, relatively unemotional, not given to excesses, emphasizing perfection, and so on. The Kwakiutl of the Pacific northwest coast, by contrast, were "Dionysian" to an extreme degree—they were violent, warlike, given to wild dancing and extremes of behavior, as in the cannibal-society dance in which the dancers were said to bite off pieces of living flesh. They were, in general, quite the opposite of the placid Zuñi. Benedict characterized the Dobuans of Melanesia, who had been studied and described by the British anthropologist Reo Fortune (1932), as being near to what we define as paranoid—because they were so suspicious and distrustful of each other, attempted to destroy each other's gardens through magic, and were remarkably sour and disapproving types in general. Although it has been subsequently shown that Benedict was far too selective in the materials she picked to demonstrate her thesis, she did in this way manage to introduce the notion of "national genius" into anthropology. This was the German tradition of Kant, Hegel, Dilthey, and Spengler that was transmitted to her in part from her own reading and in part from Boas.

While there is more to Benedict's work than is suggested above, its significance here lies in her contention that a culture is somehow the personality of its members "writ large" (Honigmann, 1972:121) but at the same time determines the personality of its members by selecting for those "temperament types" that are congruent with it. This contention does not imply, however, that there are no deviants at all and that everyone shares the same temperament:

> . . . no anthropologist with a background of experience in other cultures has ever believed that individuals were automatons, mechanically carrying out the decrees of their civilization. No culture yet observed has been able to eradicate the differences in the temperaments of the persons who compose it. It is always a give-and-take. (1934:220)

Even so, the notion of culture as a determinant of personality became the dominant orientation in culture-and-personality studies, albeit in increasingly sophisticated versions. It is also largely because of Benedict's work, following Boas, that the notion of cultures (plural) became increasingly important and the equation of culture (singular) with civilization became untenable. Benedict's *cultural relativism*, her respect for other ways of life, left no room for judging one culture as "higher" than another. There were no "stages" of development but, rather, merely different styles of life which demanded to be judged as equal. Her famous quotation from the Digger Indians at the beginning of *Patterns of Culture* makes her attitude very clear:

> God gave to every people a cup, a cup of clay, and from this cup they drank their life. . . . They all dipped in the water but their cups were different. (1934:33)

Benedict's work was stimulating and led to further work on *themes of culture* by Morris Opler (1945) and others who believed that her idea of a single overriding theme or configuration was too simple to be very useful. It also led eventually, especially during the years of World War II when it became important to know as much as possible about your enemies and allies, to studies of *modal personality* and *national character* (the type of personality or character most frequently found in a society or nation) (Inkeles and Levinson, 1954). Probably the most recent work that can be considered in this general tradition is Francis L. K. Hsu's *Kinship and Culture* (1971). Whatever else she accomplished, Benedict did more to make the term *culture* a household word than anyone before or since.

One of the more sophisticated versions of culture-and-personality studies was the creation of the psychoanalyst Abram Kardiner. In collaboration with Sapir, Ruth Benedict, Ruth Bunzel, Ralph Linton, Cora DuBois, and Carl Withers, Kardiner developed in the late 1930's and early 1940's a new and important approach to the question of culture-and-personality differences. He postulated a *basic personality structure* which he believed would be typical of the members of any given culture. To show how this basic structure occurred, he divided *institutions* into two types, primary and secondary. *Primary institutions*—mostly

PRIMARY INSTITUTION	EGO STRUCTURE (son)	SECONDARY INSTITUTION	CHECKS
Patriarchal Family Absolute to power of father Impose discipline Exploit Frustrate needs (subsistence)	Hatred—repressed Submission Ingratiation	Fear of ghosts—cause illness Immobility of lineage cult Loyalty to dead Concept of illness due to sin (displeasing a god)	Propitiation by food sacrifice Reward for repression of hatred
Basic Disciplines Oral—Nursed long Anal—Continent at 6 months Sexual—Object and aim taboos	 Obedience to discipline rewarded Denial of importance of sex	Cleanliness Insistence on compulsive act as part of cure Oedipus Tales—repressed female hatred	One intercourse keeps woman pregnant
Sibling Inequality	Sibling hatred Aggression repressed Aggression expressed Crime Acquiescence	Fear of magic Blood brotherhood—homosexuality *Ombiasy:* warrior Law Belief in fate *Tromba—mpamosavy*	Taboo against use in lineage Can control fate Can control property Severity of punishment Fate can be controlled Neurosis-Psychosis
Subsistence Economy Plenty Communal land	Work for reward of love and subsistence No food anxiety No differentiation of labor	Smooth working of economy Submission rewarded No rituals for rice Emphasis on diligence	
Prestige Economy Social Immobility Property Laws	Uselessness of strife Jealousy Property as means of enlarging ego Deification-Lineage cult	Deification and control over others *Tromba*—fate Rage of gods Law	Many checks on ostentation Illness and absence of support Punishment Malevolent magic

KARDINER'S OUTLINE FOR LINKING PRIMARY AND SECONDARY INSTITUTIONS IN TANALA SOCIETY.
(From Kardiner, 1939)

those having to do with the treatment of very young children and more or less on the Freudian model—were considered to be the most important in the formation of basic personality. *Secondary institutions* were those which came into play to satisfy the basic personality needs created by primary institutions. These included such things as rituals, religion, folktales, and other so-called *"projective systems."* This idea was a powerful innovation, allowing Kardiner and his associates to demonstrate the effects of one cultural system on another, mediated by basic personality structure.

The best example of this interaction between personality and institutions, which in fact stimulated Kardiner to construct his scheme, can be found in Freud's *The Future of an Illusion* (1928). In this book Freud suggests that the experiences of early childhood determine later religious beliefs. That is, if parents in a given culture are nurturant and benevolent to infants and children, the character of the supernaturals in that culture will reflect "projections" of such experiences. This suggestion gave Kardiner the clue to how culture, in general, could affect personality development, in general. Thus, benevolent, kindly, attentive parents do not produce, directly, images of benevolent, kindly supernaturals but, rather, a personality type that is satisfied and gratified by the belief that supernaturals are of that character. The ritual, then, by its very performance, is believed to bring about a desired gratification because, after all, is that not the way gratification has been obtained from parents (as opposed to gratification obtained by begging or beseeching the supernaturals to intervene on one's behalf)? It is basically a simple idea:

primary institutions   →   personality type   →   secondary institutions

The most fundamental problem with this scheme, which Kardiner himself realized, was how to explain the existence of the primary institutions (which, it should be observed, are arbitrarily defined as primary in the first place). Without such an explanation, the scheme does no more than attempt to explain one aspect of culture and/or personality by another in a strangely circular manner—precisely the same problem encountered in Ruth Benedict's more simple-minded scheme. Nonetheless, the ideas set forth by Kardiner and associates were, and are, of potentially great value. It may eventually prove possible in this way to explain religious practices as we explain anything else—that is, in terms of actual causes and effects. For a long time it was believed that religion was not a proper subject for anthropological investigation because it simply did not lend itself to this kind of investigation. Note, however, that if a completely satisfactory explanation is forthcoming from this tradition it will be a result of the merger of psychology and anthropology.

A contemporary, more sophisticated, and more productive version of Kardiner's approach has been mostly associated with John W. M. Whiting of Harvard. This work combines statistical cross-cultural investigations and learning theory along with the approach mapped out by Kardiner. It also opens up possibilities for overcoming the major objection to Kardiner's scheme—the arbitrariness and inexplicability of the primary institutions. Whiting's scheme is as follows (Whiting and Child, 1953:310):

$$\binom{\text{maintenance}}{\text{systems}} \rightarrow \binom{\text{child-training}}{\text{practices}} \rightarrow \binom{\text{personality}}{\text{variables}} \rightarrow \binom{\text{projective}}{\text{systems}}$$

Thus, where Kardiner and his associates had arbitrarily lumped together as primary institutions such diverse things as child-rearing, property, economy, and so on, Whiting and his coworkers have separated child-rearing practices from *maintenance systems*, the latter being defined as:

By maintenance systems we mean the economic, political, and social organizations of a society—the basic customs surrounding the nourishment, sheltering, and protection of its members, which seem a likely source of influence on child training practices. (Whiting and Child, 1953:310)

While this might appear a simple modification it is, in fact, as Harris (1968:45) has pointed out, a modification of great significance. It offers a solution to the problem of the origins of child-rearing practices, precisely the weak point in the Kardiner scheme; and it also promises to bridge the gap between the materialist and idealist positions. Maintenance systems, in this scheme, can be taken as those fundamental technoenvironmental features that are the most primary and basic of all—for example, temperature, type of soil, amount of moisture, kinds of crops that can be grown or types of animals present, tools available for exploiting these, and the like. The belief that these technoenvironmental features are primary and causal in explanations of cultural phenomena constitutes the core, as we shall see, of the materialist position. Thus Whiting's position, although considered here under the rubric of cultural idealism, has a foot in the materialist camp. And he can, then, for example, attempt to show a relationship between a harsh environment in which women must work hard (maintenance system), the amount and kind of care they can give their infants (child-rearing), the resulting personality type (personality variable), and the character of their supernaturals (projective system); indeed, such a relationship has been found in studies already done. Or one might link average temperature to sleeping arrangements, to care of infants, to personality, and to the projective system; this too has been done. While these studies are not as yet definitive, they are remarkably promising attempts (Harrington and Whiting, 1972; Whiting, Kluckhohn, and Anthony, 1958; Whiting, 1964). They demonstrate, again, the utility of using personality variables in the study of culture.

Notice that this approach violates the basic argument of the functionalists in that it deals with various aspects of culture, which Whiting and associates call "customs," and it takes them out of context in order to compare them. In this respect it tends to go back to the era of "shreds and patches." Whiting deliberately chose the term *custom* rather than "culture trait" or "culture pattern," "because the latter have been used to include nonbehavior items [items of *material culture*] of "culture" (Whiting and Child, 1953:17)." Thus he defines culture as behavior and clearly separates it from artifacts:

For our purpose a canoe and a technique of paddling are events of quite different order. The building of a canoe and the technique of paddling are both behavior phenomena, but the canoe itself is not, and we need a cultural concept which will clearly exclude artifacts from its meaning. (Whiting and Child, 1953:17)

This is a departure from the definition Malinowski employed which, following Tylor in this respect, did not make this distinction:

It [culture] obviously is the integral whole consisting of implements and consumers' goods, of constitutional charters for the various social groupings, of human ideas and crafts, beliefs and customs. (Malinowski, 1944:36)

Or, again:

This social heritage is the key concept of cultural anthropology. It is usually called culture. . . . Culture comprises inherited artifacts, goods, technical processes, ideas, habits, and values. (Malinowski, 1931:621)

Although Whiting shares with the cultural materialists a definition of culture which emphasizes behavior, he is nonetheless more of an idealist than a materialist. He does not insist that anthropologists should study only overt, observable behavior, he employs psychological constructs such as personality and projective systems, and he is, in general, interested in mental as well as material phenomena. For Whiting, cognitive factors are, in principle at least, as legitimate and as amenable for study as are the more overt behavior patterns insisted upon by the materialists. Thus he occupies a kind of middle ground between two widely differing contemporary points of view.

Two other definitions are of special interest because they have come to be associated with major theoretical approaches in anthropology. These are the behavioral and cognitive definitions of culture. The *behavioral definition* focuses upon observable patterns of behavior within some social group. For this approach, "the culture concept comes down to behavior patterns associated with particular groups of peoples, that is to 'customs,' or to a people's 'way of life' " (Harris 1968:16). The *cognitive definition*, on the other hand, excludes behavior and restricts the culture concept to ideas, beliefs, and knowledge. While most early definitions *included* the cognitive dimensions, they were not restricted to them. (Spradley, 1972:6)

The Whiting definition of culture embraces both cognitive and overt behavioral factors. It eliminates material things—tools, houses, clothing, and other artifacts and possessions. The materialists, especially Harris (1964:22), would include material things but exclude cognition. As both materialists and idealists would agree that cognition is, indeed, behavior, their argument on this score is methodological rather than theoretical. But to insist that definitions of culture should exclude artifacts, however, is an important theoretical innovation. We shall return to it in the following chapter. The concept of culture itself remains central, of course, no matter which part of the argument one accepts.

A revision of Whiting's scheme in 1963 introduces another important consideration—ecology—and opens up still further possibilities (see the diagram overleaf). This scheme is more in line with Whiting's recent work on values (Whiting, Chasdi, Antonovsky, and Ayres, 1966) but is still not without problems, as Beatrice Whiting points out:

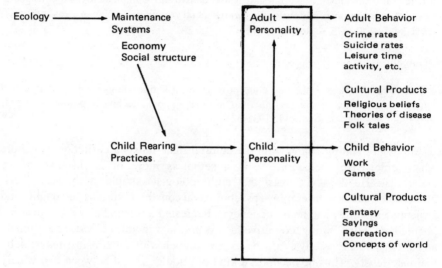

WHITING'S 1963 CULTURE-PERSONALITY-BEHAVIOR SCHEME. (B. Whiting, 1963:5)

To summarize the conceptual background in another way, the researchers viewed ecology, economics, and social and political organizations as setting the parameters for the behavior of the agents of child rearing. They viewed child behavior as an index of child personality and adult behavior and beliefs and values as indices of adult personality. The causal relationships implied in this scheme are open to discussion, and such discussions, with present available knowledge, ultimately end with a problem similar to that of the priority of the chicken or the egg. (B. Whiting, 1963:5)

Robert and Barbara LeVine have added a still further dimension (see their diagram) to the Whiting model, and a useful one, but it does not resolve the problem of causality mentioned above. This general scheme, and LeVine's later elaboration of it in his book *Culture, Behavior, and Personality* (1973) holds great promise for further studies of religious belief and ritual, as well as for other cultural phenomena. It also promises to strengthen the relationship between anthropology and psychoanalytic theory.

Anthony F. C. Wallace, another scholar who engages in culture-and-personality studies, has concentrated much more on cognitive processes than most others. His definition of culture, although stressing behavior as Whiting's does, more explicitly refers to cognitive factors also:

Those ways of behavior or techniques of solving problems which, being more frequently and more closely approximated than other ways, can be said to have a high probability of use by individual members of society. (1970:7)

It is this problem-solving character of culture that has occupied Wallace's attention mostly, but he has also done extensive work on the questions of culture and mental illness and the distribution of personality characteristics.

This tradition of culture-and-personality studies, in which Melford Spiro must also be placed, owes a great deal to the work of A. Irving Hallowell (1955). It also, as we shall see later, attempts a broad evolutionary approach to problems of culture and the individual which emphasizes the importance of biology as well as psychology. One feature of Wallace's view that sets him apart from Spiro and LeVine is that he is not so dependent upon psychoanalytic theory.

The majority of all culture-and-personality studies to date, from Benedict right down to the present time, have used culture as an *independent variable* (the one that is manipulated in an experiment) to explain one or more *dependent* (in this case personality) *variables* (the one whose behavior is assumed to follow from the manipulation of the other). This procedure is perfectly acceptable and we now have much information on how culture influences personality. But it is unfortunate that the reverse has so rarely been attempted—that is, using personality variables as independent variables and studying different aspects of culture as dependent variables. In spite of Melford Spiro's suggested reorientation of culture-and-personality studies (1972), calling for just this, very little to date has even been attempted along these lines.

Not all anthropologists in the 1930's and 1940's jumped on the bandwagons of

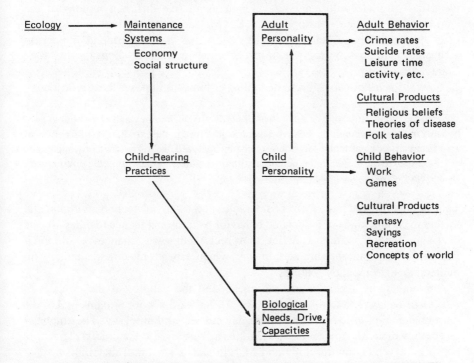

THE LEVINE EXPANSION (LEVINE AND LEVINE, 1966) OF THE WHITING CULTURE-PERSONALITY-BEHAVIOR SCHEME, AS PRESENTED IN LEVINE (1973).

culture-and-personality or social anthropology. Some, of course, merely ignored the theoretical disputes entirely and went on their way collecting data, writing ethnographic reports, and salvaging what ethnographic information they could. A few, actually a very few, rejected both of the new approaches in favor of a modified evolutionism.

Cultural Materialism

One of these, Julian Steward, was among the first anthropologists to emphasize ecology as a determining influence on culture and on the evolution of culture. His work with *"primitive bands"* was of great significance to anthropology in that he established the band as a meaningful unit of social organization for cross-cultural work and demonstrated causal explanations for the existence of various types of such bands. He did this by showing how, despite different technologies and environments associated with different primitive bands, there were underlying ecological conditions that produced similar types and subtypes. He made a similarly important discovery linking population density and agricultural techniques with Pueblo social organization. He also identified parallel evolutionary developments in five different regions of the world—Peru, Mexico, Mesopotamia, Egypt, and North China—a finding of great theoretical importance. Steward's work has had a profound impact on archaeology and has, in fact, been instrumental in bringing about the so-called "new archaeology."

Steward's *cultural ecology*, as described by himself, imposes these procedures:

First, the interrelationship of exploitive or productive technology and environment must be analyzed. . . . Second, the behavior patterns involved in the exploitation of a particular area by means of a particular technology must be analyzed. . . . The third procedure is to ascertain the extent to which the behavior patterns entailed in exploiting the environment affect other aspects of culture. (Steward, 1955:40-41)

This scheme allowed him, with considerable success, to link technoenvironmental factors to certain kinds of associated behavior patterns and thence to other aspects of culture. Since these things are linked in precisely this way, change—evolution if you will—can occur only in a certain way, which depends most fundamentally on the technoenvironmental features.

Although more recent work has questioned the validity of the concept of *patrilocal* bands (Lee and DeVore, 1968:7), Steward's work remains one of the most challenging influences on present-day cultural anthropology. The emphasis on ecology or technoenvironmental features as basic is also the crucial element in both Leslie White's culturology and Marvin Harris's cultural materialism.

Leslie White, like both Malinowski and Radcliffe-Brown, was determined to make anthropology a science. Like Malinowski, he wanted a science of culture, not of society. He was adamantly opposed to biological or psychological *reductionism*. He refused to give up the concept of culture and took a position, similar to Kroeber's superorganicism, which came to be known as *culturology*. As we have already noted in the case of Kroeber, this position holds that culture has an existence independent of human beings. Thus, if one wishes to explain some aspect of culture he must explain it in terms of some other aspect of culture. He must not, whatever he does, according to White, attempt to explain it in terms of psychology, biology, sociology, or anything other than culture:

. . . Culture is a continuum of interacting elements [traits], and this process of interaction has its own principles and its own laws. To introduce the human organism into a considera-tion of cultural variations is therefore not only irrelevant but wrong; it involves a premise that is false. Culture must be explained in terms of culture. Thus, paradoxical though it may seem, "the proper study of mankind" turns out to be not Man, after all, but Culture. The most realistic and scientifically adequate interpretation of culture is one that proceeds as if human beings did not exist. (L. White, 1969:141)

White does concede that human beings are necessary as "carriers of cultural traditions" (White with Dillingham, 1973:37) even though they need not be taken into account to explain changes in that tradition. Like Kroeber, White refuses to concede that human beings—no matter what their genius—have anything at all to do with the cultural process:

. . . Francis Galton and William James espoused the theory that periods of great cultural development are due to genius. But this theory leaves wholly unexplained why geniuses should be abundant at certain times. In short, the genius theory provides no valid explana-tion at all. It explains culture change in terms of genius, but it leaves genius unexplained. It explains the known facts of culture in terms of the unknown (or unascertained) facts of biology. The reason for simultaneous inventions is perfectly simple and clear from a culturological point of view. . . . Human beings are necessary as carriers of cultural traditions; they are not necessary for an explanation of changes in these cultural traditions. This of course cannot be emphasized too greatly. If we look at a process of evolving culture and think of cultural growth, we find that when cultural evolution reaches a certain point, a certain threshold, certain syntheses of cultural traits become possible; and by becoming possible they become inevitable. (White with Dillingham, 1973:36-37)

This view is obviously so extreme that not everyone has been willing to accept it completely. Both Kroeber and White have been accused of the *reification* of culture—that is, of making a material thing out of something that is in reality only a mental thing.

Leslie White's commitment to cultural evolution expressed itself in his so-called "basic law of cultural evolution":

Other factors remaining constant, culture evolves as the amount of energy harnessed per capita per year is increased, or as the efficiency of the instrumental means of putting the

CARRIERS OF CULTURAL TRADITION. This bowling game, *bocce*, is part of the Italian-American culture in many United States cities; this photograph was taken in rural Argentina in 1966. (Photograph by Richard Wilkie)

energy to work is increased. Both factors may increase simultaneously of course. (1969:368)

White viewed himself as being in the direct line of evolutionary theory from Morgan to Tylor. He is also in the direct line of Frederick Engels and Karl Marx, a fact that was used in an unprincipled and unscientific attack on him during the period of national paranoia in which he did most of his productive work. His link to Marx can be seen very clearly in the following:

Technology is the hero of our piece. This is a world of rocks and rivers, sticks and steel, of sun, air and starlight, of galaxies, atoms and molecules. Man is but a particular kind of material body who must do certain things to maintain his status in a cosmic material system. The means of adjustment and control, of security and survival, are of course technological. Culture thus becomes primarily a mechanism for harnessing energy and of putting it to work in the service of man, and, secondarily, of channelling and regulating his behavior not directly concerned with subsistence and offense and defense. Social systems are therefore determined by technological systems, and philosophies and the arts express experience as it is defined by technology and refracted by social systems. Cultural systems like those of the biological level are capable of growth. That is, the power to capture any energy is also the ability to harness more and still more of it. Thus cultural systems, like biological organisms, develop, multiply, and extend themselves. (L. White, 1969:390-391)

The most fundamental assumption of Marxist philosophers is that nonideological factors determine social organization and ideology. One of the clearest statements of this proposition can be seen in the following by Marvin Harris, the most important and vociferous contemporary proponent of this general point of view:

We are led inexorably to conclude that thoughts about institutions are constrained by the institutions under which men do their thinking. Now there arises the question, whence come the institutions? Marx attempted to answer this question by giving separate consideration to different varieties of institutions. He split the nonideological aspects of sociocultural life into two parts: the economic structure ["the real foundation"] and the "legal and political superstructure." He came to distinguish, therefore, three major sociocultural segments: (1) the economic base; (2) the legal-political arrangements, which in modern terms correspond to social structure, or social organization; and (3) "social consciousness" or ideology. Marx and Engels then boldly proclaimed that it was in the economic base that the explanation for both parts of the superstructure—social organization and ideology—were to be found.

Why was it not the other way round? Why not the dominance of social organization over economics? The answer there is contained in the phrase which associates "relations of production" with "a definite stage of development" or man's "material powers of production." It is the stage of development of the material powers of production which renders the "relations of production" *independent* of man's will. For no group of men can will into existence whenever and wherever they choose, the apparatus of production—*coup de poing*, plows, or Bessemer converters—except in a *definite order of progression*. That order of progression corresponds precisely to what the combined efforts of archaeologists and ethnographers have revealed it to be. The unbroken chain of technological innovations which connects digital computers with Oldowan choppers does not admit of deviations or leaps (although the rate of change might conceivably vary rather widely). Stone tools *had* to come before metal tools; spears *had* to come before bows and arrows; hunting and gathering *had* to precede the plow; the flint strike-a-light *had* to be invented before the safety match; oars and sails *had* to precede the steamboat; and handicrafts *had* to precede industrial manufacture. Indeed, none of the major opponents of cultural materialism has ever seriously questioned these facts.

The Boasians, for example, frequently pointed out that technology is cumulative and that objective measures or progress are possible in this realm. Thus, the only point at issue [aside from details concerning the order of emergence of certain innovations] is whether "the mode of production in material life determines the general character of the social, political and spiritual" aspects of sociocultural life. This, it will be seen at once, is an eminently empirical issue, not to be answered by logic alone. (Harris, 1968:231-232)

The Marxist idea then, in its most basic form is as follows:

economic base → legal-political arrangements → social consciousness
(technoenvironmental) (social organization) (ideology)

The influence of Marx on Leslie White is not mere conjecture; neither is the neglect of Marx by social scientists in the United States. It is a most interesting, if unpleasant and shortsighted chapter in the history of American anthropology.

White attended the New School in New York, where he took courses in anthropology from one of Boas's early students, Alexander Goldenweiser. He then moved to the University of Chicago where he studied with Edward Sapir, taking his Ph.D. degree in 1927. His first job was at the University of Buffalo, where he read Lewis Henry Morgan for the first time. He was profoundly impressed by Morgan, in spite of having been told by his Boasian professors that evolutionism was defunct, and he soon went on to read Marx and Engels. This study led him, in turn, to make a trip to the Soviet Union in 1929. Upon his return he took a position at the University of Michigan, where he eventually created a strong department of anthropology and trained a number of brilliant students.

White's discussion of culture emphasized its dependence upon the ability of human beings to *symbolize*. He argued that it was the ability to create and use symbols that set human beings apart from other animals and enabled them to carry on their elaborate cultural way of life. A symbol, White said:

. . . may be defined as a thing the value or meaning of which is bestowed upon it by those who use it. I say "thing" because a symbol may have any kind of physical form; it may have the form of a material object, a color, a sound, an odor, a motion of an object, a taste. The meaning, or value, of a symbol is in no instance derived from or determined by properties intrinsic in its physical form: the color appropriate to mourning may be yellow, green, or any other color; purple need not be the color of royalty; among the Manchu rulers of China it was yellow. The meaning of the word "see" is not intrinsic in its phonetic (or pictorial) properties. . . . The meanings of symbols are derived from and determined by the organisms who use them; meaning is bestowed by human organisms upon physical things or events which thereupon become symbols. Symbols "have their signification," to use John Locke's phrase, "from the arbitrary imposition of men." (L. White, 1969:25)

This was, and is, a point of great significance, as many people had argued up to White's time that there was no essential difference between the minds of animals and people except one of degree. Although this issue remains not completely understood, recent research into the symbolic and language competence of chimpanzees indicates that man is, indeed, very different in this respect (Gardner and Gardner, 1971; Premack and Premack, 1971; Premack, 1972). White's insistence upon this point stimulated a great deal of thought on the matter and helped to further refine our views about the nature of culture.

Julian Steward and Leslie White were virtually the only proponents of evolution during the period when most other anthropologists were turning to structural-functionalism and psychological anthropology. Steward's ideas were rather quickly accepted and incorporated into the mainstream of anthropology. White, on the other hand, did not have such an easy time of it, in large part owing to his obvious identification with Marx, a stigma that Julian Steward managed to avoid. Marx was simply not acceptable to most American scholars during this period of time for reasons that had nothing whatever to do with his intellectual or scholarly work—another example of the relationship of government to social-science research. The denial of more general acceptance to White must be traced in part, however, to the extremity of his position and also, perhaps, to his abrasive and dogmatic style of writing. Most anthropologists are not so willing as are Leslie White and others of his general persuasion to dismiss human beings and their beliefs and ideas as irrelevant to the processes of change and evolution.

Some of the practitioners of White's culturology, mostly his students, believe not only in material determinism and evolution, but also, like the earlier evolutionists, in "progress." Progress is defined by them, or at least by some of them, as "increase in organization, higher energy concentration, and with a qualification. . . . towards increasing heterogeneity" (Sahlins and Service, 1960:8). However reasonable this definition may sound, and however much it appears that change actually has been in this general direction over time, it still remains no more than an article of personal or national faith that it is "progress." It is progress by definition, as can be seen more clearly, perhaps, when the more specific statements of these modern-day evolutionists are considered. For example:

> Culture, continuing the life process, appropriates free energy and builds it into an organization for survival, and like life, culture moves to maximize the amount of energy exploitation. (Sahlins and Service, 1960:9)

One might well ask why the minimization of energy exploitation should not be progress? Or why not simplicity of organization? To argue that some change constitutes progress because it seems to have, in fact, occurred over time is to sadly ignore what might have happened in the past or what could happen in the future.

Marvin Harris shares many of the fundamental assumptions of culturology and cultural ecology, but does not share the belief in progress. According to Harris, as we have noted, the major shortcoming of all the approaches to culture we have so far examined, except those of White and Steward, is that they are *idealistic* as opposed to *materialistic*. They attempt to explain culture, or some particular aspect of culture, in terms of thoughts or ideas, rather than in terms of the (presumably) prior and more fundamental environmental or technoenvironmental (material) features:

> . . . If there had been an orderliness in human history, it cannot, as the Enlightenment philosophers supposed, have originated from the orderliness of men's thoughts. Men do not think their way into matrilineality, the couvade, or Iroquois cousin terminology. In the abstract, can a good reason be found why anyone should bother to think such apparently improbable thoughts? And if one man had thought of them, whence arose the compulsion and the power to convince others of their propriety? For surely it could not be that these improbable ideas construed as mere spontaneous products of fancy occur simultaneously to dozens of people at a time. Obviously, therefore, thoughts must be subject to constraints; that is, they have causes and are made more or less probable in individuals and groups of individuals by prior conditions. (Harris, 1968:231)

Harris believes there are a number of important issues in anthropology in which his position is vindicated and the idealist position is shown to be in error. The question of India's sacred cattle is perhaps the best example. It has long been held by students of India that if the Indians did not hold cattle to be sacred, and did not allow them, therefore, to compete with humans for food and space, there would be less hardship and starvation in the country than there is. That is, if it were not for their religious beliefs (ideology), the Indians would be better off economically (materially). Harris attempted to show in an article entitled ''The Cultural Ecology of India's Sacred Cattle'' (1966), that, in fact, if the topic was approached from a technoenvironmental framework, it was possible to demonstrate that Hindu ideology had little or nothing to do with it. The presence of large numbers of cattle could be adequately explained in purely ecological or technoenvironmental terms—the cattle, he argued, provided energy to till the fields, milk, hides, dung for fuel, and the like, did not really compete with humans for food, and thus had an over-all positive rather than a negative function in the Indian ecosystem. If Harris is right, the instance would be a demonstration of his position discussed above, and the prior causal significance of technoenvironmental factors and the relative insignificance of ideology. Although the issue has not been settled, there are many who are not convinced and who still subscribe to the original view that the Hindu beliefs are in this case dysfunctional (Bennett, 1967; Heston, 1971; Freed and Freed, 1972).

There are similar arguments that have to do with the explanation for the *potlatches* of the northwest coast of America (Codere, 1950), ''primitive'' warfare (Vayda, 1961), communal hunting territories (Leacock, 1954; Knight, 1965), and more. In all of these cases there continue to be opposed points of view and most anthropologists are by no means convinced of the superiority of the cultural materialist's arguments.

It is not completely clear in Harris's work just what role he ascribes to ideas. At times he appears to be insisting that ideas have no place at all in how humans relate to their technoenvironments. For example, in his otherwise encyclopedic work, *The Rise of Anthropological Theory* (1968), he simply dismisses Max Weber's monumental study, *The Protestant Ethic and the Spirit of Capitalism* (1930), on the grounds that it deals with only a single case (1968:285). Indeed, he does not even include Weber in the bibliography. Inasmuch as Weber's thesis was that capitalism could not have arisen in Europe without the ideology of Protestantism, a clear example of power ascribed to ideas, Harris's treatment of this work is open to question.

Surely there has to be a feedback of some kind between people, their ideas, and their environment. To argue that human thoughts have no causal significance at all—that is, to say ''stone tools *had* to come before metal tools; spears *had* to come before bows and arrows . . .'' (1968:232), is rather like saying the cause of the bow and arrow was simply the prior existence of trees. Spears, if indeed they came before the bow and arrow as it now appears they did, were converted into arrows and applied to bows through the mental acts (ideas) of people—and the same mental ability that enabled someone to make the conversion also permitted others to grasp the utility of the idea and to use the bow and arrow themselves. Harris's view that culture must be defined simply as behavior, and that human behavior is determined solely by technoenvironmental factors, like all such behaviorist views, tends to reduce human beings to the status of mere pawns in some great mysterious game, the rules of which can be determined by factors totally unrelated to the pieces themselves. For those unwilling to accept *a priori* the absolute primacy of technoenvironmental factors, the claim that they alone determine both social organization and ideology is not well substantiated as yet. The study of culture involves recognizing that the thoughts, as well as the acts, of human beings are important variables in the invention, transmission, and further evolution of mankind and culture. That they are important can be seen in the fact that at least since Turgot, through Arnold, Tylor, Boas, Malinowski, Benedict, Steward, White, Harris, and the thousands of diverse others, investigators have found it necessary to cling to the culture concept in one form or another. Why, for example, does Steward find it necessary to speak of *cultural* ecology? Why, if ecology is the study of an organism's relation to its total environment, need there be one ecology for others but a different one—*cultural ecology*—for humans? Why is it necessary to specify *human* ecology as contrasted with any other? Why speak, as we have in recent years, of *human* geography or its synonym, *cultural* geography? Why does Marvin Harris specify that it is *cultural* materialism rather than some other kind?

The answer, it would appear, is that humans possess an awesome ability to act upon the environment as well as be acted upon by it. At least part of this ability does seem to be the result of man's ability to symbolize, which if shared at all by other animals, is shared in a most rudimentary form. Symbolization is fundamentally a psychological phenomenon, not a technoenvironmental feature. While one who so wishes may attempt to study cultural phenomena without considering the symbolic processes associated with culture, the study inevitably must be limited to a passing glance rather than a full view.

Just as Harris's materialism allies him with Steward and White, so his views oppose him dramatically to many others in the anthropological profession. Part of the reason is simply his materialism, but another part lies in his views on psychologizing. The issues are seen most clearly in the current controversy over *emic* rather than *etic* approaches.

The terms *emic* and *etic*, as well as the distinction between them, were the creation of the distinguished linguist Kenneth Pike (1954). In brief, emic statements refer to distinctions or meanings as they are perceived by the actors themselves—the people themselves, if the reporter is an anthropologist or linguist studying them. Etic statements are those whose meanings can be verified by independent investigators using similar operations—what the people being observed may personally believe about them is simply not relevant to their truth or falsity.

Harris believes that virtually all ethnographic reports suffer from the failure to distinguish clearly between emic and etic statements. That is, the monographs contain some etic statements and some emic statements, indiscriminantly mixed so that the reader cannot know which is which. There is little doubt that this confusion does, in fact, occur. Indeed, the goal of the "new ethnography," to which we will shortly return, is to eliminate this problem by focusing strictly on emic categories until they are clearly understood, and only then begin speaking about etics. Harris conceded that emics are not necessarily less empirical or subject to scientific study than are etics. But he also believes that all past ethnographic work has been biased towards emics (1968:576).

What is most unfortunate about this bias, from Harris's point of view, is that emic statements get hopelessly confused at times with what he regards as improper psychological statements and categories. Because this confusion then encourages explanations based upon mental states it is, in Harris's view, to be avoided at all costs. Harris goes on to show, with several examples, that even "structural" anthropologists—like Radcliffe-Brown, his followers, and Leslie White—depend heavily upon psychologically derived terms. They speak constantly of such things as "fear," "evasion," "feelings," "sentiments," "jealousy," "shame," and an infinite variety of others, in spite of their antipsychological theories. It is entirely possible to argue that as this vocabulary has characterized anthropology from its very beginning, and still continues, as Harris himself admits, it might be fundamental to ethnographic description. One might still object to it, not on the grounds that it should not be done at all, but, rather, that it should be done better than it has been. Harris, of course, true to cultural materialism, thinks it should not be done at all.

It is not clear what an anthropological monograph completely devoid of psychological terms would look like. Although Harris's *The Nature of Cultural Things* (1964) attempts to demonstrate a method of investigation that would presumably yield such a monograph, no one has as yet actually produced one. In any case, it is Harris's antipsychological stance, more than any other thing, that separates him most sharply from other current developments in anthropology. There are three such current trends we need to mention: the so-called "structuralism" of Levi-Strauss, the "new ethnography," and what is being termed "symbolic anthropology."

Structuralism

Claude Levi-Strauss, by far the greatest French anthropologist ever, was born in Belgium in 1908. He was a student at the University of Paris where he took a degree in Philosophy. From 1934 to 1937 he was Professor of Sociology at the University of São Paulo, Brazil. During this time he read Robert Lowie's *Primitive Society* (1920), his first introduction to anthropology. In 1938-1939 Levi-Strauss undertook an expedition into central Brazil. Little is known of this except that it formed the basis for his writings on the Nambikwara and Tupi-Kawahib Indians. After a short tour of military service in France, Levi-Strauss arrived in 1941 at the New School for Social Research in New York. During 1946-1947 he served as French cultural attaché in the United States. From 1948 to 1958 he was at the University of Paris and he was also, during most of this time and until 1960, Secretary General of the International Council of Social Sciences. In 1958 he was appointed to the newly created chair of Social Anthropology at the Collège de France. In 1968 he was awarded the highest scientific distinction in France, the Gold Medal of the Centre National de la Recherche Scientifique (Leach, 1970). He was named a foreign associate of the United States National Academy of Sciences in 1967 and, in 1973, was elected to the French Academy, an organization founded in 1635 and limited to only 40 members. His influence is so great that he has become one of the best-known anthropologists in the history of the discipline.

Historically, Levi-Strauss is in the same tradition of anthropology as Emile Durkheim, Marcel Mauss, and Radcliffe-Brown. But he has extended the tradition into the very realm that Durkheim and Radcliffe-Brown most abhorred, the psychological. This, among other things, places him in the cultural idealist tradition and thereby opposes his position to that of the materialists. To understand this difference let us use as an example, following Harris, the contrasting explanations for the division of labor in society.

Adam Smith (1776) had explained the existence of a *division of labor* in purely economic terms—greater specialization of labor provides a more efficient means of production and hence cheaper goods for all—hence, it was believed, to greater "happiness" for all. Durkheim (1893) challenged this purely materialistic view by demonstrating that the division of labor was not, in fact, associated with greater "happiness." He then substituted for the efficiency in Smith's original explanation the functional importance of social solidarity and the reduction of competition:

> The division of labor thus emerges as a social arrangement not for increasing productivity, but for reducing competition. Its principal effect is to increase the amount of heterogeneity among the parts of the social organism, thereby multiplying and intensifying their mutual dependence. In other words, the *function* of the division of labor is to preserve social solidarity. (Harris, 1968:476)

Marx, too, had given prominence to rivalry and competition. But for him this social problem could not be resolved merely through the division of labor but, rather, only through the struggle between *social classes*. Durkheim, who shared the interest in rivalry and competition, took an entirely opposite view—one that in Harris's opinion was most unfortunate as it put him directly into the idealist camp. Durkheim rejected the idea of class struggle and in doing so he also rejected economic explanations. Thus he began a mode of explanation completely independent of technoeconomic factors:

Durkheim's unique contribution was thus the founding of a science of culture which could explain sociocultural phenomena without getting involved in techno-economic causation. Henceforth it would suffice merely to investigate the manner by which a given trait or institution contributed to the maintenance of solidarity among the members of the social organism. (Harris, 1968:476)

Here we see, if Harris is correct, the origins of the French sociological tradition that was later to result in both Radcliffe-Brown's functionalism and Levi-Strauss's structuralism, sharing at the very least the idealism to which Harris is so adamantly opposed. But to understand the idealism of Levi-Strauss we must also understand his psychological bent which he does not share with Radcliffe-Brown.

Durkheim, like Radcliffe-Brown, wanted a science of society devoid of psychology. Indeed, the thrust of one of his major works, *Suicide* (1897), was to prove that suicide could be explained purely sociologically, with no recourse to the individual or psychology. Yet, as Alex Inkeles has shown, Durkheim did employ an implicit psychological theory:

. . . despite his intention to go "directly" to the causes of suicide, "disregarding the individual as such, his motives and his ideas," Durkheim was in the end forced to introduce a general theory of personality as the intervening variable between, on the one hand, the state of integration of social structures and, on the other hand, the varying rates of suicide he sought to explain. To the question of how the origin of suicide could lie in the degree of integration of a social structure, he replied by referring to man's "psychological constitution," which, he said, "needs an object transcending it." This object is lacking in the weakly integrated society, and consequently "the individual, having too keen a feeling for himself and his own value . . . wishes to be his own only goal, and as such an objective cannot satisfy him, drags out languidly and indifferently an existence which henceforth seems meaningless to him." (Inkeles, 1959:252)

This is the same kind psychologizing that Harris has noted. In this case the object "transcending" man's "psychological constitution" is no more or less than the social order itself. And the social order transcending individual people is the result of the *"collective conscience,"* defined by Durkheim in *The Division of Labor in Society* (1893) as follows:

The totality of beliefs and sentiments common to average citizens of the same society forms a determinate system which has its own life; one may call it the *collective* or *common conscience*. No doubt, it has not a specific organ as a substratum; it is, by definition, diffuse in every reach of society. Nevertheless, it has specific characteristics which make it a distinct reality. It is, in effect, independent of the particular conditions in which individuals are placed; they pass on and it remains. It is the same in the North and in the South, in great cities and in small, in different professions. Moreover, it does not change with each generation, but, on the contrary, it connects successive generations with one another. It is, thus, an entirely different thing from particular consciences, although it can be realized only through them. (1893:79-80)

However ambiguous the concept of the "collective conscience" may appear, it has been an extremely influential idea. It can, of course, be substituted for culture. "The totality of beliefs and sentiments common to average citizens of the same society" is, in fact, one of the most common definitions of culture. It is necessary to understand the idea of the collective unconscious if one is to attempt to understand Levi-Strauss. But there is also one further figure in the French sociological tradition we must mention because of his influence on Levi-Strauss.

Marcel Mauss was Durkheim's nephew, but he was also a professional associate of Durkheim's and, after Durkheim's death, became the most prominent scholar in this particular tradition. In his most famous work, *The Gift* (1924), Mauss attempted to explain much of sociocultural life through what he called "collective representations," a notion with obvious ties to the collective conscience. But Mauss was also interested in bringing psychological studies more into line with sociological ones, a position which, of course, Durkheim would not have considered. Mauss was interested in such things as obligation, motive, and in general the meaning of gift-giving to the participants themselves. Mauss believed he had uncovered one of the fundamental bases of social life in the universal process of gift-giving. Out of his interest in this, particularly his interest in the "inside" view, Mauss came to realize that there may be absolutely fundamental "structures" of some kind in the mind that would be prior to the collective representations and would determine them. It is here that we find the most important link with the contemporary work of Levi-Strauss.

Mauss attempted in *The Gift* to reduce all varieties of gift-giving to one "elementary form," the principle of reciprocity. That this principle is importantly psychological as well as sociological can be seen in Mauss's use of terms like "obligation," "motive," "generosity," "morals," and the like. He wished to show that the gift-exchange of primitive societies could not be explained in terms of the purely economic motives of "civilized" society but was motivated rather by the more basic principle of reciprocity. Upon this principle, he believed, ultimately depended all social solidarity. He further held, following the early evolutionists, that contemporary "primitive" societies were representative of archaic or past forms of life and thus could tell us about our own history and development.

Levi-Strauss, in his first famous work, *Les Structures Elémentaires de la Parenté* (1949) (*The Elementary Structures of Kinship*), extended Mauss's notion of reciprocity to one further commodity that could be exchanged—women. He argues that the purpose of *incest taboos*, a universal feature of all human societies that has long puzzled anthropologists, was simply to bring about an exchange of women. Kinship systems, then, also a universal feature of human life, can be studied from the point of view of how they represent different systems of exchanging women and what implications follow from different modes of exchange. For instance, there are societies in which it is permissible, and indeed even preferred, to marry a *cross cousin*, but in which at the same time *parallel cousins* are taboo as marriage partners—one cannot marry the opposite-sex child of one's father's brother or mother's sister (children of siblings of the same sex being parallel cousins), but can marry the opposite-sex child of father's sister or mother's brother (children born to siblings of different sex are cross cousins). In our own system of kinship (except in rare cases) all of these cousins would be prohibited as marriage partners. Thus the exchange of women between groups following different rules would result in different networks of kin and in different forms of social organization.

But not only were there sociological advantages to be derived from reciprocity, there was also, Levi-Strauss argued, a fundamental human psychological "need" for it. And the only way to properly understand this need, he continued, was to appeal to the "fundamental structures of the mind." In order to learn about these fundamental structures of the mind, Levi-Strauss turned to studies of child development, particularly to studies of the development of thought. He found what he believed to be an important clue in the duality established by the fact that we all must experience the difference between "self" and "other." This experience, he thought, made reciprocity a part of the search for psychological security. Harris has objected to Levi-Strauss's search for elementary mental structures as merely the same procedure as positing "instincts" whenever an explanation is needed (1968:491). But while it is true that if there are indeed such things as elementary structures of the mind, we are not very close to understanding them, nevertheless in all fairness to Levi-Strauss we must observe that the search for such elementary structures is very different from simply making up a new instinct whenever one is required. There is a long and rapidly growing tradition of studying how both children and adults think, and how they think must surely have something to do with how they experience each other and the world around them. There is also a relationship between Levi-Strauss's search for elementary structures of the mind and the concept of the "unconscious" as formulated by Freud and Jung, although Levi-Strauss has yet to make clear how he himself perceives the relationship. More important, perhaps, is the relationship between the structuralism of Levi-Strauss and that of Piaget (1970:106), as well as that between Levi-Strauss and the "universal grammar" of the linguist Noam Chomsky. Consider, for example, what Chomsky says of the study of universal grammar:

. . . The study of universal grammar, so understood, is a study of the nature of human intellectual capacities. It tries to formulate the necessary and sufficient conditions that a system must meet to qualify as a potential human language, conditions that are not accidentally true of the existing human languages, but that are rather rooted in the human "language capacity," and thus constitute the innate organization that determines what counts as linguistic experience and what knowledge of language arises on the basis of this experience. Universal grammar, then, constitutes an explanatory theory of a much deeper sort than particular grammar, although the particular grammar of a language can also be regarded as an explanatory theory. (Chomsky, 1972:27)

Levi-Strauss has been influenced by modern *structural linguistics*, by *depth psychology*, and by *cybernetics*, none of which were completely available to Durkheim and Mauss. He believes there may be universal and fundamental "structures of the mind," which through their operation determine the form and content of human acts. One of the most fundamental of these structures, Levi-Strauss maintains, is the tendency of the mind to operate in terms of binary oppositions (that is, to continually divide things into two categories—to dichotomize). This tendency gives the clue, he thinks, that enables us to understand many things which have heretofore eluded understanding. Levi-Strauss has attempted to apply his mode of analysis to these main topics: (1) kinship analysis (*The Elementary Structures of Kinship*, 1949), (2) the logic of myth (*The Raw and the Cooked*, 1969; *From Honey to Ashes*, 1973), and (3) primitive classifications (*The Savage Mind*, 1966). He has in each area made valuable contributions and stimulated much further work. Although he has more critics than admirers in anthropology, Levi-Strauss does not lack for the latter. His *Festschrift, Echanges et Communications* (Pouillon and Maranda, 1970) is the largest volume of its kind ever published. No less a figure than Edmund Leach, a most distinguished member of the British structural-functional school, has become a defender of Levi-Strauss and has also attempted the same kinds of analyses (Leach, 1967; 1969; 1970). This is not to say that Leach accepts uncritically everything Levi-Strauss says, or that Levi-Strauss is necessarily correct. There is a long way to go before a truly convincing case will be made for this type of analysis. The implications for a theory of culture, however, are profound.

Levi-Strauss uses what is essentially the comparative method of the early evolutionists. He believes that the study of existing "primitives" tells us something about the past, something about our own development:

. . . The anthropologist respects history, but he does not accord it a special value. He conceives it as a study complementary to his own: one of them unfurls the range of human societies in time, the other in space. And the difference is even less great than it might seem, since the historian strives to reconstruct the picture of vanished societies as they were at the points which for them corresponded to the present, while the ethnographer does his best to reconstruct the historical stages which temporally preceded their existing form. (Levi-Strauss, 1966:256)

Yet, at the same time, as Leach points out, Levi-Strauss has a way of looking at history and at the past that differs from most others: ". . . Levi-Strauss insists that when history takes the form of a recollection of past events it is part of the thinker's present, not of his past" (Leach, 1970:16). Likewise, Levi-Strauss omits the value judgments of the early evolutionists:

The presuppositions of 19th-century anthropologists were protohistorical, Evolutionist or Diffusionist as the case might be. But Levi-Strauss' time sense is geological. Although,

A BORORO WOMAN. The headstrap-supported basket contains firewood and an axe; another adult and child are in the shaded background. This tribe lives in the region where western Brazil adjoins Bolivia. (Smithsonian Institution; National Anthropological Archives)

like Tylor and Frazer, he seems to be interested in the customs of contemporary primitive peoples only because he thinks of them as being in some sense primeval, he does not argue, as Frazer might have done, that what is primeval is inferior. In a landscape, rocks of immense antiquity may be found alongside sediments of relatively recent origin, but we do not argue on that account that one is inferior to the other. So also with living things (and by implication human societies). (Leach, 1970:17)

Thus, for Levi-Strauss, there is no essential difference between the minds of primitive men and those of contemporary men. It is to his credit that he so quickly rejected the idea of "stages" of intellectual development. The human mind, for

Levi-Strauss, has always worked in the same way and what was present in the past is with us still in one form or another: "for the thinking human being all recollected experience is contemporaneous; as in myth, all events are part of a single synchronous totality" (Leach, 1970:16). But since Levi-Strauss has yet to demonstrate this, and since it so clearly relates to concepts such as the collective conscience, the unconscious, archetypes, archaic remnants, and the like, it is easy to see why the critics react so strongly. Even so, the question of the human mind and its organization remains one of our greatest puzzles:

> Just as the human body represents a whole museum of organs, each with a long evolutionary history behind it, so we should expect to find that the mind is organized in a similar way. It can no more be a product without history than is the body in which it exists. By "history" I do not mean the fact that the mind builds itself up by conscious reference to the past through language and other cultural traditions. I am referring to the biological, prehistoric, and unconscious development of the mind in archaic man, whose psyche was still close to that of the animal. (Jung, 1968:57)

While we may be unable to accept the assertions of Freud, Jung, or Levi-Strauss on the nature of the mind, we cannot, as some would have us do, simply throw out the problem. And it may be the case that we are getting much closer to the time when we will be better able to solve it.

The New Ethnography

Linguistics has led the way in recent years to what is often called the "new ethnography" (Sturtevant, 1964). The new ethnography has to do primarily with the controversy mentioned earlier over "emic" as opposed to "etic" approaches.

The most important claim of the "new ethnographers" is that they will be able to give more precise descriptions of cultural phenomena than heretofore possible—cultural descriptions that will be modeled on linguistic ones. Just as the linguist works with standard units—in terms of *phonemes*, *morphemes*, *phonology* and *grammar*—so, they claim, will the ethnographer be able to find the proper units for comparison. Thus, rather than imposing our own units and classifications on other cultures, arbitrarily forcing them, as it were, to have such things as economics, politics, or religion as we have done since the very beginning of anthropology, we will be able to elicit their meaningful units and classifications. Perceiving these will give us the "inside" view, the subject's own view of the world and things as opposed to our own ethnocentric and egocentric views. In terms of aims this approach is not fundamentally very different from those of Boas, Malinowski, and most other fieldworkers (Berreman, 1966). The claim for a new ethnography is based primarily on the availability of new linguistic methods; the approach is most often termed *ethnoscience*. Using this method we have already found that other people do not always classify things around them as we do. Where we, for example, have general categories like "plants" and "animals," for some people there are only certain kinds of plants and animals. Where we have color terms like *scarlet*, *maroon*, and *pink*, many people would lump all of them under a single term. Likewise, where we lump a number of relatives together under the term *uncle* or *aunt*, many people would distinguish terminologically between father's brother and mother's brother, between father's sister and mother's sister. We distinguish between natural and supernatural, between magic and science, between logical and illogical, and between other pairs, whereas other people do not. But although ethnoscientists argue that only by first ascertaining the categories other people use will we eventually (perhaps) be able to derive universal categories, the opponents of ethnoscience argue that, carried to its logical extreme, ethnoscience would result in purely relativistic descriptions of particular cases. Insofar as the units and categories of one culture are found to be relative to that culture and no other, there would be no basis for comparison and hence no science. Spiro, in his study *Burmese Supernaturalism*, has stated such a point of view:

> As between the "emic" and "etic" approaches, then, my approach is unabashedly etic. The former approach leads to a descriptive and relativistic inquiry whose interest begins and ends with the parochial. The latter approach leads to a theoretical and comparative inquiry in which the parochial is of interest as an instance of the universal. If the former issues in ethnography, the latter (although based on ethnography) issues in science. Since I am interested in science, the explanations offered in this study use concepts which are analytic rather than substantive; their reference is usually to a theoretical construct rather than to an ethnographic category; and their domain is usually the class "supernaturalism" and not merely Burmese supernaturalism. (1967:6)

Harris, as we have noted, although hostile to what he sees as an emic bias in anthropology, does not believe that emic studies need, necessarily, be more subjective or unscientific than etic studies. Many have noted that to date most ethnoscientific studies have concerned themselves with exceedingly small domains which some regard as basically trivial—local classifications of colors, plants, insects, disease, and the like. Furthermore, they have been mostly unconcerned with whether or not any new scientific insights can be derived from such studies. In this respect they are like the purely descriptive ethnographic efforts of the historical particularists. This limited character may be a result of the difficulties of actually doing ethnoscientific research in the field, for such work is extremely time-consuming and demanding. It may also turn out that the results are not worth the effort required. But it would be of great importance for the study of culture to have thorough emic data from as many cultures as possible. With such data it would then be possible to see to what extent there are real similarities and differences in the ways people classify, attach meanings to things around them, and communicate with one another. It would also be of great benefit to know how people in various cultures express their innermost thoughts, feelings, and states of mind. Recent studies are pointing the way and opening up new horizons for this type of research (Spradley, 1972; Tyler, 1969).

Symbolic Anthropology

One further recent development in the study of culture must be noted. This is the so-called "symbolic anthropology" of Clifford Geertz, David Schneider, Victor Turner, and others. The most fundamental point of agreement among all scholars in this new development is that culture is primarily a system of symbols. This proposition places them firmly in the idealist tradition and opposes them to the materialists who wish to define culture strictly in terms of behavior. As an example of what the symbolic approach implies, consider Geertz's definition of religion:

. . . (1) a system of symbols which acts to (2) establish powerful, pervasive, and long-lasting moods and motivations in men by (3) formulating conceptions of a general order of existence and (4) clothing these conceptions with such an aura of factuality that (5) the moods and motivations seem uniquely realistic. (1966:4)

Notice that this definition is heavily psychological, as of course it must be if one is to deal with symbols at all. To understand the symbolic system of any given group, whether it be the religious system or some other cultural system such as kinship, politics, or economics, necessarily requires dealing with the mind, both conscious and unconscious. In so far as Geertz, Schneider, and Turner deal with symbols and the unconscious they are linked to Freud, Jung, and Levi-Strauss. But symbolic anthropology is much more solidly grounded in careful, objectively described fieldwork— in *empiricism*—than is Levi-Strauss's structuralism. And it also deals, at least in the hands of some, in a much more realistic way with the problem of emic versus etic descriptions. This advantage is seen the most clearly, perhaps, in the work of the British anthropologist Victor Turner:

I found that I could not analyze ritual symbols without studying them in a time series in relation to other "events," for symbols are essentially involved in social process. I came to see performances of rituals as distinct phases in the social processes whereby groups became adjusted to internal changes and adapted to their external environment. From this standpoint the ritual symbol becomes a factor in social action, a positive force in an activity field. The symbol becomes associated with human interests, purposes, ends, and means, whether these are explicitly formulated or have to be inferred from the observed behavior. The structure and properties of a symbol become those of a dynamic entity, at least within its appropriate context of action. (Turner, 1967:20)

If this is so, we might well expect failure for the study of symbols as pursued by Levi-Strauss in his later works, *The Raw and the Cooked* and *From Honey to*

Ashes, in which he analyzes folk tales and other material drawn from a variety of cultures and sources, and thus totally removes it from context. The difference here between Turner and Levi-Strauss lies in the fact that Turner attempts to understand the meaning of a symbol by seeing what it means to those who actually use it, and in the context in which it is used. Levi-Strauss, on the other hand, more similar to Freud and Jung, attributes symbolic meaning to things on the basis of his beliefs about how the mind operates.

Turner believes that the structure and properties of ritual symbols must be inferred from these classes of data: (1) external form and observable characteristics; (2) interpretations offered by specialists and laymen; (3) significant contexts largely worked out by the anthropologist (Turner, 1967:20). Thus the meaning of symbols is entirely understood through observation and questioning. This approach combines comparisons of emic with etic descriptions—observations of overt behavior with statements pertaining to "inner states" and meanings. It also compares the interpretations of anthropologists with those of the persons being studied.

When applied to individual cases this type of analysis spreads out to include both technoenvironmental and biological factors. The best illustration of this quality, which must suffice for our purposes here, comes from Turner himself:

Here is an example. At *Nkang'a*, the girl's puberty ritual, a novice is wrapped in a blanket and laid at the foot of a *mudyi* sapling. The *mudyi* tree *Diplorrhyncus condylocarpon* is conspicuous for its white latex, which exudes in milky beads if the thin bark is scratched. For Ndembu. this is its most important characteristic, and therefore I propose to call it "the milk tree" henceforward. Most Ndembu women can attribute several meanings to this tree. In the first place, they say that the milk tree is the "senior" (*mukulumpi*) tree of the ritual. Each kind of ritual has this "senior" or, as I will call it, "dominant" symbol. Such symbols fall into a special class which I will discuss more fully later. Here it is enough to state that dominant symbols are regarded not merely as means to the fulfillment of the avowed purposes of a given ritual, but also and more importantly refer to values that are regarded as ends in themselves, that is, to axiomatic values. Secondly, the women say with reference to its observable characteristics that the milk tree stands for human breast milk and also for the breasts that supply it. They relate this meaning to the fact that *Nkang'a* is performed when a girl's breasts begin to ripen, not after her first menstruation, which is the subject of another and less elaborate ritual. The main theme of *Nkang'a* is indeed the tie nurturing between mother and child, not the bond of birth. This theme of nurturing is expressed at *Nkang'a* in a number of supplementary symbols indicative of the act of feeding and of foodstuff. In the third place, the women describe the milk tree as "the tree of a mother and her child." Here the reference has shifted from description of a biological act, breast feeding, to a social tie of profound significance both in domestic relations and in the structure of the widest Ndembu community. (1967:20-21)

Symbolic analyses of this kind are a recent development in cultural anthropology. They hold great promise for the understanding of culture and *cultural systems*. The work of all those who at the moment can be classified as symbolic anthropologists is by no means uniform. David Schneider's insightful analysis of American kinship as a symbolic system (1968) departs importantly from the scheme laid down by Geertz in his theoretical paper on "Religion as a Cultural System" (1966), and it is also different from Turner's work. Nonetheless, the work of all three of these anthropologists can easily be seen as part of a single emerging tradition. Symbolic anthropology constitutes an important new step in the continuing development and refinement of the culture concept and the study of culture.

The overwhelming importance of the operation of the mind to symbolic anthropologists can be seen in Schneider's definition of culture:

A particular culture, American culture for instance, consists of a system of units (or parts) which are defined in certain ways and which are differentiated according to certain criteria. These units define the world or the universe, the way the things in it relate to each other, and what these things should be and do.

I have used the term "unit" as the widest, most general, all-purpose word possible in this context. A unit in a particular culture is simply anything that is culturally defined and distinguished as an entity. It may be a person, place, thing, feeling, state of affairs, sense of foreboding, fantasy, hallucination, hope, or idea. In American culture such units as uncle, town, blue (depressed), a mess, a hunch, the idea of progress, hope, and art are cultural units. (1968:2)

It should be obvious that Levi-Strauss's structuralism, the new ethnography, and symbolic anthropology are all heavily psychological—or mentalistic, if you prefer. Thus, with the culture-and-personality tradition, they constitute a type of approach which can be characterized as cultural idealism and contrasted with cultural materialism. It should be equally obvious that neither cultural idealism nor cultural materialism are monolithic. There are several different forms of each.

Summary

In the 1920's and 1930's, along with British structural-functionalism, two new traditions of anthropology developed—culture-and-personality and cultural materialism. The former attempted to make explicit use of psychological variables, the latter totally rejected them and concentrated instead on the causal priority of technoenvironmental factors. Culture-and-personality studies were only incidentally interested in questions of evolution, whereas a newer, more sophisticated evolutionism characterized the cultural materialists. Culture-and-personality can be seen as part of a wider type of anthropology, cultural idealism. The idealist camp, in addition to culture-and-personality scholars, includes the so-called new ethnographers, the structuralists who follow Levi-Strauss, and the symbolic anthropologists. The division into cultural materialists and cultural idealists is not a completely satisfactory one. There are some scholars, such as John W. M. Whiting, who in some ways fit into both camps, or at least promise to bridge the gap. Most importantly, the distinction between materialists and idealists is made on the basis of whether or not they will accept ideas or mental processes as legitimate data for study.

In spite of their differences, the idealists and the materialists share a vital concern with evolution and the evolutionary process. This resurgence of interest in evolution, along with other developments, has brought up new considerations to which we now turn.

Further Readings

There are several good general collections and books on culture-and-personality: Kaplan's *Studying Personality Cross-Culturally*; Hsu's *Psychological Anthropology*; Honigmann's *Personality in Culture*; Wallace's *Culture and Personality*; the volume edited by Kluckhohn, Murray, and Schneider, *Personality in Nature, Society and Culture*; and LeVine's recent *Culture, Behavior and Personality*.

For works dealing with child rearing, personality, and culture see Kardiner's *The Individual and His Society*, Whiting and Child's *Child Training and Personality*, Beatrice Whiting's collection *Six Cultures: Studies of Child Rearing,* Spiro's *Children of the Kibbutz*, Bateson and Mead's *Balinese Character: A Photographic Analysis*, and Williams's recent book, *An Introduction to Socialization*.

Cultural materialism is the main theme of Marvin Harris's *The Rise of Anthropological Theory* although it is also a history of anthropology. Harris also presents his position in *The Nature of Cultural Things*. Leslie White's position is ably presented in his famous work *The Science of Culture*, Steward's in his book *Theory of Culture Change*.

There are two good collections on ethnoscience and cognitive anthropology—Spradley's *Culture and Cognition: Rules, Maps and Plans*, and Tyler's *Cognitive Anthropology*. Schneider's position on symbolic anthropology is best presented in his brief volume *American Kinship: A Cultural Account*, Turner's in his *The Forest of Symbols*, and Geertz's in his papers "Religion as a Cultural System" and "The Impact of the Concept of Culture on the Concept of Man." Many books on Levi-Strauss are now available in addition to the works of Levi-Strauss himself. Leach's *Levi-Strauss*, and his edited collection *The Structural Study of Myth and Totemism*, are perhaps somewhat more straightforward and understandable than most.

CHAPTER V BEHAVIORAL EVOLUTION

The culture concept has been influenced by events and discoveries outside the field of cultural anthropology itself. The relationship between archeology, physical anthropology, and cultural anthropology, which has always existed, has been strengthened by recent developments in all these fields. Developments in paleoanthropology, ethology, and cybernetics have been equally or more important in bringing about a new view of man and culture. All of this accretion has combined in recent years to bring about a substantial change in the way human beings have always thought about themselves. A broad, new, conjunctive approach to the study of man and culture is emerging, one in which the relationship between human biology and culture can be better understood. We can see clearly now that biological and cultural evolution are not separate processes as has been implicitly assumed in the past. The developing new view of man and culture also holds the promise of overcoming the narrow disciplinary foci we have used in the past. It is also obvious now that to truly understand the process of evolution and man's position in the over-all scheme of things we need to overcome our tendency to fragment and compartmentalize, and instead to attack the questions using whatever theories, concepts, and methods are required to do the job. It is an exciting time for students of man and culture, what with the wealth of new information and the many new ideas about how it all fits together.

We have discussed the history of the culture concept up to now almost as if it were unrelated to developments outside cultural anthropology. In fact, except during the earliest period when the concept of culture first emerged, this is precisely the way the concept developed. This historical process is related to Ernest Becker's thesis in *The Lost Science of Man*, and worth noting.

Becker has argued that the science of man, and by this he means essentially the general idea that it was possible to study man scientifically at all, began as a "grand vision." The purpose of this grand vision—this science of man—was to enable man to overcome the moral crisis brought about by the breakdown of medievalism and the absence of anything to take its place. In order to have a sound basis for a new social order, it appeared necessary to understand what had happened to the old, and what kinds of laws or rules governed human progress in general. Thus the concepts we still employ—culture, society, social system, and their likes—began to emerge. But, Becker asserts, this grand vision got lost along the way. The science of man became bogged down by the tendency of its practitioners to fragment, to invent new concepts and then found new disciplines around them. Thus sociology took for its subject matter, as we see so clearly in Durkheim and Radcliffe-Brown, the concepts of society and social system. Political science attempted to carve out its own distinctive subject matter. Psychology took the psyche as its proper subject matter. Workers in all of these newer sciences were at the same time careful not to intrude on the subject matter of economics, which was somewhat older and better established. Anthropology took the concept of culture. An attempt was made, then, however unconsciously or unknowingly, to create a science of culture that would have its own distinctive subject matter and that would not be reducible to other like disciplines such as biology, psychology, or whatever. This attempt had the effect, alas still with us, of creating independent departments of specialists ("fetishists," in Becker's terms), which came to exist largely for their own self-interest—hence the grand, all-encompassing science of man, which was to solve the moral crisis resulting from industrialization, became lost. While it is obvious that universities must be organized in some fashion for administrative purposes and logistics, there is an unfortunate tendency for organizations to solidify and maintain themselves in ways that are not necessarily conducive to the most efficient pursuit of knowledge. However strong this need and tendency, recent developments both inside and outside anthropology once again demand a complete science of man.

The history of the study of culture reflects an overwhelming attempt to demonstrate *cultural* influences as opposed to others. Anthropologists have consistently argued against race as a factor in producing different cultural traditions or as a factor affecting intelligence or evolution. They have, likewise, tended to oppose purely biological explanations for the development of intelligence, personality, or cultures. They have opposed genetics as the major factor in explanations for human or cultural differences, and they have opposed instinct theories as well. Kroeber's attempt to establish culture as a "superorganic" phenomenon, one totally unrelated to psychology or biology, is the best and simplest example of these oppositions. The result has been that we have studied culture, for the most part, independently of biology, genetics, physiology, and so on. The relationship of cultural anthropology to psychology has not been quite so distant, as we have seen, but even here there has been great resistance. Biologists and geneticists, as well as psychologists and others, have been guilty of the same thing—they have studied their subject matter as if it were unrelated to culture. Even archeologists and physical anthropologists for a time tended to drift away from the cultural anthropologist. We now recognize that this trend is no longer possible, that fragmenting the science of man has been responsible for a terribly distorted view of man and culture, psychology and genetics, biology and evolution, in addition to helping the science of man to become "lost." This realization has led, in recent years, to a new approach to a science of man. This approach is sometimes called "behavioral anthropology," "evolutionary anthropology," "biological anthropology," "Darwinian anthropology," and even "human biology." We refer to it here as "behavioral evolution," this being the term used by A. Irving Hallowell, one of the early proponents of such a view, in a pioneering paper:

> In this paper I have attempted to give the broad outlines of a *conjunctive* approach to human evolution. The organic, psychological, social, and cultural dimensions of the evolutionary process are taken into account as they are related to underlying conditions that are necessary and sufficient for a human level of existence. I have also devoted some attention to earlier opinions to bring into sharper focus the problems that need reconsideration in the light of contemporary knowledge. "Behavioral evolution" is, perhaps, the term which best defines the framework of a conjunctive approach. (Hallowell, 1963:440)

This conjunctive approach to human evolution, culture, society, and personality puts all of these subjects in an entirely new light. It has been brought about by five recent developments: (1) the "rediscovery" of Darwin and evolution, (2) new discoveries in the field of *paleoanthropology*, (3) the increasing importance of *ethological* studies, particularly those dealing with nonhuman primates and carnivores, (4) the accumulation of more and more cross-cultural data on a larger number of human groups, and (5) the discovery of cybernetics.

Evolution and Behavior

As we have seen, when the early evolutionary theories were mostly discredited by the newer generations of anthropologists, the concept of evolution itself was neglected. Psychologists likewise, when the recapitulation hypothesis was discredited, turned away from the study of evolution. This general attitude toward evolution was unfortunately encouraged by the discovery and rapid development of genetics—Darwin had written before the science of genetics was established. Within a short time after his death, critics began to challenge much of what Darwin had said, especially his views on the inheritance of acquired characteristics (which were very similar to Lamarck's), but even his theory of natural selection. By the early 1900's the geneticists had attained a dominant position that they held until fairly recently (Freeman, 1970).

To understand the significance of this turn it is necessary to understand that the early theories of biological evolution, both Darwin's and Lamarck's, importantly emphasized *behavior* as a significant variable in the process of evolution. This emphasis is most obvious in the Lamarckian view, where the behavior of the organism is what is believed to bring about the subsequent changes in the species (the giraffe has a long neck because its ancestors had to stretch to reach the trees on which they fed, for instance); but behavior is equally important in the theory of natural selection. Darwin had argued that inasmuch as all species had more young than could survive there was a factor of *overproduction*. There was also, he observed, *variation*—that is, individuals of the same species are not identical in every way. Overproduction meant that there was *competition* for things, including the opportunity to reproduce. Because there was variation, some creatures did better than others in this competition, wherefore their characteristics survived and those of others did not. Clearly, in this scheme, the behavior of creatures is of great importance.

The geneticists, in their early and most enthusiastic period, virtually did away with behavior as a relevant consideration and attempted to explain evolution simply as a result of a kind of genetic programing that operated independently of the behavior of the animal. George Gaylord Simpson has put it very nicely:

Samuel Butler said that a hen is an egg's way of producing another egg. Thus in the Darwinian epoch he foreshadowed a reorientation of evolutionary studies that did later occur. Without expressing it in that way, the evolutionary scientists of Butler's and earlier times held the common-sense view that an egg is a hen's way of producing another hen. They were trying to explain the evolution of the hen, not of the egg. It was the geneticists, after 1900, who came around to Butler's view that the essence of the matter is in the egg, not in the hen. (Simpson, 1958:7)

The result of turning away from behavior was to turn away from Darwinism as well. The turn also contributed to the separation of genetics and biology from the study of culture. Now there is a new *synthetic theory* that incorporates the more useful features of Darwin, of genetics, and of various other views and that, most importantly, once again recognizes behavior as a factor of great significance (Campbell, 1966; Freeman, 1970; Hallowell, 1963; Roe and Simpson, 1958). Darwin has thus been rediscovered and the evolutionary theory ''has emerged saliently as the unifying paradigm of all the biological sciences, from biochemistry to ecology'' (Freeman, 1970:51).

Paleoanthropology

Perhaps even more dramatic with respect to a new view of man and culture are the recent discoveries from paleontology and archeology. These have raised questions about the fundamental definitions of man and culture, definitions that had been for the most part unchallenged for a long period. What, after all, in evolutionary perspective, *is* a ''man?'' If we find, in the course of archeological excavations, the bones of creatures which are more or less like those of modern man but not exactly like them, how do we determine whether or not they are ''men'' as opposed to nonmen? Until fairly recently this issue was not regarded as

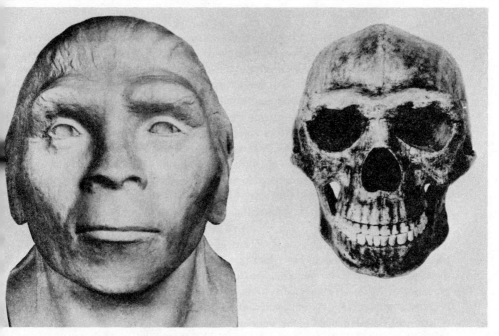

HOMO ERECTUS (SINANTHROPUS; PEKING MAN). Reconstruction of the head and skull of a woman, made by Franz Weidenreich with the assistance of Lucile Swan. (Courtesy of The American Museum of Natural History)

critical. Remember that well into the nineteenth century no human fossils had been found at all. The first fossil formally recognized as such was a *Neanderthal* found in 1856. Even the true significance of this fossil lay in limbo for another thirty years—until two similar skeletons were uncovered in association with the remains of extinct animals and a number of crude stone tools (Daniel, 1962; Howell, 1965; Oakley, 1964). Neanderthals, however, are classified along with modern man as *Homo sapiens*. The classification is based upon morphological features, one of the most important of which is the size of the skull and brain case. Thus Neanderthals, being recent and large-brained, did not importantly affect our definition of man. Things became considerably more difficult after the 1890's, when a young Dutch doctor and student of early man, Eugene DuBois, discovered what turned out to be a more primitive fossil human—*Java man*. This fossil was subsequently termed *Homo erectus*, since it was quite different from anything previously known, but still basically human in form. This discovery caused so much controversy in anthropological circles and was subject to so much disbelief that DuBois locked up his finds and refused to let others see them. After other *Homo erectus* finds were made, in Java, China, Algeria, and East Africa, DuBois was eventually given credit for his find and *Homo erectus* was seen to be a separate, far-ranging, and successful species (Howell, 1965). Although Java man created a sensation when first discovered, and although it was more ''primitive'' or ''ape-like'' than

Neanderthal, it still did not seriously shake our beliefs about what the fundamental criteria for being human were—Java man was bipedal, had humanlike dentition, and had other physical features similar to those of modern man. More importantly, however, Java man proved to have approximately 1000 cubic centimeters of brain, 900-1000 cubic centimeters being an implicitly held "critical point" for man as opposed to apes (modern man ranges from 1000 to 2000 with a mean of 1300). That is, if one had a fossil find otherwise humanlike, it was considered human only if it also had not less than 900-1000 cc. of brain case. One further reason the finding of Java man did relatively little to shake our established beliefs about human evolution is that the fossils could not be adequately dated, since the geology of Java was so little known at the time of DuBois's discovery. Although Java man was established as older than Neanderthal, just how much older was not clear until many years later.

Archeological sites, however, do not always contain fossil materials. In the absence of such evidence, how does one establish that the site was occupied by humans as opposed to some other creature? The common solution was to use the presence of tools—if there were tools, they must have been made by humans, because it was universally believed that only men made and used tools. Evidence of fire, too, could be used in the same way. Brain size was linked with these latter two criteria. To make fire and to make and use tools, it was long believed, required having a brain of the proper "human" size. For a long time nothing much happened to challenge this view.

But this way of thinking received a severe jolt with the discovery, in recent years, of an entirely unprecedented group of fossils, the *Australopithecines*. The first of these, the famous Taung baby, was discovered in 1924 by the anatomist Raymond Dart in South Africa. At first, as in the case of Java man, the scientific community reacted with surprised disbelief. Part of the skepticism stemmed from the fact that Dart's find was a child only five or six years of age. To establish it as an entirely new and radically different fossil it was necessary to find more evidence, preferably adults. Then, in the 1930's, the paleontologist Robert Broom found enough materials to reconstruct several adult skulls along with various other body bones. Broom's fossils were slightly different from Dart's original, but close enough to establish the authenticity of the Australopithecines. Since these early discoveries there have been many more such finds; and they come now from East Africa as well as South Africa. Although there are many professional disputes over whether certain finds are older than others, whether certain types are different species or merely variants of a single species, and the like, both the general features of the Australopithecines and the crude dates of their appearance are quite clear—and the implications for theories of man and culture are most profound.

In the Australopithecines we have creatures who are erect and bipedal, with a humanlike pelvis and leg formation. The dentition and the skull are remarkably manlike although the creature is so old it was first thought that it had to be an ape. Current dates, well-established in terms of the relatively sophisticated dating

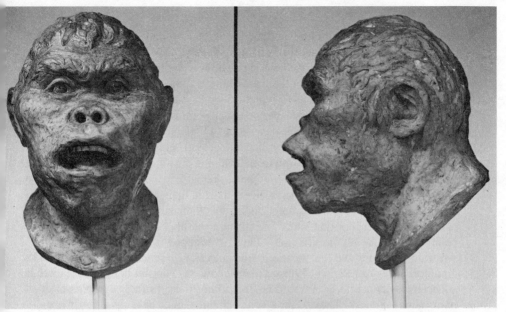

AUSTRALOPITHECUS. Restoration made by Harry Shapiro. (Courtesy of The American Museum of Natural History)

techniques of modern archeology, paleontology, and geology, date some of the Australopithecines to roughly 3.5 millions of years ago. The dates for *Homo erectus*, and also for the first evidence of the use of fire, go back approximately 500,000 years. Neanderthals have been traced back to about 100,000 years and modern man to approximately 50,000 years. Keep in mind that less than 150 years ago the few people who believed the earth might be somewhat more than 6000 years old were considered radical!

Australopithecus was a relatively small-brained creature, with a brain size averaging around 500 cc. What made the Australopithecines such an unprecedented and startling discovery was the evidence that they must have hunted small game and apparently made and used bone and stone tools. This evidence obviously challenged the prevailing view that the large brain of *Homo erectus* or *Homo sapiens* was a necessary requirement for making and using tools. Since tools were routinely taken as evidence of culture, their tools meant that the Australopithecines must have possessed the rudiments, at least, of culture. Thus we are now forced to believe that tool-making and tool-using actually preceded the large brain and, in fact, appear to be factors involved in the evolution of the brain. As a consequence, then, in a specifically biological frame of reference, man becomes in important measure a *product of culture*—of his own thought and behavior, that is—as well as the creator of it. The large brain, *and* culture, contrary to what we always believed, must have evolved *together* over a long period of time, with the behavior associated with tool-using feeding back on the organism itself and helping to bring about a change in dentition, in the shape of the face and skull, in the pelvis, and hence in the size of the brain (Campbell, 1966; Howell, 1965; Hallowell, 1963; Pfeiffer, 1969; Roe and Simpson, 1958; Spuhler, 1959). The fossil record is far more complicated than this, of course, but it now demands that we face up to issues we could formerly ignore. Not the least of these is the relationship of man to his environment and technology.

As matters stand at the moment, we must point out, there is no unequivocal evidence that Australopithecines made stone tools. Some authorities argue that the evidence indicates *Homo habilis*, still another fossil, as the most logical candidate for the first *tool-maker* as opposed to *Australopithecus* who may only have been a *tool-user*. *Homo habilis*, they say, had a cranial capacity of 680 cc., a more manlike skull than *Australopithecus*, teeth that are likewise more manlike, a more fully developed hand that was functionally able to make tools, an entirely modern collarbone, and a foot that was more modern that that of *Australopithecus*. It is believed that *Homo habilis* may have overlapped somewhat in time with Australopithecines and that Australopithecines and *Homo habilis* may have had a common ancestor (Napier, 1969). Others, however, do not believe that there is sufficient evidence to establish that *Homo habilis* is, in fact, a new species of man (genus *Homo*). They believe *Homo habilis* may be only a subspecies of *Australopithecus* (Campbell, 1969). Arguments like this between specialists, it is important to realize, constitute much of what anthropology is all about. But bear in mind that the general picture emerging from the fossil record is not subject to dispute. Clearly, some relatively small-brained, erect, bipedal "protoman" was responsible for making and using tools millions of years before we had thought it possible.

Ethology

It is strange that although people knew for a long time that animals other than men used tools and made things—for what, after all, is involved in the spider's construction of a web, a bird's making a nest, a primate's using a stick to probe for insects or a rock to break things, a hermit crab's using a discarded shell, and the like—they continued to define themselves as *the* tool-makers and to assume that this capacity set man apart clearly and completely from other creatures. It is true, however, that we knew surprisingly little about the behavior of animals in their natural state.

Paleontology is not the only development to bring about changes in the way we think about ourselves and culture. In recent years the science of ethology has made tremendous contributions to our thought along these lines. Indeed, the Nobel prize for medicine in 1973 was shared by three ethologists—Konrad Lorenz, Nicholas Tinbergen, and Karl von Frisch. We now have, for the first time, solid data that bear upon the behavior of many species of animals *in their natural environment*, and it seems incredible, in looking back, that until about forty years ago we had virtually no such information. Furthermore, even the information that might have been available was not ordinarily used by students of man. Although there are over 200 species of monkeys and apes, we had no adequate observations of any of them in their natural environment until 1931 when, under the tutelage of Robert M. Yerkes, H. W. Nissen did a field study on the chimpanzee (Carpenter, 1964:3). Even so, it was not until the 1950's that such studies became an accepted and important part of anthropology, biology, and psychology. Man, defined by himself as the tool-making, unique, and distinctive culture-bearing creature, had apparently no need for such information! Indeed, some even today do not believe that such information has any relevance whatsoever to understanding the behavior of men; others, at the opposite extreme, naively believe one can generalize directly from animals to men. In between are those more cautious scholars who recognize that while one cannot generalize directly from animal to human behavior, one can learn a great deal about behavior in general. This information about behavior in general is, in turn, most helpful in trying to understand human behavior in particular. We study chimpanzees, gorillas, monkeys, wolves, lions, or whatever, not because *our* behavior is like theirs but, rather, because the behavior of our ancient prehuman forebears must have been more similar to that of certain present-day animals than it is to our own present-day behavior. Likewise, we do not study contemporary hunting and gathering peoples because they behave as our ancestors did, but because they must behave more nearly as our ancestors did than we do. These assumptions are fundamental to any study of man and culture in phylogenetic perspective—but they must not be abused; as anthropologist Alexander Alland has said:

A renewed interest in the application of Darwininan biology to human behavior has developed in the last several years. This interest has opened an exciting field for theory and research specifically because it operates without the assumption that, since men are animals, they must behave like other animals. Instead, those interested in this approach search for both continuities and discontinuities in those processes which gave rise to man and which continue to influence his development.

Books like *African Genesis*, *The Territorial Imperative*, *On Aggression*, and *The Naked Ape* (there are several more) obscure the real scientific progress that has been made in this area. These books oversimplify both Darwinism and the human condition. Their focus on hypothetical biological determinants of human social existence does not offer a plausible theory of human origins. Furthermore, these authors have been singularly unable to offer insights into the reasons for behavioral differences between groups, or to explain the complexities of human social patterns.

It is important to salvage those aspects of biological theory which can contribute to an understanding of man. The works named represent an intellectual dead end at a time when the complexities of human behavior can and must be probed in depth. The political and ecological situation in the world has reached a level of crisis appproaching disaster. Outworn analyses such as those which equate war with innate aggression can only offer comfort to those who wish to maintain the *status quo*. (1972:2-3)

Recent studies of animal behavior have told us many things we did not previously know and have also caused us to consider much more systematically and deeply some of the things we thought we already knew. The exciting work done on the chimpanzee by Jane van Lawick-Goodall, for example, has made us aware of a number of new facts. Chimpanzees make and use simple tools. They have been observed picking twigs, stripping the leaves from them, and then using what remains to dip into termite nests to get the termites for food. They also have been observed making sponges of soft leaves in order to drink water they could not otherwise have reached. They routinely make nests to sleep in at night. What is more, we know now for the first time that chimpanzees, contrary to what has always been believed about them, occasionally hunt and kill other animals for food. We have detailed information on the sexual life of chimpanzees which has exploded many of the myths that formerly surrounded the subject. The chimpanzees, far from fighting over sexually receptive females or allowing them to mate only· with the dominant male, rather calmly take turns (van Lawick-Goodall, 1971:96).

George B. Schaller's work with the mountain gorilla is another case in point. Probably no animal in history had been subject to so many myths, distortions, and outright fabrications as this peaceful, placid beast. And, again, the information sheds new light on former beliefs:

Some scientists have maintained that monkey and ape groups remain together over long periods of time because the males have continuous and ready access to receptive females. But from my observations it seems that gorilla groups remain stable, on the whole, even though there may be no receptive females for months at a time, indicating that sex is of little or no importance here. Gorillas always gave me the impression that they stay together because they like and know one another. The magnanimity with which Big Daddy shared his females with other males, even though some were only temporary visitors, helped to promote peace in the group. (Schaller, 1964:122)

Similarly, with respect to the widely advertised belief that territoriality is an "instinctive" phenomenon:

The fact that several gorilla groups occupy the same section of the forest, and that, when groups meet, their interactions tend to be peaceful was of considerable interest to me. Once it was generally thought that each monkey and ape group lived in a territory, the boundaries of which were defended vigorously against intrusions by other members of the same species. But the gorilla certainly shares its range and its abundant food resources with others of its kind, disdaining all claims to a plot of land of its own. (Schaller, 1964:201)

This is not to say that territoriality is not important in many animals; it is, but what is emerging clearly from ethological studies is that all of those phenomena we have tended to take for granted—sexual exclusiveness, territoriality, instinctive aggressiveness, and the like—are immeasurably more complex than we had heretofore imagined. Previous views of animal behavior have been oversimplified, as well as previous views of man and culture. We have, until recently, attributed remarkable abilities to *Homo sapiens* with no regard for the complexities of animal social organization, tool-using, or "proto-culture" that preceded them. It was as if man had suddenly emerged, from an ancestor that possessed none of these characteristics at all, as a radically different, dominant, large-brained, culture-bearing creature. While chimpanzees and gorillas do not tell us directly of our own behavior, they suggest much about the kinds and ranges of behavior that must probably have been involved in the evolution of our behavior.

But studies of the behavior of monkeys and apes, however much they are closer to men than other animals are, must not be taken as the only ones of relevance. As Schaller has made clear, from an ecological point of view there are cogent reasons to study other kinds of animals, particularly group-dwelling carnivores:

When trying to deduce the social system used by *Australopithecus* and other early hominids, anthropologists have usually looked for clues among nonhuman primates. This is logical on phylogenetic grounds but not on ecological ones. Social systems are so strongly influenced by the ecological conditions under which an animal lives that even the same species may behave differently from area to area as Rowell (1967) has shown for several primates and Kruuk (1970) for hyenas. Monkeys and apes are essentially vegetarians living in groups which confine themselves to small ranges. Man and his precursors, on the other hand, have been widely roaming scavengers and hunters for perhaps two million years, a way of life that has diverged so drastically from the nonhuman primates that similarities in the social systems of the two may well be accidental. More can probably be learned about the genesis of man's social system by studying phylogenetically unrelated but ecologically similar forms than by perusing nonhuman primates. The social carnivores provide an obvious choice. (Schaller, 1972:378)

Studies of such animals as lions, hyenas, jackals, wild dogs, and wolves have suggested, among other things, that it is the social behavior of these animals, and nothing else, that enables them to exploit the particular environments they inhabit (Kruuk, 1972:275). This is strong evidence for those who hold that cooperation and the evolution of sociability are of far greater importance in evolution than a creature's innate aggressiveness or some kind of situation of "all against all." These studies have demonstrated nothing conclusive as yet, but, again, they show the enormous complexity of the issues and they force us to consider our assumptions more carefully.

Nor are the relevant studies confined only to nonhuman primates and carnivorous predators. The behaviors of all creatures—insects, amphibians, reptiles, and birds—are all of great interest now to students of man. Again, not because they necessarily tell us about *human* behavior per se, but because they tell us so much about *behavior* itself, particularly those forms of behavior we label communication, adaptation, sociability, territoriality, and even what we term "intelligence." Information from both paleontology and ethology is coming in so fast at the present time one has difficulty keeping abreast of it. It combines to put us on the threshold of a new, comprehensive, and significant science of man.

Cross-Cultural Studies

Ethnography is generally defined as the scientific description of human life. Ethnography can easily be thought of as the ethology of humans. As in the case of ethological studies in general, it may seem incredible now to realize how little we actually knew about "human beings in their wild state" until well into the twentieth century. Remember that the only sources of information available to the early evolutionists—and to all scholars before them—were the usually biased accounts of travelers, missionaries, prospectors, traders, and adventurers. Systematic, scientific studies of non-Western peoples began in earnest only in the twentieth century—in fact, only about fifty years ago. That all theories of behavior, society, culture and evolution were based upon the behavior of Western Europeans or on biased accounts of other people is a fact of great significance in the history of science and should not be ignored. The related factor of assuming that existing "primitive" people could be taken as representative of our prehistoric ancestors is perhaps of no less importance.

In recent years we have accumulated a wealth of detailed ethnographic information on a substantial number of different cultures all around the globe. We know from this information, plus the archeological record, that currently existing hunters and gatherers are marginal types not representative of those hunting and gathering populations who existed in previous times and who exploited the vast herds of miscellaneous ungulates that populated their environments in such staggeringly large numbers. The Eskimo, Australian Aborigines, African Bushmen, and other hunter-gatherers that we have studied most intensively all occupy relatively remote and sparse environments. Their requirements for making a living are a far cry, for example, from the requirements of those who lived in close proximity to the estimated thirty million bison that inhabited the North American continent at the time of first European contact (McHugh, 1972). Archeological evidence indicates that many of our ancestors must likewise have been blessed with an abundance. Nonetheless, the information acquired from studies of existing hunter-gatherers has often been a critical factor in allowing archeologists to interpret the meaning of their finds. To have some idea, say of the way contemporary people make use of stone tools or housing sites, how and why they move over the land, what kinds of refuse they leave behind, and other such things, is obviously of value when an investigator is confronted by limited evidence of such activity in the past. This kind of combination of ethnography with archeology is a part of the exciting "new archeology" that is still developing.

Ethnographic studies have gone much further, however, to give us insight into the workings of culture and cultural evolution and the essential human condition. It was, for example, as we have seen, the cross-cultural record that converted Freud's brilliant but parochial and essentially culture-bound psychoanalytic theory into a newer, more powerful, more comprehensive and more useful theory which, however inadequate some might consider it, still remains the only

BUSHMEN, KALAHARI DESERT; THREE GIRLS DANCING. (Photograph by Richard B. Lee)

psychological theory of personality "adequate thus far to cope with the enormous complexities of the human psyche" (Spiro, 1972:574).

Although anthropologists have been accused in the past, perhaps rightly so, of concentrating too exclusively on the differences between human cultures and thus neglecting the similarities, it is also the case that the information to establish true human universals has come from the cross-cultural record. We now recognize, for example, that if there be such a thing as an Oedipus complex, it results not from memory traces in the species, not from biology, but rather from universally similar factors of infancy, childhood, the family, and the requirements of child-rearing. We know that human beings, for reasons which are now beginning to become clear, have chosen only a few from an infinite number of possible kinship systems (Murdock, 1949). We know, likewise, that however much cultures may differ in their specifics, each human culture has a normative dimension and constitutes, in that sense, a moral order. And we know that such things as aggression, territoriality, war, and the like are not absolute human universals but are dependent upon circumstances of technology, environment, personality, culture, and history. We

UGANDAN BOW-HARPIST. (Bunyole, 1970; photograph courtesy of Michael and Susan Whyte)

NEW GUINEA, EASTERN HIGHLANDS. Man dressed for a ceremonial dance. (Photograph by Joan D. Langness, 1971)

also know that most of those various behavior patterns that we have attempted to define as "normal" or "abnormal" are, in fact, relative to the cultural context in which they occur and that, with the exception of only the most extreme pathologies, no definite scale exists whereby we can measure behavior in such terms. Homosexuality, excessive drinking, suicide, homicide, infanticide, cannibalism, and other such "problems" all take on a new dimension when seen in cross-cultural terms. The same thing is true of competence, happiness, efficiency, intelligence, and similar concepts. We are by no means very close to understanding this vast panorama of behavior, but at least we are now aware that it exists and we have a much better understanding of its dimensions than ever before. If critics condemn anthropologists for having neglected their own culture and their own social problems for the esoteric and bizarre, let these critics tell us where else we would have acquired *any* valid information on the richness and beauty of human life as it has expressed itself around the world. Or perhaps we would somehow be better off not knowing of the infinite wonder of human life?

Cybernetics

One development of recent years that has helped to bring about the new view of culture and evolution is the discovery of cybernetics—essentially the study of the control functions of communication. In at least three ways, the development of cybernetics has influenced the science of man: by challenging the absolute laws of Newtonian physics and thus demonstrating that the social sciences need not be less scientific than physics, by opening our eyes to the complexities of feedback and thus allowing us to see the process of evolution in a more useful perspective, and by providing us with computers that enable us to handle masses of data not otherwise manageable.

According to Newtonian physics, which had dominated science for at least two hundred years, the universe operated according to precise, rigid laws in which the future depended strictly upon the past; everything was deemed perfectly predictable and there were, in principle, no uncertainties. It was this model that students of man—anthropologists, sociologists, psychologists, political scientists, and others—attempted to emulate in their attempts to become scientific. It is this model that influenced Boas and Durkheim, Radcliffe-Brown and Malinowski, and virtually all others. For years, members of the so-called "hard sciences" argued that the various social sciences could never become sciences at all—that human behavior was fundamentally unpredictable and hence that the study of it could not be the same as the study of the laws of the universe. The new view of physics, arising out of the Heisenberg *"principle of uncertainty"* (S. F. Mason, 1962:557), and utilizing as it does statistics and probability theory instead of absolutes and immutables, renders this criticism untenable and thus opens up new possibilities for a true science of man which is just that—a science:

Newtonian physics, which had ruled from the end of the seventeenth century to the end of the nineteenth with scarcely an opposing voice, described a universe in which everything happened precisely according to law, a compact, tightly organized universe in which the whole future depends strictly upon the whole past. Such a picture can never be either fully justified or fully rejected experimentally and belongs in large measure to a conception of the world which is supplementary to experiment but in some ways more universal than anything that can be experimentally verified. We can never test by our imperfect experiments whether one set of physical laws or another can be verified down to the last decimal. The Newtonian view, however, was compelled to state and formulate physics as if it were, in

fact, subject to such laws. This is now no longer the dominant attitude of physics . . . .
(Wiener, 1954:7)

Cybernetic explanations, according to anthropologist Gregory Bateson (1972), have peculiarities which make them much more useful to social and behavioral scientists than the explanations of classical physics. First of all, they deal with "form" rather than with the "substance" that the laws for energy and matter were concerned with. That is, cybernetic explanations are interested in the relations between things rather than in what actually composes or makes up the things. They are similar in this way to Levi-Strauss's structuralism, which is not surprising inasmuch as Levi-Strauss was influenced to some extent by cybernetic theory. Cybernetic explanations are also interested in the order of things rather than in what is being ordered. But they are thus interested in order not purely for its own sake but rather for the information that is associated with or emerges from the order—what message is conveyed, that is. Such explanations are further concerned with "context" in a way that physics is not. There is, of course, a hierarchy of contexts within which communications must be understood. The same message can obviously mean different things in different contexts. This becomes absolutely crucial for studies of emics where we are led to "understand" in terms of larger and larger contexts. As Bateson says, "without context there is no communication" (1972:408). Cybernetic explanations are negative rather than positive:

Causal explanation is usually positive. We say that billiard ball B moved in such and such a direction because billiard ball A hit it at such and such an angle. In contrast to this, cybernetic explanation is always negative. We consider what alternative possibilities could conceivably have occurred and then ask why many of the alternatives were not followed, so that the particular event was one of those few which could, in fact, occur. The classical example of this type of explanation is the theory of evolution under natural selection. According to this theory, those organisms which were not both physiologically and environmentally viable could not possibly have lived to reproduce. Therefore, evolution always followed the pathways of viability. As Lewis Carroll has pointed out, the theory explains quite satisfactorily why there are no bread-and-butter-flies today. (Bateson, 1967:29)

Thus cybernetics deals with "restraints." The assumption is that without restraints of some kind, change would be regulated only by chance.

. . . For example, the selection of a piece for a given position in a jigsaw puzzle is "restrained" by many factors. Its shape must conform to that of its several neighbors and possibly that of the boundary of the puzzle; its color must conform to the color pattern of its region; the orientation of its edges must obey the topological regularities set by the cutting machine in which the puzzle was made; and so on. From the point of view of the man who is trying to solve the puzzle, these are all clues, i.e., sources of information which will guide him in his selection. From the point of view of the cybernetic observer, they are *restraints*. (Bateson, 1967:29)

Likewise, there are restraints that result from "feedback." That is, the information one receives from having attempted something not only enables one to try it again somewhat differently, but also reduces the chances of trying still other things. The concept of feedback has helped us to understand that human evolution was not a completely predetermined process independent of the actions of organisms but, rather, depended upon the actions of organisms for its continuation. Adaptive change, such as that required by evolution, has many dimensions. It involves responding, learning, ecological succession, biological change, and so on, depending upon how we wish to view it. But in all cases, if it is to be truly adaptive change, it must involve trial and error, and there must be a way of comparing one attempt with another. Because some errors must always be made, and because errors are "always biologically and/or psychically expensive" (Bateson, 1972:274), certain things continually drop out of the system and thereby change the context. A new situation exists and the process continues.

This view of evolutionary change is far more sophisticated than that held by Darwin or the early cultural evolutionists. It combines with the other recent developments we have mentioned to put us on the brink of a comprehensive, meaningful, and, we must hope, useful science of man. This newly emerging view combines features of all of the views that have gone before it. It is, above all, evolutionary. It recognizes the importance of history and diffusion. It insists upon the crucial significance of an ecological point of view. It recognizes the significance of technoenvironmental factors, but it does not believe that these are the sole determinants of cultural phenomena or cultural change. Finally, it recognizes what Bateson has recently termed the "ecology of mind" (1972)—that is, the question of how ideas interact both with themselves and with the environment to produce a viable system. Thus it goes well beyond arguments involving history versus science, idiographic versus nomothetic, functionalism versus historical reconstruction, sociology versus psychology, group versus individual, idealism versus materialism, and the like. It retains as a most useful convenience, however, the concept of culture—albeit in a revised form. In its simplest form it might look something like the diagram.

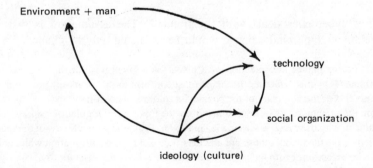

NEW GUINEA, HIGHLANDS. Men doing each others' hair. (Photograph by L. L. Langness)

People inevitably exist in some environment. Out of their interaction with their environment emerges a technology. Technology, we can say, is not the absolutely unique possession of human beings, since animals, too, in some sense have technologies. The spider's web, the nests of birds, the use of simple tools by many creatures, and other such things are examples of technology. But in humans technology is developed to an extraordinary degree. Out of man's interaction with his environment and the emerging technology are implications for the way he can order himself with relation to others—his social organization. All of these things in turn—his interaction with his environment, technology, and social organization, feed into ideology. The scheme does not just stop at that point, however, for ideology, in its turn, has implications that feed back into all of the other dimensions. However much technoenvironmental factors are determinants of behavior, the relationship between human beings and their environment and technology is mediated by their ideas and beliefs about themselves, their fellows, and, indeed, the universe itself. The Mennonites, a religious group in the United States, resist automobiles, television, and modern technology in general not because they are unaware that such things exist, but rather because of their religious beliefs. And we know that people have often died rather than change their beliefs. Likewise, as the venerable historian Arnold J. Toynbee has recently pointed out (1973), there is surely some relationship between people's attitudes towards the world and how they have treated it. Witness a Judeo-Christian attitude:

And God blessed them, and God said unto them, Be fruitful, and multiply, and replenish the earth, and subdue it: and have dominion over the fish of the sea, and over the fowl of the air, and over every living thing that moveth upon the earth. (Genesis I, 28)

Compare this with the following attitude expressed by the Shahaptian medicine man Smohalla:

My young men shall never work. Men who work cannot dream, and wisdom comes to us in dreams. . . . You ask me to plough the ground. Shall I take a knife and tear my mother's bosom? You ask me to dig for stone. Shall I dig under her skin for her bones? You ask me to cut the grass and make hay and sell it and be rich like white men. But dare I cut off my mother's hair? (quoted in Haines, 1955:169)

Or consider one of the many comments of the remarkable Nez Perce leader Chief Joseph:

The white men were many and we could not hold our own with them. We were like deer. They were like grizzly bears. We had a small country. Their country was large. We were contented to let things remain as the Great Spirit made them. They were not, and would change the rivers if they did not suit them. (quoted in Brown, 1970:304)

Characteristics of Man as an Animal

We are now beginning to recognize fully man's kinship with the rest of nature. And in the same way we recognize the continuity of biological and cultural evolution. We observe that man is an animal; then as an animal he is a *mammal*, a *primate*, and a *hominid*. Each of these classifications imply certain things for the way man relates to his environment and to other creatures.

Being a mammal, man shares with all other mammals certain features or "adaptive complexes" (Campbell, 1966) that are generally regarded as particularly important in understanding evolution and culture. Mammals have the ability, for example, for constant and lively activity. This capacity contrasts mammals with both reptiles and amphibians, which become relatively inactive at night and during periods of cold weather. The difference would presumably give the mammals an advantage over reptiles and amphibians, and it would also have allowed mammals to move northward into colder latitudes and thus exploit more of the earth's surface. This kind of capacity for constant activity is made possible through the phenomenon of *homoiothermy*—the ability to maintain a constant and appropriate body temperature. This ability may date back as much as 150 million years (Campbell, 1966).

To maintain a constant body temperature it is necessary to have a reliable supply of food for energy. Mammals solved this problem in part by evolving a new kind of dentition. Whereas reptiles have what is called *homodont* dentition, mammals have *heterodont* dentition. A snake's teeth are nearly all of the same shape (fangs excepted) and have the same function—namely to trap. Mammalian teeth, on the other hand, are more specialized, some being for tearing, others for chewing, cutting, or grinding. With such teeth many more kinds of food could be exploited than had heretofore been possible, and the efficiency of the digestive process was increased as well.

Still another factor of great importance for the mammals was reproductive economy. Reptiles maintain themselves by producing large numbers of eggs, only a few of which hatch offspring that live to maturity. The mammals, by retaining and nourishing the egg inside the mother, cut down on losses and thus improve reproductive economy. There is a postnatal factor here as well as a prenatal one. It is of the utmost importance for the development of culture. Mammals are fed by the mother for long periods of time after they are born. Remaining in close association with the parent, instead of being abandoned to shift for themselves as the offspring of reptiles are, they are relatively safe. More important by far is that this long period of dependency allows for a much greater transfer of learned behavior:

The intimate relationship between generations resulting from suckling and caring for the young makes possible the transmission of learned behavior by imitation. Behavior patterns learned by trial and error have been recognized among lower vertebrates and invertebrates, but the simplicity and origin of such behavior puts it into a different class from that of mammals. It is the transmission of complex learned behavior by imitation that makes it unnecessary to learn solely from direct experience—a dangerous process. . . . Instead, the experience of generations can be assimilated in a short time with reduced danger to the young. Thus the mammals have the great advantage [shared to some extent by birds] of being able, as it were, to "inherit" [by imitative learning from parents] "acquired" [i.e., learned] behavior characters. The inheritance of acquired characters makes possible a high rate of evolution of those characters, and thus the behavior patterns of mammals have evolved fast and increased in complexity in such a way as to put them in that respect at a different level from all other living organisms. (Campbell, 1966:49)

The "different level" here is culture. It is in this factor of increasing postnatal dependence upon adults that we find the real basis for what becomes in hominids an overwhelmingly cultural mode of existence.

The greater ability to imitate, and to learn in general, is largely due to the increase in brain size we find in mammals. Even relatively ordinary mammals like the sheep, for instance, have large brains in proportion to their body weight when compared with reptiles. This ratio of brain weight to body weight increases in the primates; within the primates it increases very dramatically in hominids, especially in *Homo sapiens*. Not only does the brain increase in size, but in addition most of the increase is in the cortex, the part of the brain that seems to be involved specifically in both memory and problem-solving activities. It is this high brain-to-body ratio, along with the period of infant dependency, that allows for the extragenetic transmission of information, the most fundamental requirement for culture.

Being not merely a mammal but a primate and the most highly developed of primates, man shares with other primates further things of great significance for an understanding of man. Foremost of these is the ancient but more highly developed and exceedingly useful five-fingered hand. The evolution of the hand was accompanied by a host of other changes. Evolution is an exceedingly complicated process, even the slightest change in one organ being accompanied by corresponding changes in many others. This is not very well understood as yet although we have many ideas as to how changes most probably occurred. Consider what John Pfeiffer has to say on the hand:

> The retreat of the snout was also accompanied by the loss of prosimian tactile whiskers or "feelers." The hands acquired a considerably richer supply of nerve cells and fibers concerned with the sense of touch. Hands and sense organs evolved together, each development accelerating the other in an involved feedback relationship. Fingers became more and more mobile, capable not only of moving faster but also of assuming a far greater variety of positions. Devices designed originally for grasping and holding on were used increasingly to get food and, even more important, to pick up objects, bring them closer, and turn them around to examine from all angles. The ability to manipulate in this way was new in the history of terrestrial life, reached a high point in the monkey family. (Pfeiffer, 1969:30)

In comparison with other mammals, primates have in general much greater maneuverability of the limbs, with a well-developed collarbone enabling them to move the arm in all directions. There is also a much improved sense of balance and improved motor control. Primates typically bear one offspring at a birth, a development which, it is believed, must be associated with dwelling in the trees; it would be difficult or impossible for a mother to get around in the trees with large numbers of infants. Also, with fewer infants, much better care can be given them. The primate mother, then, with only two teats placed high on the chest and having the ability to use forelimbs and hands, can hold her infant, observe it carefully, and fondle it in a way no nonprimate mother can. This situation may have much to do with the development of emotional attachments between them which could, perhaps, then be generalizable to other animals later in life. In the primates we see continued cortical expansion, a still greater period of infant dependency, the development of stereoscopic vision, a complicated social organization, and other factors that are found in a somewhat modified form in hominids.

The argument is that hominids evolved out of creatures similar though not identical to contemporary primates, and this evolution was associated with changes in behavior and environment leading eventually to *Homo sapiens*. The omnivorous nature of primates, particularly their chewing and digestive processes, it is argued, made it possible for them to evolve from forest-living to plains-living creatures. The necessity for this adaptation may have been a change in climate, but there may have been other factors as well. The flexibility of primate food habits allowed an adaptation in food-finding behavior such that the early hominids could bring about a fundamental change in their environment by spreading out into other climates and temperatures. Among other things, there appears to have been a change towards cooperative hunting, a development of central importance for further human evolution. And it is believed there must have been developing also at this time an increasingly complicated technology, mode of communication, and social organization. The facts of all these developments are by no means complete; indeed, much of the evidence is scanty. But that a process of this kind occurred, involving creatures of this kind, over an exceedingly long period of time, is no longer open to serious dispute. It is the details of occurrence that are not clear, not the process or the fact.

Being not merely a primate but a hominid, man has certain characteristics as a hominid that must not be overlooked. First, man is the most generalized of animals. He has no highly specialized organs, no heavy fur, no hooves, no wings, no multiple stomach like the ungulates, no weapon teeth, no natural body armor. In sum, evolving man did not make the dangerous specializations, like the dinosaur or saber-tooth tiger, that led to extinction.

Humans have a distinctive form of sexual behavior characterized by an absence of oestrus. Most animals mate only at certain times of the year. Indeed, often the males and females of a species are not together at all except during the brief mating season. Some animals have one breeding period a year, others have more than one. Humans can and do breed at any time during the year. Accordingly, humans experience no such period of sexual excitement and disruption of social behavior as is found in many other primates—no period of "sexual mania." This sexual behavior appears to be associated with a longer period of child-rearing without loss of reproductive ability, with the possibility of a more permanent male-female relationship, and with sexual drives more readily subject to cortical rather than purely hormonal control. All of these characteristics, in turn, are presumably related in ways that are not well understood to the presence of the permanent breast in humans, to a manner of copulation in which the partners can face and embrace each other, and to the capability for female orgasm, which is not generally believed to occur in nonhuman creatures. There are hints here, it is believed, as to the factors involved in bringing about the complex emotional life of human beings.

Still other factors are also related to sex. In many species the female is much smaller than the male. This difference in size allows, in creatures like the baboon, a greater number of females to survive in a limited amount of territory and hence to better maintain the size of the group. In humans, as we know, the difference in size between males and females is not very great. The reasons for this smaller difference in humans are not completely clear, but they may have to do with the need for the female pelvis to be large enough to accomodate the large-brained human fetus, and with the fact that human males do not need a larger size to cope with predators or with each other. All of these distinctive human characteristics are related, in turn, to the phenomenon of fetalization—that is, to the fact that man retains in the adult form characteristics that are found in the fetal form of lower animals. Physically, humans have become increasingly infantilized—this infantile physique can be seen in the smallness of the human face and the large brain case, and also in such features as the long neck, small teeth, thin nails, thin skull bones, and the like. What appears to be involved here is that in order for brain and intelligence to grow, humans need more time for learning—it simply takes more time to become human than to become some other kind of mammal. It is the brain and learning which gain an advantage by this slowed-down process.

The human hominid begins extrauterine life equipped with a basic human structure and a few reflexes, but with no complex given patterns of behavior that can emerge despite *socialization*. As a human, an individual must learn goals and also the techniques for attaining them. Contrast this need for learning with the rather complex behavior patterns of honeybees or other social insects (Allee, 1958) that do not seem to involve learning. Or contrast it, if you will, with the behavior of salmon, driven somehow to the precise spot where they were hatched, even after having traveled thousands of miles in the ocean and even though their parents died before they were hatched. Humans, although they have the same basic drives that other animals have, do not have these more elaborate patterns that emerge without learning.

Finally, man alone, as we have previously noted, has developed the capacity for *symbolic* behavior. The human brain—developed to such a remarkable culmination from the large and complex brain of the mammals—allows humans to invent and transmit symbols and thus creates a vast chasm between humans and other animals. And it is symbols of course, that make culture possible. Although we know that some nonhuman creatures have a simple technology, that they can communicate, might be said to have the rudiments of a cultural way of life and even perhaps the rudiments of the ability to symbolize, they cannot truly be said to live in a symbolic cultural world as we humans do.

Reviewing the catalogue of human characteristics—diet and dentition, primate reproduction and nurturance, brain development, generalized capacities rather than specializations, infantile physique, learned rather than reflex behavior patterns, capacity to use symbols—we see that culture is not a more happenstance sort of thing—it is a necessary, inevitable, and indispensable human requirement. The necessity for culture is a result of the unique psychobiological characteristics of the human animal. Humans have drives as all animals do, but being primates, and above all, hominids, they have no biologically given ways of satisfying the drives—they must invent, modify, and transmit extragenetically the symbolic means which enable them to survive and, indeed, to reflect upon and appreciate their survival. There is no better statement of this necessity for culture than that by the anthropologist Clifford Geertz:

. . . there is no such thing as a human nature independent of culture. Men without culture would not be the clever savages of Golding's *Lord of the Flies* thrown back upon the cruel wisdom of their animal instincts; nor would they be the nature's noblemen of Enlightenment primitivism or even, as classical anthropological theory would imply, intrinsically talented apes who had somehow failed to find themselves. They would be unworkable monstrosities with very few useful instincts, fewer recognizable sentiments, and no intellect: mental basket cases. As our central nervous system—and most particularly its crowning curse and glory, the neocortex—grew up in great part in interaction with culture, it is incapable of directing our behavior or organizing our experience without the guidance provided by systems of significant symbols. What happened to us in the Ice Age is that we were obliged to abandon the regularity and precision of detailed genetic control over our conduct for the flexibility and adaptability of a more generalized, though of course no less real, genetic control over it. To supply the additional information necessary to be able to act, we were forced, in turn, to rely more and more heavily on cultural sources—the accumulated fund of significant symbols. Such symbols are thus not mere expressions, instrumentalities, or correlates of our biological, psychological, and social existence; they are prerequisites of it. Without men, no culture, certainly; but equally, and more significantly, without culture, no men.

We are, in sum, incomplete and unfinished animals who complete and finish ourselves through culture—and not through culture in general but through highly particular forms of it; Dobuan and Javanese, Hopi and Italian, upper-class and lower-class, academic and commercial. Man's great capacity for learning, his plasticity, has often been remarked, but what is even more critical is his extreme dependence upon a certain sort of learning: the attainment of concepts, the apprehension and application of specific systems of symbolic meaning. Beavers build dams, birds build nests, bees locate food, baboons organize social groups, and mice mate on the basis of forms of learning that rest predominantly on the instructions encoded in their genes and evoked by appropriate patterns of external stimuli: physical keys inserted into organic locks. But men build dams or shelters, locate food, organize their social groups, or find sexual partners under the guidance of instructions encoded in flow charts and blueprints, hunting lore, moral systems, and aesthetic judgments: conceptual structures molding formless talents.

We live, as one writer has neatly put it, in an "information gap." Between what our body tells us and what we have to know in order to function, there is a vacuum we must fill ourselves, and we fill it with information (or misinformation) provided by our culture. The boundary between what is innately controlled and what is culturally controlled in human behavior is an ill-defined and wavering one. Some things are, for all intents and purposes, entirely controlled intrinsically: we need no more cultural guidance to learn how to breathe than a fish needs to learn how to swim. Others are almost certainly largely cultural: we do not attempt to explain on a genetic basis why some men put their trust in centralized planning and others in the free market, though it might be an amusing exercise. Almost all complex human behavior is, of course, the vector outcome of the two. Our capacity to speak is surely innate; our capacity to speak English is surely cultural. Smiling at pleasing stimuli and frowning at unpleasant ones are surely in some degree genetically determined (even apes screw up their faces at noxious odors); but sardonic smiling and burlesque frowning are equally surely predominantly cultural, as is perhaps demonstrated by the Balinese definition of a madman as someone who, like an American, smiles when there is nothing to laugh at. Between the basic ground plans for our life that our genes lay down—the capacity to speak or to smile—and the precise behavior we in fact execute—speaking English in a certain tone of voice, smiling enigmatically in a delicate social situation—lies a complex set of significant symbols under whose direction we transform the first into the second, the ground plans into the activity. (Geertz, 1965:112-114)

Summary

The concept of culture—foreshadowed by Turgot and others, introduced into English by Matthew Arnold and Edward Tylor, pluralized by Boas, clarified by Kroeber and Sapir, spurned by Radcliffe-Brown, but popularized by Benedict, utilized more importantly by Malinowski, White, Harris, Schneider, and scores of others—remains the key concept of anthropology. The most recent emphases in definitions of culture have to do with its symbolic qualities and our utter dependence, as human beings, on the complicated symbolic systems—cultural traditions—we have inherited from our ancestors. While many different definitions of culture are still in use, and while there is no general agreement on any one definition, there are two main trends—one, illustrated best by Marvin Harris, stresses culture as behavior; the other, best represented by Clifford Geertz, emphasizes symbolization.

Comparably, there are those who still argue that technoenvironmental factors are basic, causal, and relatively unaffected by human thought or belief; and there are those who believe that no adequate understanding can result unless human cognitive abilities are taken more fully and consciously into account. It would seem to be growing more and more obvious that both of these factors must be considered in explanations of evolution and culture. Thus the new conjunctive approach we have briefly sketched includes in one form or another all of the major approaches that went into making anthropology what it is today. We recognize evolution; indeed, evolution has become the most central unifying feature of modern social and biological sciences. We recognize that there was and is diffusion. History is regarded as crucial, both oral and written. Psychological factors are an integral feature of this new view. Social organization is recognized as basic. The new ecological perspective includes not only environmental and technological variables but also insists on recognizing the input of the creature itself.

This new view has implications for methods, so that cultural anthropologists now not only work more closely with linguists, archeologists, and physical anthropologists, but also depend upon biologists, physiologists, nutritionists, botanists, geologists, chemists, psychiatrists, and a host of others as well. The emphasis is on problems rather than on disciplines, on cooperation rather than "fetishism."

Further Readings

A. I. Hallowell's paper, "Personality, Culture and Society in Behavioral Evolution," also *Instinctive Behavior*, edited by Schiller, Allee's *The Social Life of Animals*, and Roe and Simpson, *Behavior and Evolution*, must likewise be consulted. *Evolution after Darwin*, edited by Sol Tax, is also of great interest. Simpson's *The Meaning of Evolution* remains an excellent work on evolution in general. For human evolution see Campbell's book of that title and also Pfeiffer's *The Emergence of Man*. *Evolution and Human Behavior* by Alland is also of note.

For ethology, the volume edited by Eibl-Eibesfeldt, *Ethology*, is outstanding. But see also *Instinctive Behavior*, edited by Schiller, Allee's *The Social Life of Animals*, and Tinbergen's *Social Behaviour in Animals*. Studies of a single species of particular interest include Mech's *The Wolf*, McHugh's *The Time of the Buffalo*, Schaller's *The Year of the Gorilla*, and Jane van Lawick-Goodall's *In the Shadow of Man*. Jolly's *The Evolution of Primate Behavior* is quite exceptional for primates in general.

For work on early man consult Howell, *Early Man*; Howells, *Mankind in the Making*; and Campbell, *Human Evolution*.

For cybernetics and its importance see Wiener, *The Human Use of Human Beings: Cybernetics and Society*, and also Bateson's *Steps to an Ecology of Mind*. *Steps to an Ecology of Mind* is also of immense value on the question of man's relationship to his environment.

The significance of cross-cultural studies as such has not really been treated in a single volume. But, again, see Hallowell's paper mentioned above, and Geertz's collection of essays, *The Interpretation of Cultures*.

CONCLUSION THE SCIENCE OF MAN
REGAINED?

Dell Hymes, one of our most distinguished anthropologists, has recently asked, "If anthropology did not exist, would it have to be invented? If it were reinvented, would it be the anthropology we have now?" The answer to both of these questions, he says, is "no" (1972). Hymes is expressing here a sentiment that is currently shared by many in the anthropological profession. It reflects the mood of discontent that many people in our society have experienced in recent years. It also reflects the frustration many feel over the failure of social sciences, including anthropology, to do very much to bring about the changes we believe are not only desirable but necessary. Finally, it reflects the insightful thesis of Ernest Becker, mourning the "lost science of man." But Hymes does not really have in mind the anthropology of Becker—in the sense of anthropology as a general, comprehensive science of man—he refers rather to anthropology in the sense of Becker's "fetishism."

Hymes questions the anthropology of contemporary academia, of universities, departments, disciplines, budgets, associations, meetings, committees, "smoke-filled rooms," and all the trappings of institutions and organizations that so easily lose sight of their true reasons for being and become "establishment" and self-serving. This is the anthropology that divides itself neatly into physical, cultural, social, archeology, and linguistics, and assumes that a knowledge of any one or more of these subdivisions, with little or no help from any outside sources, constitutes an adequate understanding of the "science of man." Why, Hymes asks, should anthropology be "what anthropologists do"? Why should it not be, as Becker suggests too, for the sake of mankind's self-knowledge and liberation rather than for the continuation of the departments themselves?

Hymes, like Becker, deplores an anthropology that is self-serving and parasitic, an anthropology that makes no contribution to change and towards helping to bring about a genuine world community in which the dignity and well-being of *all* peoples are assured. This would be a world in which, however much people differed from one another either physically or culturally,

148

there would be no "savages," no "barbarians," no "civilized" elite but, rather, equal human beings with an appreciation of the true wonder of their mutual differences. It would also be a world in which there was no poverty, no unnecessary disease, no indiscriminate violence and destruction, no senseless killing, no gross inequities, and an end to those problems that are at least potentially soluble through the actions of human beings. Perhaps such a world is simply not possible; but most of us would like to believe that it is.

Anthropologists have made some contributions to such a world. But they have also helped at times to inhibit change, not out of malice but, rather, because of "fetishism." The idea that scholars can reduce complex problems to narrower and simpler ones merely by definition, and then specialize in them independently of the work of others, may make for an easier way to proceed; but it unfortunately does little to solve problems or to advance knowledge. Some idea of how this "fetishism" has worked in anthropology can be gained from the following:

> The plain fact is that there are such things as "political anthropology," "economic anthropology," "anthropology of religion" only because there is such a thing as "anthropology." They exist because of the organization of academic life, not the organization of reality. Guiana does not have one politics for anthropologists, another for economists; there is no theory of religion that is anthropological, as opposed to sociological, or to the understanding of religion developed by students of the history of religions. If religion is a single subject, it is the same subject for all. Too often our publications and careers have been built on the ploy of a putative contribution to the "anthropology of X" or "X anthropology." These are sometimes legitimations of new topics, no doubt, but legitimations required by a border-guard mentality. (Hymes, 1972:38)

Although this censure ignores the obvious fact that for many years, and indeed, until quite recently, there were few sociologists, psychologists, economists, or students of religion, or the like, who were interested in going into the field to look at the cultures anthropologists were studying, it is nevertheless a point well taken. "Fetishism," we observe, has by no means been unique to anthropology. But this tendency, among others, must be overcome if we are to achieve a genuinely comprehensive and useful science of man.

Disciplinary fetishism is not the only reason we have not done better than we have. The organization of universities and the vested interests of individuals do not, we must remember, exist in a vacuum. They are part of the wider society. There is a natural tendency for all social or political systems to resist change. This resistance has been a key factor in changing the original vision of a science of man, devoted to the interests of man, into the disciplinary hodge-podge it has currently become. On the one hand, although some funds have been available in recent years to social scientists, the amount of such support is not very great when compared to the amounts spent on "hard sciences" research, or even on cancer research alone. Furthermore, when it comes to social and political change, the problem is often in the implementation of change rather than in the lack of knowledge about what might be done—or even what ought to be done.

It is extremely important to be aware of the paradox here. On the one hand, recent developments in a variety of fields demand intellectually that we recognize a new, synthetic, unified science of man (whether it be called anthropology, behavioral evolution, or whatever); but on the other hand and at the same time, powerful but nonintellectual forces—the organization of universities, the tendencies toward fetishism on the part of individuals, and the resistance of the political machinery—are preventing us from realizing the full potential of the new view of man that is so rapidly developing.

Amidst all of the developments, or lack of them, we should bear in mind that the basic problems that brought about the idea of a science of man—the problems of moral crisis that Becker speaks of—have neither been solved nor disappeared. Indeed, the problems we now face, moral and otherwise, are if anything greater, more complicated, more threatening, and more urgent than ever before. Because they are so, the science of man will be—must be—regained. The materials for such a science, however briefly they are indicated in this book, are rapidly accumulating.

The new science of man will be roughly of the type suggested in this book. It will certainly be cognizant of the ecological, technological, psychological, and cultural factors we know to be of such crucial importance. It will be widely shared so that all peoples, everywhere, will be aware of it and benefit from it—for it is obvious now that the problems of one area of the world are inevitably and inseparably the problems of all. The most important integrating feature of the new science of man will be an evolutionary frame of reference. What this science comes to be called is not in itself of great significance. The anthropologists' contribution to this, as I have attempted to indicate, is the concept of culture. This cultural dimension of the human condition holds the key "for the future of evolution on this planet." As Hymes has put it:

. . . It was perhaps the achievement of Tylor to help establish the notion of culture in terms of mankind as a whole . . . , and of Boas to help establish the study, in their own terms, of human cultures. . . . Our task may be to establish the study of the *cultural* as a universal and personal dimension of human efforts toward the future. (Hymes, 1972:34)

Anthropology departments are, of course, not very likely to simply disappear in the immediate future. Nor are they very likely to fragment, since recent developments like the shortage of jobs and funds will most probably work against such a tendency. This constraint need not be to the disadvantage of a science of man, in that anthropology remains, as it has always been, by far the most comprehensive of all the sciences of man. Thus, using current anthropology as a base, it should be possible to move freely outward to the concepts and methods of other fields. Doing this means, of course, the complete abandonment of fetishism:

> The true coherence of anthropology, then, is personal. It is not official or bureaucratic. The issue is not between general anthropology and fragmentation, but between a bureaucratic general anthropology, whose latent function is the protection of academic comfort and privilege, and a personal general anthropology, whose function is the advancement of knowledge and the welfare of mankind.
> Herein lies a fundamental part of "reinventing" anthropology. Each anthropologist must reinvent it, as a general field, for him or herself, following personal interest and talent where best they lead. The legitimate purpose of anthropological training is to facilitate this process. It has no other. (Hymes, 1972:47-48)

GLOSSARY

a priori Prior to experience, presumptively, reasoning from axioms. That kind of reasoning which deduces consequences from axioms presumed to be true without verification by experience.

age-area hypothesis The notion that a culture trait diffuses outward in the various directions from its origin point at an equal rate. Thus the distance of a trait from its origin point can be taken as an indication of its age.

animism The notion that the phenomena of life are produced by an immaterial *anima*, or soul, which is distinct from matter. Tylor's minimum definition of a religion.

anthropology The science of man in the widest sense. Often divided into social or cultural anthropology, physical anthropology, archeology, and linguistics.

anthropomorphic Attributing human form or personality to nonhuman beings or nonliving things.

antiquarian Someone who studies antiquities.

archeology That branch of anthropology that studies artifacts and other material remains of older cultures.

artifact Something made by man.

Australopithecus A fossil manlike creature who lived in Africa during the Pleistocene era.

basic personality structure A matrix in which character traits develop. Not to be confused with national character or modal personality. See Kardiner, 1945:24.

behavior Observable interactions between an organism and its environment. Or, as for the physicist, a change of state over time.

behaviorist One who believes the only legitimate object of psychological, anthropological, or sociological investigation is observable behavior (as opposed, for example, to mind, ideas, or thoughts).

civilization A human condition or state of being presumably elevated in some way above other states or conditions of being. Opposed to the condition of being primitive or barbarous. A quantitatively high level of cultural or technological complexity.

153

clan   A unilineal descent group, either patrilineal or matrilineal, within which the specific genealogical connections with the founding ancestor are unknown so that many of the members are unable to say precisely how they are related to one another. The founding ancestor can be either real, or imaginary, such as an animal or plant.

collective conscience   From Durkheim. "The totality of beliefs and sentiments common to average citizens of the same society, which forms a determinate system which has its own life . . ."

comparative method   A procedure by which different classes of phenomena (deemed on various criteria to be comparable) are examined to determine their similarities and differences and the causes of these similarities and differences.

configuration (of culture)   The basic integrative "theme" of a culture. That overriding orientation that gives to a culture its distinctive "stamp" or character. See Benedict, 1934.

convergent evolution   The process by which similar cultural traits in different cultures are believed to have originated independently and evolved through dissimilar phases.

coup de poing   A simply flaked triangular stone tool, one of the first formal implements; probably used for a variety of purposes.

couvade   The imitation of some of the concomitants of childbirth by the father, at around the time of birth. This may include retiring into bed, seclusion, and the observance of food taboos, all of which are believed to help the child.

cultural anthropology   The branch of anthropology that has as its subject matter the study of culture (as contrasted with the study of physical, biological, or other characteristics).

cultural ecology   From Julian Steward. This term attempts to recognize that "the mutual relations between organisms and their environment," the most usual definition of ecology, must especially emphasize, in the case of man, his basic, adaptive characteristic—culture.

cultural materialism   An approach, in anthropology, whereby technoenvironmental and technoeconomic variables are assumed to be primary and independent variables causing cultural variability. Social organization and ideology are considered to be dependent variables.

cultural relativism   The belief that there is no single scale of values for all cultures, hence that particular customs, beliefs, practices, and other items must be judged relative to the cultural context in which they appear.

cultural system   A portion or aspect of a culture, selected and isolated for analysis with emphasis on its systemic quality. Thus we speak of the religious system, political system, kinship system, etc.

culture   There is no standard, commonly accepted definition. The most important criteria are that culture is shared behavior and ideas which are cumulative, systemic, symbolic, and transmitted from generation to generation extragenetically.

culture-and-personality   That area of research that attempts to bring together the study of culture and the study of personality, the effects of one upon the other. Culture being an anthropological concept and personality a psychological one, this is an interdisciplinary approach to human variability.

culture area   A region in which a majority of cultural traits and practices are shared by the different groups that live within its boundaries. In the Great Plains culture area, for example, inhabitants shared buffalo hunting, the horse, tepee, and other items.

culture center The place where a particular trait or complex is found in its defined and most ideal form.

culture circle The area, geographically, within which a culture complex is found.

culture climax The point in space at which a type of culture (Plains culture, Northwest Coast culture, or the like) has its maximum intensity.

culture complex The fundamental and organically related culture traits that are found within a culture circle. Often spoken of as the cattle complex of East Africa, the pig complex of Melanesia, and the like.

culture trait The simplest, most basic unit into which a culture can be broken down and analyzed.

culturology The study of cultural phenomena "in their own right." This term is used by Leslie White, its foremost proponent, to distinguish the study of culture from sociology.

cybernetics The study of control and communication in living and mechanical systems.

deductive Said of the process of reasoning from generals to particulars, or inferring particulars from known or assumed generalizations. Contrasted with *inductive*.

dependent variable In controlled experimentation, the dependent variable is the one whose behavior is assumed to be predictable from another called the independent variable.

depth psychology That branch of psychology which explains behavior in terms of the unconscious.

descent A relationship mediated by a parent between a person and an ancestor; *ancestor* is defined as a genealogical predecessor, of the grandparental or earlier generation.

diffusion The process by which an item of culture spreads from one area to another. Essentially, borrowing by one culture from another.

division of labor The division of a task into parts, each of which is performed by a separate person. This should not be equated directly with specialization.

ecosystem The total system of components that meaningfully interact and affect one another and characterize a given population.

emic Descriptive of the meaning of something as it is perceived and understood by the participants in a culture rather than by the observers or outsiders.

empiricism The practice or principle of basing conclusions solely upon experience. In science it implies conclusions drawn from observation and experiment only.

ethnocentric Assuming or believing that one's own group's standards, mode of living, values, beliefs, and the like are superior to those of others.

ethnohistory A method for studying the history of a culture through the use of written and oral traditions.

ethnology In its most comprehensive usage, the science of peoples and cultures. Ethnology is contrasted with ethnography in that the latter is purely descriptive whereas the former is analytic and seeks to find generalizations.

ethnoscience Basically, the system of beliefs and knowledge about the world and things held by groups of "nonscientifically" oriented people. The term is also used for a particular *method* for ascertaining what a people's beliefs are and how they are organized.

ethology The comparative study of animal behavior.

etic Descriptive of the meaning of something as it is perceived and understood by an observer (outsider) rather than by the participants themselves.

evolutionary stages Arbitrarily defined steps or levels through which, it is proposed, people must have passed in the process of evolution. Most usually savagery, barbarism, and civilization, the latter being considered a "higher" stage.

evolutionists Name given to a group of early anthropologists who believed in a theory of evolutionary stages through which they thought peoples and cultures must pass on their way to becoming "civilized."

Festschrift A volume of essays written and edited in honor of a distinguished scholar, usually upon his sixtieth birthday or upon his retirement.

fetishism The worship of inanimate objects. Irrational reverence or respect for something as sacred or powerful.

functionalism A theoretical position in anthropology that attempts to explain social or psychological phenomena in terms of the contribution they make to sociological or psychological well being.

geographical determinism A theoretical position that holds that cultural or social phenomena can be explained by geographical conditions.

grammar The established or understood rules of speech or writing.

heterodont Having teeth of different kinds.

historical particularism Name given to the outlook of a group of early American anthroplogists who believed that in order to understand cultural phenomena it was necessary to understand the particular histories of the cultures in which they were found. Franz Boas and his students are said to have held this position.

Hominidae The family of primates that includes man and fossil species related to him.

homoiothermy The phenomenon of maintaining the body at a constant temperature by means of an internal regulator of some kind.

homodont Having teeth which are all of the same kind.

Homo erectus A fossil species of the genus *Homo* who lived from approximately 250,000 to 1 million years ago.

idealism A philosophical position which holds that the objects of external perception are ideas of the perceiving mind. Contrasted with *materialism*.

idiographic Said of a study that attempts to establish a particular or specific factual proposition as opposed to a general one. See *nomothetic*.

idolatry The worship of idols or images—usually artifacts.

incest taboo The prohibition of incest—that is, of sexual relations and/or marriage —within the family or a group of kin.

independent invention The presence of similar or identical things in different cultures in consequence of specific invention in numerous places rather than by diffusion from one invention site to all other sites of occurrence.

independent variables   The causal variables that are manipulated in experiments and whose values determine the values of the *dependent variables*.

inductive   Said of the process of inferring a law or generalization from a number of particular cases. Contrasted with *deductive*.

Kulturkreise   The presumed origin points for the major culture complexes that are believed to have then diffused outward. Associated with Wilhelm Schmidt and the German diffusionists.

linguistics   The comparative study of languages.

maintenance systems   The subsistence economy and social structure that combines to enable the family to maintain itself over time. See B. Whiting, 1963:5.

mammal   An animal of the zoological class Mammalia, characterized by the possession of glands in which milk is secreted for the nourishment of offspring.

material culture   The tangible elements of a culture, consisting of artifacts; physically existing objects.

materialism   The philosophical position that nothing exists except matter, its movement, and its modification. Also, the position that consciousness is due to the operation of material agencies. Contrasted with *idealism*.

matriarchy   A society in which authority is primarily held by females. Hypothetical, it appears, as no such society is actually known.

matrilineal descent   Descent traced through the female line.

migration   Movement from one place to another, either permanently, or recurrently as with the seasons.

modal personality   The most representative personality in a given culture.

monogenesis   Development of all life from a single cell, or of all human beings from a single pair.

morpheme   A discrete unit of sound with a definite meaning and function. The smallest structural unit of a language that has meaning.

Neanderthal man   A type of fossil man, demonstrably different from modern man, first found in 1856 in the Neander Valley (now a nature reserve about 10 km. east of Düsseldorf).

new ethnography   A data-gathering technique developed in recent years for eliciting emic data and consciously separating it from etic data.

national character   The most representative character type to be found in a nation. Essentially the same as *modal personality*.

nomothetic   Said of a study that attempts to derive general propositions that will hold for a number of cases rather than one case. Contrasted with *idiographic*.

Oedipus complex   From psychoanalytic theory. The situation (largely unconscious) in which a son is in love (strong sexual desires being involved, according to psychoanalysts) with his mother and is jealous of his father (with resulting feelings of guilt and emotional conflict). When considering daughters rather than sons, this is termed the Electra complex.

paleoanthropology   The study of human fossil remains.

parallel evolution   A situation in which the same cultural feature evolves in the same manner in more than one culture.

patriarchy   A society in which authority is held primarily by males.

pattern of culture   The combination of distinctive themes or characteristics which give direction and purpose to a culture.

phoneme   A basic sound in a language, one that is recognizable regardless of variations in its position and can be assigned a symbol. The English language, for example, is said to have 45 phonemes.

phonology   The study of speech sounds.

physical anthropology   The systematic study of the physical and biological characteristics of human beings. Human biology.

Pleistocene   A geological period, roughly the most recent 2,000,000+ years, which has seen substantial climatic change involving periodic glaciations and in which the development of man and culture took place.

polygenesis   Development of mankind from several independent pairs of ancestors.

potlatch   A ceremonial destruction or giving away of property to enhance one's status, practiced among the Indians of the Pacific Northwest.

primary institutions   Those customs or ways of behavior that have to do with child-rearing and basic subsistence. See Kardiner, 1945:23.

primate   A zoological order that includes lemurs, tarsiers, monkeys, apes, and man.

primitive band   The most fundamental social group beyond the individual family. The type of social organization found where hunting and gathering form the basis for subsistence.

principle of uncertainty   In the study of the behavior of particles, there is always some uncertainty in specifying positions and velocities. From this discovery by Heisenberg, physicists have come to hold the position that nature behaves in such a way so that it is fundamentally impossible to make an absolutely precise prediction of what will happen, and therefore that we can deal only with probabilities.

projective systems   Those systems of thought that are developed from nuclear traumatic experiences in the life histories of individuals—such things as religion, folklore, and the like. See Kardiner, 1945:39.

psychic unity of mankind   The belief that the minds of men are basically similar no matter where they are found and that, given the proper conditions, people have the capacity to develop similarly.

psychological anthropology   The name applied to an attempt to understand cultural phenomena by invoking psychological theories and variables.

racial determinism   The belief, totally discredited in anthropology, that cultural differences can be explained by racial characteristics.

reductionism   The practice or principle of explaining something by "reducing" it to another level. Thus, explaining a cultural variable by reducing it to a psychological level of explanation, or explaining behavior by reducing it to the level of physiology or instinct.

reify   To convert something, mentally, into a thing (Latin *res*) when it is not a thing but, rather, a concept.

relativism (cultural)   See *cultural relativism*.

salvage ethnography   The attempt to find out as much as possible about a disappearing culture by interviewing the surviving members before they either disappear or forget what the culture was like.

secondary institutions   Those institutional behaviors, like religion and folklore, that are the result of primary institutions and the psychological phenomenon known as projection. See Kardiner, 1945:23.

shamanism   Religious and curing practices based upon the idea that a spirit or power can be invoked to possess a person (shaman) and thus endow him with supernatural powers of various kinds.

social anthropology   The study of social structure or organization (mostly in preliterate societies) rather than culture. Identified primarily with A. R. Radcliffe-Brown and his followers.

social class   A level within a society, distinguished primarily by economic condition but also by occupation, education, and the like. Examples: lower class, middle class, working class.

socialization   The process involved in the transmission of culture from one generation to the next.

structuralism   In anthropology, the attempt to analyze the underlying principles of organization rather than the content, as in studying the social structure of a group rather than its culture, or the underlying structures of the mind rather than the actual content of the mind as expressed in dreams or myths. Structuralists seek to understand the relationships between things rather than the things themselves.

structural linguistics   That type of linguistic analysis which attempts to study the unconscious structure of language rather than conscious linguistic phenomena. It takes the relations between the terms as the important datum rather than the terms themselves; it assumes that the underlying structure is systemic; and it aims to discover general laws of language.

subsistence   The means of supporting life. Livelihood. The techniques for insuring a supply of food.

superorganicism   That position in anthropology that holds culture to be superorganic, a thing in and of itself, acting independently of individual human beings. Usually identified with A. L. Kroeber and Leslie White.

survival   A culture trait present in a previous period and still present in a contemporary culture where it does not appear to belong.

symbol   Something that stands for something else and whose meaning is neither obvious nor intrinsic. The characters in the alphabet are examples of symbols.

symbolic anthropology   An approach that attempts to analyze cultures as systems of meaningful symbols that enable human beings to organize their lives and survive.

themes of culture   The basic integrating patterns of behavior that give a culture its character and direction.

theonomy   Government by God: divine rule. Being subject to the authority of God.

trait   See *culture trait*.

tribe   A distinct social or political group that is autonomous and claims a particular territory as its own.

ungulate   A hoofed animal.

unilineal evolution   A form of evolution in which the attainment of each stage depends upon having passed through the previous stage.

REFERENCES

Alland, Alexander, Jr. 1967 *Evolution and Human Behavior*. Anchor Books, New York.

1972 *The Human Imperative*. Columbia University Press, New York.

Allee, W. C. 1958 *The Social Life of Animals*. Beacon Press, Boston.

Arnold, Matthew 1869 *Culture and Anarchy*.

Avebury, Lord *See* Lubbock, John.

Bachofen, J. J. 1861 *Das Mutterrecht*.

Barnett, H. G. 1953 *Innovation: The Basis of Cultural Change*. McGraw-Hill, New York.

Bateson, Gregory 1967 "Cybernetic Explanation." *American Behavioral Scientist*, Vol. 10, No. 8, pp. 29-32.

1972 *Steps to an Ecology of Mind*. Chandler, New York. (The Ballantine paperback edition, also 1972, differs.)

Bateson, Gregory, and Margaret Mead 1942 *Balinese Character: A Photographic Analysis*. Special Publication of the New York Academy of Sciences, New York.

Becker, Ernest 1971 *The Lost Science of Man*. George Braziller, New York.

Benedict, Ruth 1934 *Patterns of Culture*. Houghton Mifflin, New York.

Bennett, John W. 1967 "Discussion and Criticism, On the Cultural Ecology of Indian Cattle." *Current Anthropology*, Vol. 8, No. 3, pp. 251-252.

Berreman, Gerald D. 1966 "Anemic and Emetic Analyses in Social Anthropology." *American Anthropologist*, Vol. 68, No. 2, Part 1, pp. 346-354.

Berry, William B. N. 1968 *Growth of a Prehistoric Time Scale*. Freeman, San Francisco.

Bidney, David 1967 *Theoretical Anthropology*, second, augmented edition. Schocken Books, New York.

Boas, Franz 1887 "The Occurrence of Similar Inventions in Areas Widely Apart." *Science*, Vol. IX, pp. 485-486.

1896 "The Limitations of the Comparative Method of Anthropology." Reprinted in Boas, *Race, Language and Culture*, Macmillan, New York, 1940, pp. 271-304.

Bowers, Alfred W. 1950 *Mandan Social and Ceremonial Organization*. University of Chicago Press.

Brace, C. L., G. R. Gamble, and J. T. Bond 1971 *Race and Intelligence*. Anthropological Studies, No. 8, American Anthropological Association.

Brace, C. Loring, and Frank B. Livingstone 1971 "On Creeping Jensenism." In C. L. Brace *et al.*, ed., *Race and Intelligence*.

Brown, Dee 1970 *Bury My Heart At Wounded Knee*. Bantam Books, New York.

Buel, J. W. 1889 *The Story of Man*.

Büttikofer, J. 1893 "Notes." *American Anthropologist*, Vol. VI, pp. 337-339.

Campbell, Bernard 1966 *Human Evolution*. Aldine, Chicago.
    1969 "Just Another 'Man-Ape'?" In Hermann K. Bleibtreu, ed., *Evolutionary Anthropology*, Allyn and Bacon Inc., Boston, pp. 162-166.

Carmack, Robert M. 1972 "Ethnohistory: A Review of Its Development, Definitions, Methods and Aims." In B. J. Siegel, ed., *Annual Review of Anthropology*, Annual Reviews, Inc., Palo Alto, California, pp. 227-246.

Carpenter, C. R. 1964 *Naturalistic Behavior of Nonhuman Primates*. The Pennsylvania State University Press, University Park, Pennsylvania.

Chase, Stuart 1948 *The Proper Study of Mankind*. Harper, New York.

Chomsky, Noam 1972 *Language and Mind*. Harcourt, New York.

Codere, Helen 1950 *Fighting with Property*. Monographs of the American Ethnological Society, Vol. 18, J. J. Augustin, Locust Valley, New York.

Daniel, Glyn 1962 *The Idea of Prehistory*. Penguin.

Driver, H. E., and Alfred L. Kroeber 1932 "Quantitative Expression of Cultural Relationships." *University of California Publications in American Archaeology and Ethnology*, Vol. 31, No. 4, pp. 211-256.

Dudley, Edward, and Maximillian E. Novak, ed. 1972 *The Wild Man Within*. University of Pittsburgh Press, Pittsburgh, Pennsylvania.

Durkheim, Emile 1893 *The Division of Labor in Society*. Free Press, New York, 1964.
    1897 *Suicide*. J. Spaulding and G. Simpson, trans. Free Press, Glencoe, Illinois, 1951.

Eggan, Fred 1950 *Social Organization of the Western Pueblos*. University of Chicago Press.

Eibl-Eibesfeldt, Irenäus 1970 *Ethology: The Biology of Behavior*. Holt, New York.

Evans-Pritchard, E. E. 1940 *The Nuer*. Oxford University Press.

Fenichel, Otto 1945 *The Psychoanalytic Theory of Neurosis*. Norton, New York.

Ferree, Barr 1890 "Climatic Influences in Primitive Architecture." *American Anthropologist*, Vol. III, pp. 147-158.

Firth, Raymond 1936 *We, the Tikopia*. Allen and Unwin, London.
    1957 "Introduction: Malinowski as Scientist and as Man." In Raymond Firth, ed., *Man and Culture*, Harper and Row, New York, pp. 1-14.

Fortes, Meyer 1945 *The Dynamics of Clanship among the Tallensi*. Oxford University Press.
    1949 "Preface." In *Social Structure Studies Presented to A. R. Radcliffe-Brown*. Clarendon Press, Oxford, pp. v-xiv.
    1969 *Kinship and the Social Order: The Legacy of Lewis Henry Morgan*. Aldine, Chicago.

Fortune. Reo F. 1932 *Sorcerers of Dobu*. Routledge, London.

Frazer, James G. 1890 *The Golden Bough*.

Freed, S. A., and R. S. Freed 1972 "Cattle in a North Indian Village." *Ethnology*, XI, No. 4, pp. 399-408.

Freeman, Derek 1970 "Human Nature and Culture." *In Man and the New Biology*, Australian National University Press, Canberra, pp. 50-75.

Freud, Sigmund 1918 *Totem and Taboo*. A. A. Brill, trans.

1920 *A General Introduction to Psychoanalysis*. Garden City Publishing Co., Garden City, New York, 1928.

1928 *The Future of an Illusion*. W. D. Robson-Scott, trans. Institute of Psychoanalysis, London.

1935 *The Ego and the Id*. Authorized translation by Joan Riviere. Hogarth Press, London.

1939 *Moses and Monotheism*. Vintage Books, New York.

Frobenius, Leo 1898 *Die Weltanschauung der Naturvolker*.

Gardner, B. T., and R. A. Gardner 1971 "Two-Way Communication with an Infant Chimpanzee." In Alan M. Schreier, Harry F. Harlow, and Fred Stollnitz, ed., *Behavior of Non-Human Primates*, Academic Press, New York.

Geertz, Clifford 1965 "The Impact of the Concept of Culture on the Concept of Man." In John R. Platt, ed., *New Views of the Nature of Man*, University of Chicago Press, pp. 93-118.

1966 "Religion as a Cultural System. In Michael Banton, ed., *Anthropological Approaches to the Study of Religion*, Association of Social Anthropologists Monograph No. 3, pp. 1-46.

1973 *The Interpretation of Cultures*. Basic Books, Inc., New York.

Ginsberg, Herbert, and Sylvia Opper. 1969 *Piaget's Theory of Intellectual Development*. Prentice-Hall, Englewood Cliffs, New Jersey.

Gluckman, Max 1963 *Order and Rebellion in Tribal Africa*. Free Press, New York.

Gosse, P. H. 1857 *Omphalos*.

Graebner, F. 1911 *Die Methode der Ethnologie*.

Gronewold, Sylvia 1972 "Did Frank Hamilton Cushing Go Native?" In Solon T. Kimball and James B. Watson, ed., *Crossing Cultural Boundaries*. Chandler, New York, pp. 33-50.

Haddon, Alfred C. 1930 "Introduction." In E. B. Tylor, *Anthropology*, Watts and Co., London.

1934 *History of Anthropology*. Watts and Co., London.

Haines, Francis 1955 *The Nez Perce Tribesmen of the Columbia Plateau*. University of Okalhoma Press, Norman.

Hall, G. Stanley 1904 *Adolescence*.

Hallowell, A. Irving 1955 *Culture and Experience*. University of Pennsylvania Press, Philadelphia.

1963 "Personality, Culture and Society in Behavioral Evolution." In Sigmund Koch, ed., *Psychology: A Study of a Science*, McGraw-Hill, New York, pp. 429-509 (Volume 6).

Hanke, Lewis 1959 *Aristotle and the American Indians*. Indiana University Press, Bloomington.

Harrington, Charles, and John W. M. Whiting 1972 "Socialization Process and Personality." In Hsu, 1972, pp. 469-507.

Harris, Marvin 1964 *The Nature of Cultural Things*. Random House, New York.

1966 "The Cultural Ecology of India's Sacred Cattle." *Current Anthropology*, Vol. 7, No. 8, pp. 51-66.

1968 *The Rise of Anthropological Theory*. Thomas Y. Crowell, New York.

Hays, H. R.   1958   *From Ape to Angel: An Informal History of Social Anthropology.* Alfred A. Knopf, New York.

Herskovits, Melville J.   1924   "A Preliminary Consideration of the Culture Areas of Africa." *American Anthropologist*, Vol. 26, pp. 50-63.

Heston, Alan   1971   "An Approach to the Sacred Cow of India." *Current Anthropology*, Vol. 12, No. 2, pp. 191-209.

Hodgen, Margaret   1964   *Early Anthropology in the Sixteenth and Seventeenth Centuries.* University of Pennsylvania Press, Philadelphia.

Hogbin, Ian   1934   *Law and Order in Polynesia.* Cooper Square Publishers, New York, 1972.

Holmes, G.   1914   "Areas of American Culture Characterization Tentatively Outlined as an Aid in the Study of Antiquities," *American Anthropologist*, Vol. XVI, pp. 413-416.

Honigmann, John J.   1961   "North America." In F. L. K. Hsu, ed., *Psychological Anthropology*, Dorsey Press, Homewood, Ill., pp. 93-134.

1967   *Personality in Culture*, Harper and Row, New York.

1972   "North America." In Hsu, 1972, pp. 121-165.

Howell, F. Clark, and the Editors of *Life*.   1965   *Early Man.* Time Inc., New York.

Howells, William   1967   *Mankind in the Making*, Doubleday and Co., New York.

Hsu, Francis L. K.   1971   *Kinship and Culture.* Aldine, Chicago.

1972   (ed.) *Psychological Anthropology*, rev. ed. Schenkman, Cambridge, Massachusetts.

Huxley, Julian   1960   "The Emergence of Darwinism." In Sol Tax, ed., *The Evolution of Life*, University of Chicago Press, pp. 1-21.

Hymes, Dell   1972   "The Use of Anthropology: Critical, Political, Personal," in Dell Hymes, ed., *Reinventing Anthropology*, Pantheon Books, New York, pp. 3-79.

Inkeles, Alex   1959   "Personality and Social Structure." In Robert K. Merton, Leonard Broom, and Leonard J. Cottrell, Jr., ed., *Sociology Today*, Basic Books, New York, pp. 249-276.

Inkeles, Alex, and Daniel J. Levinson   1954   "National Character: The Study of Modal Personality and Sociocultural Systems," In Gardner Lindzey, ed., *Handbook of Social Psychology*, Vol. II., Addison-Wesley Publishing Co., Reading, Mass., pp. 977-1020.

Jarvie, I. C.   1964   *The Revolution in Anthropology.* Routledge, London.

1972   *The Story of Social Anthropology.* McGraw-Hill, New York.

Jensen, A. R.   1969   "How Much Can We Boost I. Q. and Scholastic Achievement?" *Harvard Educational Review*, 39:1-123.

Jolly, Alison   1972   *The Evolution of Primate Behavior.* Macmillan, New York.

Jung, Carl Gustav   1959   *The Archetypes and the Collective Unconscious*, Vol. 9, Part 1, *The Collected Works of C. G. Jung.* Routledge, London.

1968   *Man and His Symbols.* Dell, New York.

Kaplan, Bert, ed.   1961   *Studying Personality Cross-Culturally.* Row, Peterson, Evanston, Illinois.

Kardiner, Abram   1939   *The Individual and His Society.* Columbia University Press. New York.

1945   *The Psychological Frontiers of Society.* Columbia University Press, New York.

Kardiner, Abram, and Edward Preble   1961   *They Studied Man.* Mentor, New York.

Kennedy, John   1973   "Cultural Psychiatry." In John J. Honigmann, ed., *Handbook of Social and Cultural Anthropology*, Rand McNally, Chicago, pp. 1119-1198.

Kluckhohn, C., H. Murray, and D. Schneider   1955   *Personality in Nature, Society and Culture*. Knopf, New York.

Knight, Rolf   1965   "A Re-examination of Hunting, Trapping and Territoriality among the Northeastern Algonkian Indians." In A. Leeds and A. Vayda, ed., *The Role of Animals in Human Ecological Adjustments*, The American Association for the Advancement of Science, Washington, D.C., pp. 27-42.

Kroeber, Alfred L.   1917   "The Superorganic." *American Anthropologist*, Vol. XIX, pp. 163-213.

1923   *Anthropology*. Harcourt, New York.

1931   "The Culture-Area and Age-Area Concepts of Clark Wissler." In Stuart A. Rice, ed., *Methods in Social Science*, University of Chicago Press, pp. 248-265.

Kroeber, Alfred L., and C. Kluckhohn   1963   *Culture: A Critical Review of Concepts and Definitions*. Vintage Books, New York.

Kroeber, Theodora   1970   *Alfred Kroeber: A Personal Configuration*. University of California Press, Berkeley.

Kruuk, Hans   1972   *The Spotted Hyena: A Study of Predation and Social Behavior*. University of Chicago Press.

LaBarre, Weston   1954   *The Human Animal*. University of Chicago Press.

Langness, L. L.   1965   *The Life History in Anthropological Science*. Holt, New York.

Lawick-Goodall, Jane van   1971   *In the Shadow of Man*. Dell, New York.

Leach, Edmund   1965   *Political Systems of Highland Burma*. Beacon Press, Boston.

1966   "On the Founding Fathers." *Current Anthropology*, Vol. 7, 560-567.

1967   (ed.) *The Structural Study of Myth and Totemism*. Tavistock Publications, London.

1969   *Genesis as Myth and Other Essays*. Grossman Publishers, London.

1970   *Levi-Strauss*. Fontana/Collins, London.

Leacock, Eleanor.   1954   *The Montagnais Hunting Territory and the Fur Trade*. Memoir 78, American Anthropological Association.

Lee, Richard B., and DeVore, Irven   1968   *Man the Hunter*. Aldine, Chicago.

LeVine, Robert A.   1973   *Culture, Behavior and Personality*. Aldine, Chicago.

LeVine, Robert A., and Barbara G. LeVine   1966   *Nyansongo: A Gusii Community in Kenya*, Wiley, New York.

Levi-Strauss, Claude   1949   *Les Structures Elémentaires de la Parenté*. Presses Universitaires de France, Paris. English translation: 1969 *The Elementary Structures of Kinship*, Beacon Press, Boston.

1966   *The Savage Mind*. University of Chicago Press (first published in French, 1962).

1969   *The Raw and the Cooked*. Harper and Row, New York (first published in French, 1964).

1973   *From Honey to Ashes*. Harper and Row, New York (first published in French, 1966).

Linton, Adelin, and Charles Wagley   1971   *Ralph Linton*. Columbia University Press, New York.

Linton, Ralph   1936   *The Study of Man*. Appleton-Century, New York.

Locke, John   1690   *An Essay Concerning Human Understanding*.

Lowie, Robert   1917   *Culture and Ethnology*. Boni and Liveright, New York.

1920   *Primitive Society*. Boni and Liveright, New York.

1937   *The History of Ethnological Theory*. Rinehart, New York.

Lubbock, John (Lord Avebury) 1870 *The Origin of Civilization and the Primitive Condition of Man.* Longmans, Green and Co., London, 1912.

Lurie, Nancy Oestreich 1966 "Women in Early American Anthropology," in June Helm, ed., *Pioneers of American Anthropology,* University of Washington Press, Seattle, pp. 31-81.

McHugh, Tom 1972 *The Time of the Buffalo.* Knopf, New York.

McLennan, J. F. 1876 *Studies in Ancient History.*

Mahdi, Muhsin 1971 *Ibn Khaldun's Philosophy of History.* University of Chicago Press.

Maine, Henry 1861 *Ancient Law.*

Mair, Lucy 1934 *An African People in the Twentieth Century.* Routledge, London.

Malinowski, Bronislaw 1927 *Sex and Repression in Savage Society.* Routledge, London.

1929 *The Sexual Life of Savages in Northwestern Melanesia.* Routledge, London.

1931 "Culture." *Encyclopedia of the Social Sciences,* Vol. 4, pp. 621-646.

1935 *Coral Gardens and Their Magic.* 2 vols. Allen and Unwin, London.

1939 "Review of Six Essays on Culture by Albert Blumenthal." *American Sociological Review,* Vol. 4, pp. 588-592.

1944 *A Scientific Theory of Culture.* University of North Carolina Press, Chapel Hill.

1959 *Crime and Custom in Savage Society.* Littlefield, Adams & Co., Paterson, New Jersey (first published 1926, Routledge, London).

1967 *A Diary in the Strict Sense of the Term,* Harcourt, New York.

Marett, R. R. 1936 *Tylor.* Chapman and Hall, London.

Mason, Otis T. 1894 "Technogeography, or the Relation of the Earth to the Industries of Mankind." *American Anthropologist,* Vol. VII, No. 2, pp. 137-161.

1895 "Influence of Environment upon Human Industries or Arts." Annual Report of the Smithsonian Institution, pp. 639-665.

Mason, Philip P., ed. 1962 *The Literary Voyager or Muzzeniegun.* Michigan State University Press, East Lansing, Michigan.

Mason, Stephen F. 1962 *A History of the Sciences.* Collier Books, New York.

Mauss, Marcel 1954 *The Gift.* I. Cunnison, trans. Free Press, New York (originally published in French, 1924).

Mead, Margaret 1939 *From the South Seas.* Morrow, New York.

1959 "Apprenticeship under Boas." In Walter Goldschmidt, ed., *The Anthropology of Franz Boas.* Memoir 87, American Anthropological Association, pp. 29-45.

Mech, L. David 1970 *The Wolf.* American Museum of Natural History Press, New York.

Meggitt, Mervyn 1965 *The Lineage System of the Mae Enga of New Guinea.* Oliver and Boyd, Edinburgh.

Miller, George A. 1971 Foreword to *The Cultural Context of Learning and Thinking* (Michael Cole, John Gay, Joseph A. Glick, and Donald W. Sharp). Basic Books, New York.

Morgan, Lewis H. 1877 *Ancient Society.*

Murdock, George P. 1949 *Social Structure.* Macmillan, New York.

Murphy, Robert F. 1972 *Robert H. Lowie.* Columbia University Press, New York.

Nadel, S. F. 1942 *A Black Byzantium*. Oxford University Press, London.

Napier, John 1969 "Five Steps to Man." In Hermann K. Bleibtreu, ed., *Evolutionary Anthropology*, Allyn and Bacon, Boston, pp. 156-162.

Oakley, Kenneth Page 1964 *The Problem of Man's Antiquity*. Bulletin of the British Museum (Natural History), vol. 9, No. 5, London.

Opler, Morris 1945 "Themes as Dynamic Forces in Culture." *American Journal of Sociology*, LI, No. 3, pp. 198-206.

Penniman, T. K. 1935 *A Hundred Years of Anthropology*. Duckworth, London.

Perry, W. J. 1923 *Children of the Sun*. Methuen, London.

Pfeiffer, John E. 1969 *The Emergence of Man*, Harper and Row, New York.

Piaget, Jean 1970 *Structuralism*. Basic Books, New York.

Pike, Kenneth 1954 *Language in Relation to a Unified Theory of the Structure of Human Behavior*, Vol. 1. Summer Institute of Linguistics, Glendale, California.

Pitt-Rivers, A. L.-F. 1906 *The Evolution of Culture and Other Essays*. J. L. Myres, ed., Clarendon Press, Oxford.

Polanyi, Karl 1944 *The Great Transformation*. Holt, New York.

Pollard, Sidney 1971 *The Idea of Progress*. Penguin Books.

Pouillon, J., and P. Maranda, ed. 1970 *Echanges et Communications*, 2 vols. Mouton, Paris and the Hague.

Premack, A. J., and David Premack 1972 "Teaching Language to an Ape." *Scientific American*, 227 (4), pp. 92-99.

Premack, David 1971 "On the Assessment of Language Competence in Chimpanzees." In Alan M. Schreier, Harry F. Harlow, and Fred Stollnitz, ed., *Behavior of Non-Human Primates*, Academic Press, New York.

Radcliffe-Brown, A. R. 1922 *The Andaman Islanders*. Free Press, Glencoe, Illinois.

1952 *Structure and Function in Primitive Society*. Cohen and West, London.

1957 *A Natural Science of Society*. Free Press, Glencoe, Illinois.

Radin, Paul 1926 *Crashing Thunder, the Autobiography of an American Indian*. Appleton, New York.

Ratzel, F. 1896 *The History of Mankind*. A. J. Butler, trans. (originally published in German, 1885-1888).

Reid, Mayne 1861 *Odd People: Being a Popular Description of Singular Races of Man*.

Resek, Carl 1960 *Lewis Henry Morgan: American Scholar*, University of Chicago Press.

Richards, Audrey I. 1954 *Economic Development and Tribal Change*. Cambridge University Press.

1957 "The Concept of Culture in Malinowski's Work." In Raymond Firth, ed., *Man and Culture*, Harper and Row, New York., pp. 15-32.

Rivers, W. H. R. 1920 *Instinct and the Unconscious: A Contribution to a Biological Theory of the Psycho-neuroses*. Cambridge University Press.

Roe, Anne, and George Gaylord Simpson, ed. 1958 *Behavior and Evolution*. Yale University Press, New Haven.

Roheim, Geza 1943 *The Origin and Function of Culture*. Nervous and Mental Disease Monographs, New York.

Sahlins, Marshall D.   1960   "Evolution: Specific and General," In Sahlins and Service, 1960, pp. 12-44.

Sahlins, Marshall D., and Elman R. Service, ed.   1960   *Evolution and Culture*. University of Michigan Press, Ann Arbor.

Sapir, Edward   1916   *Time Perspectives in Aboriginal American Culture, A Study in Method*. Canada Department of Mines, Geological Survey, Ottawa, Government Printing Bureau.

1917   "Do We Need A Superorganic? *American Anthropologist*, Vol. XIX, pp. 441-447.

1924   "Culture, Genuine and Spurious." *American Journal of Sociology*, Vol. 29, pp. 401-429.

Schaller, George B.   1964   *The Year of the Gorilla*. University of Chicago Press.

1972   *The Serengeti Lion: A Study of Predator-Prey Relations*. University of Chicago Press.

Schiller, Claire H., ed.   1957   *Instinctive Behavior*. International Universities Press, New York.

Schmidt, Wilhelm   1939   *The Culture Historical Method of Ethnology*. S. A. Sieber, trans. Fortuny's, New York.

Schneider, David M.   1968   *American Kinship: A Cultural Account*. Prentice-Hall, Englewood Cliffs, New Jersey.

Schneider, Louis, and Charles Bonjean, ed.   1973   *The Idea of Culture in the Social Sciences*. Cambridge University Press, New York.

Seligman, C. G.   1924   "Anthropology and Psychology: A Study of Some Points of Contact" (Presidential Address). *Journal of the Royal Anthropological Institute of Great Britain and Ireland*, 54:13-46.

1932   "Anthropological Perspective and Psychological Theory" (The Huxley Memorial Lecture for 1932). *Journal of the Royal Anthropological Institute of Great Britain and Ireland*, 62:193-228.

Simpson, George Gaylord   1949   *The Meaning of Evolution*. Mentor, New York.

1958   "The Study of Evolution: Methods and Present Status of Theory." In Roe and Simpson, 1958, pp. 7-26.

Singer, Milton   1961   "A Survey of Culture and Personality Theory and Research." In Kaplan, 1961, pp. 9-90.

Smith, Adam   1776   *The Wealth of Nations*.

Smith, George Elliot   1928   *In the Beginning: The Origin of Civilization*. Morrow, New York.

Smith, M. G.   1960   *Government in Zazzau: 1800-1950*. Oxford University Press.

Spiro, Melford E.   1951   "Culture and Personality: The Natural History of a False Dichotomy." *Psychiatry*, 14:19-46.

1958   *Children of the Kibbutz*, Harvard University Press, Cambridge, Massachusetts.

1967   *Burmese Supernaturalism*. Prentice-Hall, Englewood Cliffs, New Jersey.

1972   "An Overview and Suggested Reorientation." In Hsu, 1972, pp. 573-607.

Spradley, James P.   1972   *Culture and Cognition: Rules, Maps, and Plans*. Chandler, New York.

Spuhler, J. N., ed.   1959   *The Evolution of Man's Capacity for Culture*. Wayne State University Press, Detroit, Michigan.

Steward, Julian 1955 *Theory of Culture Change*. University of Illinois Press, Urbana.

Stocking, George W., Jr. 1963 "Mathew Arnold, E. B. Tylor, and the Uses of Invention." *American Anthropologist*, Vol. LXV, pp. 783-799. As reprinted in Stocking, 1968

1964 "French Anthropology in 1800." *Isis*, Vol. LV, pp. 134-150. As reprinted in Stocking, 1968.

1965 "From Physics to Ethnology: Franz Boas' Arctic Expedition as a Problem in the Historiography of the Behavioral Sciences." *Journal of the History of the Behavioral Sciences*, Vol. I, No. 1, pp. 53-66. As reprinted in Stocking, 1968.

1968 *Race, Culture, and Evolution: Essays in the History of Anthropology*. Free Press, New York.

Sturtevant, W. 1964 "Studies in Ethnoscience." *American Anthropologist*, Vol. 66, part 2, pp. 99-131.

Tax, Sol, ed. 1960 *Evolution after Darwin*. University of Chicago Press.

Tinbergen, Nicholas 1953 *Social Behavior in Animals: with Special Reference to Vertebrates*. Methuen, London.

Toynbee, Arnold J. 1973 "The Genesis of Pollution." *Horizon*, Vol. XV, No. 3, pp. 4-9.

Turner, Victor 1967 *The Forest of Symbols*. Cornell University Press, Ithaca, New York.

Tyler, Stephen A. 1969 *Cognitive Anthropology*. Holt, New York.

Tylor, Edward Burnett 1861 *Anahuac or Mexico and the Mexicans, Ancient and Modern*.

1871 *Primitive Culture: Researches into the Development of Mythology, Philosophy, Religion, Language, Art and Custom*. J. Murray, London, 2 vols., 1903.

Vayda, Andrew 1961 "Expansion and Warfare among Swidden Agriculturalists." *American Anthropologist*, Vol. LXIII, pp. 346-358.

Wallace, Anthony F. C. 1970 *Culture and Personality*. Random House, New York.

Weber, Max 1930 *The Protestant Ethic and the Spirit of Capitalism*. Scribner, New York.

White, Andrew D. 1955 *A History of the Warfare of Science with Theology in Christendom*. George Braziller, New York (originally published 1895).

White, Hayden 1972 "The Forms of Wildness: Archaeology of an Idea." In Dudley and Novak, 1972, pp. 3-38.

White, Leslie A. 1940 *Pioneers in American Anthropology: The Morgan-Bandelier Letters 1873-1883*. University of New Mexico Press, Albuquerque.

1969 *The Science of Culture*, 2nd ed. Farrar, Straus, and Giroux, New York.

White, Leslie A., with Beth Dillingham 1973 *The Concept of Culture*. Burgess, Minneapolis, Minnesota.

Whiting, Beatrice B., ed. 1963 *Six Cultures: Studies of Child Rearing*. Wiley, New York.

Whiting, John W. M. 1964 "Effects of Climate on Certain Cultural Practices." In Ward H. Goodenough, ed., *Explorations in Cultural Anthropology*, McGraw-Hill, New York, pp. 511-544.

Whiting, J. W. M., E. H. Chasdi, H. F. Antonovsky, and B. C. Ayres 1966 "The Learning of Values," In E. Vogt and E. Albert, ed., *People of the Rimrock: A Study of*

170   *References*

Values in Five Cultures, Harvard University Press, Cambridge, Massachusetts.
Whiting, John W. M., and Irvin L. Child   1953   *Child Training and Personality*. Yale University Press, New Haven.
Whiting, J. W. M., R. Kluckhohn, and A. S. Anthony   1958   "The Function of Male Initiation Ceremonies at Puberty." In E. E. Maccoby, T. Newcomb, and E. Hartley, ed., *Readings in Social Psychology*, Holt, New York, pp. 359-370.
Wiener, Norbert   1954   *The Human Use of Human Beings: Cybernetics and Society*. Doubleday, New York.
Williams, Thomas Rhys   1972   *Introduction to Socialization: Human Culture Transmitted*. Mosby, St. Louis, Missouri.
Wissler, Clark   1914   "Influence of the Horse in the Development of Plains Culture." *American Anthropologist*, 16, pp. 1-25.
   1917   *The American Indian*. 3rd edition, 1938, Oxford University Press, New York.
   1923   *Man and Culture*. Thomas Y. Crowell, New York.
   1926   *The Relation of Nature to Man in Aboriginal America*. Oxford University Press, New York.

AUTHOR INDEX

SUBJECT INDEX